C000226658

Managing and Developing Community Sport

Can sport and physical activity (PA) be used to improve the communities we live in? How do community groups manage facilities that provide sport and PA? How can managers ensure the services they deliver meet the needs of their community? What role should community sport schemes play in society? Answer these questions and more in this, the first textbook to focus on the theory and practice of community-level sport management and development.

Bringing together academics and practitioners with expertise in sport management, sport development, the sociology of sport, PA programming and community coaching, this book outlines best practice and explores contemporary issues relating to:

- Community enhancement through sport and PA
- Leadership, enterprise and innovation
- Budgeting and decision making
- Event and facility management
- Corporate social responsibility (CSR)
- Monitoring and evaluation.

The book is divided into three sections: Part I provides an introduction to developing and managing community sport; Part II outlines the key issues and challenges that face those working in the sector; and Part III examines the leadership and management qualities needed to effectively manage and develop community sport.

Insightful and user-friendly, *Managing and Developing Community Sport* is written in an easy to read style and is a vital resource for sport management practitioners or students hoping to work in community-level sport.

Rob Wilson is a principal lecturer at Sheffield Hallam University (SHU), UK. His main research interests are the finance, economics and governance of professional team sports. He has presented at major European sport management conferences in recent years and has numerous publications in the sport management field. Rob is an active researcher with the Sport Industry Research Centre (SIRC) and contributes regularly to media items discussing the finances of sport and football with local, national and international media outlets.

Chris Platts is a senior lecturer at Sheffield Hallam University (SHU), UK. His PhD in the sociology of sport and exercise examined the education and welfare provisions for young footballers undertaking a scholarship in professional football academies. Before undertaking his doctoral study, Chris completed an MSc in the sociology of sport and a BSc in sport and exercise science, both at the University of Chester, UK. Chris has used this research to contribute to publications on the work of young athletes and the application of qualitative research methods.

Managing and Developing Community Sport

Edited by
Rob Wilson and Chris Platts

Routledge
Taylor & Francis Group

LONDON AND NEW YORK

First published 2018
by Routledge
2 Park Square, Milton Park, Abingdon, Oxon OX14 4RN

and by Routledge
711 Third Avenue, New York, NY 10017

Routledge is an imprint of the Taylor & Francis Group, an informa business

British Library Cataloguing-in-Publication Data
A catalogue record for this book is available from the British Library

Library of Congress Cataloging-in-Publication Data
Names: Wilson, Robert, editor. | Platts, Chris, editor.
Title: Managing and developing community sport / edited by Rob Wilson and Chris Platts.
Description: Abingdon, Oxon; New York, NY: Routledge, 2018. |
Includes bibliographical references and index.
Identifiers: LCCN 2017041887 | ISBN 9781138674318 (hardback) |
ISBN 9781138674332 (pbk.) | ISBN 9781315561356 (ebook)
Subjects: LCSH: Sports administration. | Sports—Social aspects. |
Physical education and training—Social aspects. | Public health—Social aspects. | Community development. | Recreation centers—Management. |
Community centers—Management.
Classification: LCC GV713 .M3613 2018 | DDC 796.06/9—dc23
LC record available at https://lccn.loc.gov/2017041887

ISBN: 978-1-138-67431-8 (hbk)
ISBN: 978-1-138-67433-2 (pbk)
ISBN: 978-1-315-56135-6 (ebk)

Typeset in Berling and Futura
by codeMantra

Contents

Figures and tables

FIGURES

TABLES

Contributors

David Broom
On completion of his PhD in data collection, David joined Sheffield Hallam University (SHU) in 2007 and is now Senior Lecturer in Physical Activity, Health and Exercise Science and a Postgraduate Research Tutor for Sport. He previously worked for the British Heart Foundation National Centre for Physical Activity and Health at the same time as he was completing a Masters in Physical Activity and Health. David has a broad interest in the benefits of PA for health but has examined the effects of exercise on appetite and appetite-related hormones, and has been involved in the development, monitoring and evaluation of a childhood obesity intervention.

Jim Cherrington
Jim joined the Academy of Sport and Physical Activity at Sheffield Hallam University (SHU) in September 2010, having been a Postgraduate Researcher at Leeds Metropolitan University where he undertook a visual ethnography of identity, the body and everyday life in basketball. Jim is currently investigating the relationship between mountain biking and the 'wilderness', with a specific focus on the dynamic between sport, nature and place. He is interested in methodological innovation, both in his work on visual methodologies and in terms of the promotion of creative forms of representation. He is an active researcher in the Academy of Sport, contributing regularly to work around the social impact of sport and leisure.

Chris Cutforth
Before joining Sheffield Hallam University (SHU), Chris enjoyed a successful 20-year career in the sport and leisure industry where he worked for three local authorities and Sport England at local, regional and national levels. During his time at Sport England, Chris was responsible for the management of programmes for Physical Education, school sport and young people, as well as contributing to the design and development of several national sport development initiatives. In 2006, Chris was seconded to the London Organising Committee of the Olympic and Paralympic Games, where he contributed to the development of the London 2012 Games Maker programme. Chris is currently studying for a doctorate in Higher Education at the SHU.

Andrew Finney
Having worked as a freelancer designer since his late teens with a core personal value of supporting local social enterprises and charities, Andrew started supporting the next generation of start-ups by joining the Enterprise Team at Sheffield Hallam University (SHU)

in September 2011. As the Enterprise Adviser, Andrew aims to raise the profile of enterprise and entrepreneurship within the institution to equip students and graduates with an enhanced capacity to generate ideas and the skills to make them happen. The Enterprise Team supports over 600 students and graduates a year to turn Post-it note start-up ideas into a sustainable income through multimillion-pound turnover organisations.

Stuart Flint

Currently at Leeds Beckett University, Stuart has a specific interest in the psychosocial effects of obesity; in particular, obesity stigmatisation and discrimination, conscious and unconscious attitudes, body image, attitude and behaviour change and factors that influence exercise participation. Stuart conducts research in the area of obesity and public health, and his primary area of focus examines weight stigmatisation and discrimination. His research also examines the effectiveness of interventions to reduce stigma, and he continues to research in this area with current areas of interest including obesity discrimination in the workplace. Stuart also conducts research examining unhealthy food and drink consumption, and his current work in this area includes unhealthy food and drink marketing and nudging to improve food and drink choice.

Maxine Gregory

With over ten years of experience working within research, consultancy and practice, Maxine is an evaluation expert focusing on PA, school sport and outdoor recreation, helping to measure impact and assess 'what works?' Maxine established and is Chair of the Sheffield Hallam University (SHU) Outdoor Recreation Research Group and Vice-Chair of the European Network of Outdoor Sport. Maxine is a graduate in Recreation Management (BSc) and Research Methods (MA) from SHU.

Melissa Jacobi

With a background in facility operations and management, both in terms of local authority sports centres and private sector leisure venues, Melissa also has extensive experience in contributing to the delivery and provision of voluntary sector sports clubs. With regard to research, Melissa has written a series of academic case studies focussing on initiatives such as parkrun that are utilised in teaching and is joint author on a research project aimed at establishing students' expectations and perceptions of 'feedback'. Melissa joined Sheffield Hallam University (SHU) in 2006, having completed her Maters in Sport Management at the institution.

Pippa Jones

A Great Britain international in both swimming and water polo, Pippa graduated in Physical Education and History from Warwick University. Her career started in Coventry where she was involved in setting up the Coventry Sports Trust and managing a Youth Training Scheme before progressing to sport development roles in a local authority, the Amateur Swimming Association (ASA) and Sports Coach United Kingdom. Prior to joining Sheffield Hallam University (SHU), Pippa worked for Derbyshire Sport between 2003 and 2007. Pippa is also a member of the ASA Sport Board.

Jude Langdon

Having worked in the sport, leisure and education industry for about 12 years before joining Sheffield Hallam University (SHU) in 2014, Jude is currently undertaking her masters, and her main areas of interest include enterprise in sport coaching and development, sport event management, marketing for sport development, developing school sport and the development of professional skills. Prior to joining SHU, Jude worked for Team Activ as an operations manager and as a competition manager for both School Sport Partnerships in Barnsley.

Jo Marsden-Heathcote

After 12 years' experience of working in the sport, leisure and health industry, Jo joined Sheffield Hallam University (SHU) in 2010 and has recently completed her MBA. Her research for this examined the role of employability in Higher Education curriculum. Her main areas of interest include Enterprise in Sport and Physical Activity, Sport Event Management, Management Applications and Physical Activity Development. Her background within the sport and PA sector allows for a practical application of underpinning theories and models utilising both the commercial and public sector.

Rebecca Peake

Rebecca joined Sheffield Hallam University (SHU) in 2012 from Loughborough College, where she was responsible for the leadership of a suite of BA(Hons) management qualifications in collaboration with Nottingham Trent and Loughborough University. Prior to this, Rebecca studied at Loughborough University and competed as an international athlete. Rebecca is the Collaborative Course Leader for Sport courses delivered in Hong Kong. The majority of her role at SHU is focused on the delivery, management and accreditation of Undergraduate and Postgraduate courses delivered in Hong Kong. Rebecca is currently undertaking her Professional Doctorate. The aim of her research is to determine International Sporting Success factors for Paralympic Athletics in the UK.

Chris Platts

With a PhD in Sociology of Sport and Exercise, Chris's study examined the education and welfare provisions for young footballers undertaking a scholarship in professional football academies and centres of excellence. The study included interviews with 303 players at 21 professional football clubs across England and Wales. Before undertaking his doctoral study, Chris completed an MSc in the Sociology of Sport and a BSc in Sport and Exercise Science, both at the University of Chester. Chris has used this research to contribute to publications on the work of young athletes and the application of qualitative research methods.

Daniel Plumley

Having joined the teaching team at Sheffield Hallam University (SHU) in 2011, Dan's main research interests are in the finance and governance of professional team sports and his PhD focussed on measuring financial and sporting performance in English professional football. He has presented at major European Sport Management conferences in recent years and has numerous publications in the sport management field. Dan is an active researcher with the SIRC and has also contributed to numerous media pieces in recent years discussing the finances of football with local, national and international media outlets including corporations such as the British Broadcasting Company.

Val Stevenson

Over the course of her career, Val has worked with the Youth and Probation Services and worked in, and managed, indoor and outdoor facilities and service delivery in a London

Borough, a district local authority and a county. Val has also gained experience managing her own business and worked in both the public and the private sectors. In relation to community sport and PA, Val has worked at all levels of the system—from community through to national, contributing to and writing government and national body strategies. Outside of Higher Education, her last full-time role before joining Sheffield Hallam University (SHU) was as the Director of a County Sport Partnership.

Chris Stone

Until recently, Chris was Lead Researcher at Football Unites, Racism Divides, an anti-racist youth and community organisation based in Sheffield, for which much of his time was spent on the Big Lottery-funded research project 'Football – A shared sense of belonging?' Chris was previously employed by, and continues to provide teaching support for, Sheffield Hallam University (SHU) as a lecturer within the field of Sport and Cultural Studies, where he also worked as a researcher on the Football and its Communities project commissioned by the Football Foundation. As of 2017, he has taken a research role with Liverpool Hope University on a three-year project to evaluate the socio-economic benefits of Everton in the Community.

Jayne Wilson

Specialising in strategy development, marketing planning and project evaluation, Jayne has been recently involved in the delivery of national training programmes for Sport England in the use of the Active People and Market Segmentation Data and has led the development of a number of sport and active recreation strategies for local authority partners. Jayne also delivers a wide range of continuing professional development activity to colleagues within the sport and active recreation sector.

Rob Wilson

Rob joined the teaching team at Sheffield Hallam University (SHU) in 2002. His main research interests are in the finance, economics and governance of professional team sports, and his MPhil focused on measuring the economic impact of local sport events. He has presented at major European Sport Management conferences in recent years and has numerous publications in the sport management field. Rob is an active researcher with the SIRC and contributes regularly to media items discussing the finances of sport and football in particular with local, national and international media outlets.

Donna Woodhouse

Donna worked for a number of years as a community practitioner and also wrote on women's football for *Sportal*, as well as being a contributor to *The Guardian*'s Football AllTalk website. She came to Sheffield Hallam University (SHU) in 2006 where she continues to research and publish around the social and cultural aspects of sport and leisure. Donna gained her first degree from the University of Birmingham's Department of Cultural Studies. She then completed her MA at the Scarman Centre for the Study of Public Order at the University of Leicester before receiving funding from the Football Association and European Social Research Council to complete her doctorate at the Sir Norman Chester Centre for Football Research, University of Leicester.

Preface

Over the past five years or so, as we have been carrying out our academic duties in the Academy of Sport & Physical Activity at Sheffield Hallam University (SHU), more and more conversations appear to be occurring between those of us who teach and research in the areas of Sport Development, Sport and Society and Sport Business Management, surrounding the increasing crossover between the disciplines. In responding to the demands of the sector, and particularly to the employers within it, the improvements and modifications that were being made to ensure the degrees on offer to students were being applied in nature were simultaneously pressuring us to explore the relationship between various sport and Physical Activity (PA) functions, benefits and challenges. Historically, for example, Sport Development had been considered more of a 'hands-on' role. Often, graduates would work for a National Governing Body or a Local Authority and be required to coach participants from a range of backgrounds and contribute effectively to increasing participation, particularly, but not exclusively, within groups who were under-represented in sport and PA. Project management, marketing and budget holding were less important than an ability to motivate and connect with those who were not interested in participating, let alone exploring interventions that could be of real benefit in harder to reach groups. To make gains, human nature provided solutions for quick wins or, in other words, interventions and sport and PA provision, which enabled the physically active to be, well, more physically active. Consequently, at a national level, participation in sport and PA, despite its obvious health benefits, has flatlined at best or fallen at worst. This presents a significant challenge to policymakers, leaders and managers; providers of sport and PA; communities; students; and us, as academics.

Despite this flatlining or reduction in participation, successive governments have, in real terms at least, cut public sector spending on sport and PA. Instead, governments are suggesting that society needs to come together to support community enterprises to deliver their own, more cost effective, solutions to engaging people in activity. Consequently, there has been a decrease in the number of people working in sport services, sport development and sport management within local authorities. Changes to the structure of organisations have also meant that those working in sport development are, now more than ever, expected to manage, lead and think strategically. Occurring simultaneously, there has been an increasing focus on the way in which commercial organisations (in the main driven by profit) can help deliver increases in participation, and, as a result, more people delivering the sport development agenda require business acumen.

Over the course of the past 40 years or so, we also must recognise that sport and PA have become increasingly commercialised, and, therefore, those with an interest in business and profit have focussed on the sector with greater intensity. Rather than being regarded as something that is done in your leisure time, the commercial value of the sport and PA sector developed quickly during the latter part of the 20th century, meaning a career in the 'sport business' was now a real possibility and could provide a genuine career opportunity. The areas that had been traditionally occupied by sport development programmes and schemes were not immune from this advance, and good examples that currently occupy these spaces include the exponential increase in budget gyms, private coaching companies delivering in-school and community settings and the development of social enterprise companies, all offering cost-effective provision to local community groups.

There is other evidence of the growing crossover between the areas explored in the book too. For example, a number of sport degree programmes have emerged within the UK and around the globe that have both management and development in the title, signifying that in order to be a good manager, you need to understand the ways in which sport is developed, and in order to develop people in and through sport and PA, you need to be able to manage and lead teams and individuals. From our discussions at the university, we concur, and, as noted earlier, this has been reflected in modifications we have made to our own degree programmes in recent years to benefit our own students studying in one of the largest sport departments in Europe. However, what we have yet to come across, and the reason for the development of this book, is a resource that helps a student develop his or her understanding of the synergy between these areas or a single resource that accurately provides a hands-on guide to becoming a multiskilled leader in the sport and PA sector, particularly one that provides solutions at a community level. The aim of this book, therefore, is to provide that.

WHAT WILL YOU GET FROM THE BOOK?

Fundamentally, this book is split into three parts. *Part I* provides the context on which this book is based. It's broken down into three, critical chapters, each providing a unique position on how you can understand and challenge the nature of developing and managing community sport. Our introductory chapter, by Dr Chris Platts (one of the book's editors), presents a user-friendly introduction to the study of community sport. In it, he outlines how community sport management and development have emerged. In taking a developmental approach, the chapter attempts to help you understand how the issues and topics explored in the rest of the book are the result of more long-term trends inside and outside of sport. This is followed by a chapter that examines the community sport landscape (by Chris Cutforth), complete with a series of opportunities and challenges for the sector. The final chapter of the opening section, by Drs Woodhouse and Cherrington, takes you on a journey that advocates a critical approach to community sport management that encourages you to challenge your own assumptions about 'sport', 'community' and 'management' in order to make informed judgements about the use–value of sport as a vehicle for social good.

In *Part II*, we outline the key issues and challenges that may face those who are expected to work in community sport through a variety of different lenses. We begin with an often-overlooked subject in sport management and development but one that will be crucial in all community contexts: PA. In their chapter, Dr David Broom and Dr Stuart Flint explore community-based PA interventions that are designed to improve lifestyle behaviours that consequently impact health inequalities. Physical inactivity and sedentary behaviour is associated with non-communicable diseases including obesity, coronary heart disease and Type 2 diabetes. These diseases typically start during childhood and have a significant impact on the economy, both in terms of direct and indirect costs such as healthcare and lost productivity in the workplace.

Chapter 5, again by Editor Dr Chris Platts, uses case studies from a number of areas to highlight the strengths and limitations of using sport as a medium through which we can engage groups who have been traditionally seen as 'excluded' from mainstream society. He examines new government strategy and the likely follow-up strategies from organisations such as Sport England and UK Sport to help us understand the likely future success of sport within the wider social inclusion agenda. Next, we move onto a growing agenda, stimulated by the commercial sector for community good: CSR. Dr Daniel Plumley and Editor Rob Wilson explore the emergence and growing importance of CSR in the delivery of community sport. By demonstrating the use of CSR programmes to deliver community-based initiatives, it is also possible to examine why CSR is of importance to major companies and how community managers can engage with them to deliver programmes and services in partnership with them.

Dr Chris Stone, a former PhD student from SHU and now working in the sector, provides us with Chapter 7 and a brilliant discussion of community responsibilities in the context of professional football clubs and football's governing bodies. Amongst all sports industries, football, as such a ubiquitous part of popular culture, has been uniquely positioned historically, politically and socially in terms of its community sport expectations. This chapter introduces you to the historical context of why this has become the case.

Chapter 8 presents an overview of the sport event industry from a community sport setting. Jo Marsden-Heathcote and Jude Langdon provide practical guidance for you to understand the planning and processes that are involved in event management and how to run successful community events that meet multiple objectives. We then move onto a robust discussion by Val Stevenson and Pippa Jones on the importance and impact of community coaching in our final chapter in Part II, Chapter 9. They explore the diverse roles of coaches who work in a variety of community populations and contexts. This includes coaching for young people, adults and ageing populations engaging in sport and PA.

These first two parts of the book will challenge you to think differently about sport and PA. In doing so, you will find that some of the things you took for granted about the 'power' of sport may not reflect the reality of the situation. Indeed, the first half of the book should be regarded as a critical look at sport and PA in the community. That is to say, you will find elements of Parts I and II where we are rather critical of current approaches or practices within sport and PA. This critical approach, however, is imperative if this book is to help you become a more independent and employable individual within the area of community sport and PA. These chapters will not tell you how good sport is. Rather, it will help you identify where things can be done better.

Finally, *Part III* examines the leadership and management functions that you need to possess to be an effective community leader and manager. The first of these 'functions' is detailed in Chapter 10 by Melissa Jacobi and Rebecca Peake, in their chapter on facility management. In it, they consider how the management of sporting provision in the UK has progressed through public delivery and Compulsory Competitive Tendering to the emergence of the private sector and the introduction of Management Companies and Trusts. They place significant focus on the key opportunities and challenges faced in the operation of community sport facilities such as multi-agency working and funding constraints. Chapter 11, by Editor Rob Wilson and Daniel Plumley, provides you with a detailed and applied discussion on budgeting and financial control in community sport and PA. They take you through the use of financial information, budgeting and community funding projects, which will help you plan, make decisions and control community-based organisations. It might be unlucky for some, but Chapter 12 is an excellently crafted analysis of leadership. Rebecca Peake and Melissa Jacobi provide us with a chapter that introduces key leadership and management concepts in the area of community sport. These concepts are exemplified using real organisations. The terms management and leadership are often used interchangeably; however, it is important to understand the differences between the two areas. Within the field of 'community sport', practitioners are required to demonstrate characteristics of both leadership and management regardless of organisation and geographic location. There is often an assumption that individuals in management roles are leaders, yet in case.

Our final two chapters take a look at two of the emergent areas in community sport: Enterprise, and Monitoring and Evaluation. First, Jo Marsden-Heathcote provides a unique approach to the understanding of Enterprise and Innovation in Chapter 13. This chapter considers the importance of entrepreneurship and enterprise within a community sport setting together with the influence of social enterprises within the sector, contemplating how 'being enterprising' within sport can facilitate and develop the use of innovation to overcome emerging challenges and struggles at a local level within sport. The last chapter is arguably one of the most important. Chapter 14 by Maxine Gregory and Jayne Wilson, two researchers from the university's world-renowned Sport Industry Research Centres, examine new approaches to the monitoring and evaluation of community projects and initiatives. The effective evaluation of community sport programmes is critical to inform our understanding of 'what works?' to increase sport participation for the future. A strong evidence base demonstrating 'what works, how, for whom, and why?' has the potential to shape planning and delivery for the future and to contribute to policy development. All community managers must engage with a policy framework and innovative practice, as outlined throughout this book. This final chapter provides you with an understanding of the importance of evaluation and the benefits of generating a strong evidence base, and it will consider different approaches to evaluation and discuss the challenges to evaluating community sport programmes. Areas of good practice are highlighted too.

OUR FINAL THOUGHTS...

We hope that, having begun to understand, debate and even critique some of the current approaches to sport and PA in the community, you will have developed a thirst for playing a role in improving the sector. Each of the chapters you read has been written and developed by an academic with expertise in that area. In developing the chapters, each author has also included a number of case studies that try and link the more theoretical discussions to 'real world' examples. In each chapter, the case studies not only help you to understand the theoretical debates within the chapter, but they are also examples of best practise where research and critical thinking have resulted in organisations being successful. In short, they are examples we believe others should follow and highlight that constantly evaluating what we, as a sector, do can have its rewards.

This book has been an exciting project and brings together an outstanding team of academics and practitioners from SHU's Academy of Sport and PA. It provides some challenging content in a user-friendly style and will, if engaged with as we hope, give you a unique insight into the mechanics of how to manage and develop community sport. We hope that you find the content enjoyable and engaging and that you take as much from it as the collection of authors have put into it.

— Rob and Chris

PART I

Contextualising community sport and physical activity

CHAPTER 1

Introducing community sport and physical activity

Chris Platts

SUMMARY

This chapter introduces you to some of the key terminology and fundamental debates that surround community sport and physical activity (PA). In particular, we look at what we mean by community, how community sport and PA has developed and, finally, some key issues facing the sector.

AIMS

By engaging with the remainder of this chapter, you will

- Be introduced to the debate surrounding how we define communities,
- Explore how sport and PA within a community setting has developed,
- Examine the ways in which management and development have merged within a community sport and PA setting and
- Be introduced to some of the current issues that are facing those who manage and develop sport and PA within a community setting.

WHAT IS A COMMUNITY?

On one level, asking 'what is a community?' may seem a rather basic question to open with in a book aimed at students working towards a degree. Indeed, it is likely to be a word you are all familiar with and feel comfortable using in conversations with people around you. However, writing in 1971, Bell and Newby identified over 90 different definitions of community, and, over the past 45 years or so, hundreds of authors have used their work to continue the debate. Given this book is concerned with the ways in which sport and PA is managed and developed within a community, it would be something of a blunder if we were not to highlight this debate and see if we can make some sense of it. After all, if we are unable to define what we mean by a community, how can we expect to successfully manage or develop sport and PA within it?

In defining what the concept of a community, Ken Roberts (2009, p. 40) argues it is 'a group that is wider than an extended family, but whose members are bound by kin-type relationships, among whom there is a sense of belonging, and a shared identity'. In outlining exactly what he means, Roberts (2008, p. 40) goes on to claim that 'the term is applied most frequently to territory-based "neighbourhood-communities"'. Do you agree with Roberts? If someone asked you which community you belonged to, would your first thought be the community within which you live? Although Roberts identifies geographical fields as the most obvious expression of a community, he is not arguing this is the only manifestation of a community, and this is where the complexity of defining a community begins. Sport is, in fact, a very good example of how different communities can exist without being bound together by a geographical location. A very good expression of this is the various communities of fans who may, in fact, be spread across the globe but feel the same belonging and identity Roberts outlined in his definition. Think, for example, of supporters of some of the most recognised teams in world sport: the New York Yankees, Barcelona Football Club, the Scuderia Ferrari Formula One Team, the Dallas Cowboys or Manchester United Football Club. We often call the supporters of these teams a community, joined together by their love of a team even though they may be spread far and wide geographically. The same could be applied to events such as Wimbledon, the Olympic Games, any World Cup and the Ryder or Solheim Cup where groups of people congregate because of their love of an event. When we think of a community, therefore, it is important to appreciate that it is more than simply a geographical place.

Looking again at Roberts's attempt to define community, there are three key words that help us explain what communities are, why they exist and why they can be so difficult to explain. These three words are *relationships*, *belonging* and *identity*. What Roberts suggests is that communities are, above anything else, about people. In no particular order, if we are to feel part of a community, we must be able to form relationships with others who are 'inside' that community, we must be able to identify with others who form that group or the thing that is of interest to that group and, finally, we must feel a sense of belonging to that group. Of course, this does not have to be sport. The most dedicated fans of the musician Justin Bieber, for example, have come to define themselves as 'Beliebers', identifying with each other through their excessive love of Bieber himself, his music and his shows. This community of fans regularly interact with each other via Internet chat rooms and meeting up at gigs. Helped by social media platforms, other fans have followed suit, creating communities of 'Swifties', 'Directioners', 'KatyCats', 'Smilers' and 'Beyhives'. Away from entertainment – while this list is not exhaustive – schools, religions, occupations, gamblers and gamers are all examples of groups who may label themselves as communities, bound together by relationships, an identity and a sense of belonging. As useful as these examples are for highlighting that community is not necessarily bound to a certain place, it is also useful in shedding light on the way technological advances have helped move communities away from the physical space we inhabit. People gain belonging and identity with each other through Facebook, Twitter, Instagram and Snapchat, all of which show how communities exist on global levels at the same time as local levels.

So what does this mean for us who have an interest in developing and managing sport and PA in a community? The first point is to accept that a community is hard to define and, as a result, may be viewed differentially by different people. This, of course, includes those designing, working on and evaluating any programme aimed at improving 'the community', and this has two major implications for us. First, when developing any programme designed to target a particular community, we *must* define what we mean by 'the community' for that particular programme. This has particular ramifications for those who are charged with delivering, monitoring and evaluating the programme for whom knowing who and where this programme is targeted is essential. Second, in doing this, if we accept that community is defined by the belonging, relationships and identity that people within the community feel, we must, as those aiming to develop a programme that engages those people, seek the views of the people within the community at the development stage of any programme. If you think about this logically, if community is defined by the people who constitute it, there is little point of sport development officers or sport managers who sit outside of the community designing a programme based on what they think the community is like. We explore this in greater detail in Chapter 3; however, at this stage, understanding that community is a contested term, exists in many different forms and must be considered at the start of any planning process are important lessons to remember as you progress through this book.

DEFINING COMMUNITY SPORT AND PHYSICAL ACTIVITY

If defining what we mean by community is fraught with complexity, a similar fate awaits us when trying to determine what is meant by community sport and PA. Rather than the definitions of the words being the issue here – although the separate terms of sport and physical activity are often mistaken for each other and used interchangeably[1] – it is the various forms of sport and PA that exists within a community setting that makes defining it problematic. For that reason, it is worth spending a little time understanding the various areas of sport and PA that exist within any community.

Over the past 40 years or so, sport and PA has been delivered in a community setting for one, or both, of two reasons (Harris & Houlihan, 2016). The first reason is termed 'sport-for-sport' and relates to any approach where sport and PA is delivered within a community to benefit the sport itself. This has been, perhaps, most obviously expressed in the work of National Governing Bodies (NGBs) who work in communities to, among other things, identify talented athletes who may progress onto their performance pathway or deliver sessions to raise awareness of their sport or PA, thus increasing membership at local clubs. The second reason, labelled 'sport-for-good', is when sport and PA is delivered within a community in order that the participants and, in many cases, members of the wider community derive positive benefits from such participation. Think, for example, of how sport and PA has been used in certain communities to reduce crime, drug use or antisocial behaviour. Equally, programmes that use sport and PA as a tool to try and 'bring communities together', often referred to as social inclusion, would be referred to as 'sport-for-good'. If you are thinking this appears simple, well, in many ways it is. However, as Harris and Houlihan (2016, p. 434) note, since the early 1970s in particular, community sport 'has been characterised by a turbulent policy field with frequent shifts in focus, most notably between sport for sport and sport for good'. That is to say, over the past 40 years or so, different groups of people have been responsible for writing the policies and strategies that help determine the role of community sport and PA; the problem being that different groups had different ideas about what community sport and PA should be and, in particular, what it was trying to achieve. It is perhaps because of this continuous shifting that 'over the past 20 years, community sport policy has focussed on both the use of sport to achieve broader social outcomes ['sport-for-good'] and traditional sport development outcomes ['sport-for-sport']' (Harris & Houlihan, 2016, p. 434). The problem this can leave us with is that the objectives associated with a 'sport-for-sport' approach to community sport and PA are different, even contradictory, to the objectives associated with any 'sport-for-good' approach. Let me explain what I mean by this.

If we are to deliver sport and PA within a community setting for the good of the community, the programmes we develop have to be characterised by a number of things. For example, the activities have to be inclusionary for a diverse range of people if we are looking to reduce the number of people who are socially excluded. We may be trying to improve the health of the participants, and, so, the activities need to be set at an appropriate standard for the range of people we are looking to include. The programmes need to be organised at times when the people we are looking to attract can attend, which means schedules need to be flexible, avoid work hours as well as take into account times when childcare takes place. Programmes need to cater for different groups of people who have very different lifestyles; some will be single parents, some will work shift patterns, some will be carers, some will have large families, some will commute to and from work and so on. The picture becomes even more complicated when we try to improve issues such as crime, drug use, mental health, social isolation or integration of refugees. Any activity also needs to cater for people who are physically and mentally impaired.

Although, on the face of it, 'sport-for-sport' programmes would claim that its activities need to be similarly inclusive because it is a 'sport-for-sport' approach; if the sport (or PA) is prioritised above any additional benefits, a number of issues arise. First, competitive sport is, by its very nature, an exclusionary activity that seeks to promote and celebrate ability, where 'ability' is defined using a very narrow set of criteria. Selection for squads, teams, tournaments, events and races are based largely on meeting those criteria, which, unhelpfully for any attempt at increasing participation, excludes a large number of people within society who are unable to meet those criteria. Second, the judgement of whether someone meets those criteria comes from an external source to the participant. In organised clubs, this may be a coach or manager; in some places, it could be a team captain; or in certain sports, it may be a selector. Similarly, in semi-serious leagues like 'back to netball', 'back to hockey' or 'five-a-side football', selection could be done by the organiser, but emphasis is still placed on the better athletes playing ahead of those who are deemed not good enough. Third, and perhaps most importantly, research has shown that competitive sport is not particularly useful in deriving outcomes that a 'sport-for-good' approach aims for. That is to say, there is growing evidence that using a 'sport-for-sport' approach and expecting to achieve some 'sport-for-good' outcomes is somewhat irrational. Indeed, there is not only evidence to suggest that community sport and PA cannot improve the health of the nation (Weed, 2016), but also, in fact, that participation in competitive sport can have adverse effects on health through issues such as injury, overuse (Roderick, 2006) and drug use (Waddington, 2000; Waddington & Smith, 2009). Similarly, competitive sport is not necessarily good for bringing the community together and, in places, actually reinforces divides between groups. It appears that, contrary to popular belief, competitive sport and PA may have a number of negative consequences for mental health, particularly at the elite level of competition (Malcolm & Scott, 2012).

While defining what we mean by 'sport-for-good' and 'sport-for-sport' may be slightly easier than defining what we mean by 'community', in practical terms, being clear what we want from any sport and PA programme in a community and how we might achieve it is rather more difficult to understand. As we have noted, those who have worked in these settings have continually grappled with these issues. We may suggest, of course, that the answer to how we approach sport and PA in a community is simply a matter of following the ambitions of the powerful groups who fund community sport. However, as the next section will highlight, that course of action has its own issues.

HOW HAS COMMUNITY SPORT AND PHYSICAL ACTIVITY DEVELOPED?

In order for us to understand in greater detail how difficult it is to develop and manage community sport and PA programmes, it is worth us briefly exploring the ways in which this area has developed. There are three points to highlight. First, long-term planning within this area has, historically, been particularly difficult. Second, this stems from the context within which the area of community sport and PA operates, which can be rather volatile. Finally, changes within society more generally can have a significant impact on the way in which sport and PA within a community operates.

In order to understand how sport and PA has developed within community settings, we must highlight the central role played by successive governments in shaping and re-shaping community sport and PA. The current situation with regard to government and community sport and PA is examined in greater detail in Chapter 2 of this book; however, it is widely accepted that governments have played a substantial role in determining the direction of community sport and PA from as far back as the 1960s (Coalter, 2007). Indeed, over the course of the 1960s, a number of developments would occur that are key to understanding where we are today. Perhaps the most significant of these developments was the commissioning of the Wolfenden Report by a lobbying group under the name of the Central Council for Sport and Physical Recreation (CCPR). In recent years, it has become rather common to discuss evidence regarding community sport and PA; however, the Wolfenden Report represented a rare insight into the 'state of play' regarding sport and recreation provision in the UK. Interestingly, given the topic of this book, the issues the Wolfenden Report sought to gather evidence on included sporting opportunities for young people, community sports facilities and coaching, the contribution sport could make to the wider society, the intrinsic value of sport and the ways in which sport could be organised and administered. These are all things you will come across in this book and remain aspects of community sport and PA today, which perhaps gives us all an indication into how successful (or not) we have been as a sector over the past half a century or so.

The publication of the Wolfenden Report caused something of a ripple effect culminating in, among other things, the appointment of the first Minister for Sport in 1964 and the establishment of the Sport Development Advisory Council. These are, perhaps, the first signs that community sport and PA is being viewed as something government should be involved with, and by 1972, the CCPR was granted funding powers and was known thereafter as the Great Britain Sports Council (GBSC). Although they were still operating at 'arm's length' from central government, during this period, the focus of the GBSC was largely on a 'Sport for All' agenda that aimed to create new opportunities for people from all sections of society to participate in sport, and over the course of the late 1970s and early 1980s, in partnership with Local Authorities (LAs) (another important group of organisations that you will learn more about in Chapter 2), an increasing emphasis was placed on facility development – mainly sports and leisure centres, swimming pools and artificial outdoor sports pitches.

1980s and 1990s

It was noted at the start of this chapter that issues and changes within wider society have played, and continue to play, a prominent role in shaping the way community sport and PA develops. This has always been the case, and it always will be – whatever country you are living and working in – because community sport and PA does not exist in isolation from the society of which it is a part. The 1980s (in the UK) is a particularly good decade for highlighting this process, as changes in government, unrest within society and strategic economic plans paved the way for a number of developments that impacted community sport and PA. The place to start, perhaps, is with Margaret Thatcher, who was prime minister in the UK between 1979 and 1990. According to Bloyce and Smith (2009, p. 38), 'Thatcher did not particularly like sport, and in terms of her political position her view was bolstered by the perceived problem that football hooliganism posed for her government'. During the course of the 1980s, however, a number of urban riots occurred in places such as Bradford, Bristol, Birmingham, Liverpool and London, and this placed pressure on Thatcher and her government to act (Houlihan, 2002). Despite her negativity towards sport more broadly, 'Thatcher and her government still perceived sport as a potential solution to the problems of social unrest in various inner-cities' (Bloyce & Smith, 2009, p. 38), and this was brought to life through the establishment of the Action Sport programmes in 1982. While there are arguments in both ways regarding the success of these programmes, and it is certainly worth reading the work of Houlihan and White (2002), Coalter (2007) and Bloyce and Smith (2009) on this topic, what is important for us here is the way in which the urban riots of the early 1980s resulted in what many consider the first dedicated set of sport development within a community setting.

Now, while Action Sport was being delivered through LAs using public monies, there were other economic processes emerging during the 1980s that had consequences for the way community sport management and development operates today. First among these was the encouragement of market competition (Walters & Hamil, 2013) through, among other things, the privatisation of a number of former publically owned organisations. Why is this so important for us? As you will see later in this chapter, over the past 20 years or so in particular, community sport and PA has come to be delivered increasingly by companies and organisations that sit within the private sector. This has been at the expense of LA delivery in the main. We may also argue that, as part of the process that has seen more private sector delivery of community sport and PA, there has been an increasing emphasis on the commercial side of sport and PA, which is reflected in the themes covered in the remainder of this book. Corporate social responsibility, events, finance, leadership and enterprise have all emerged from the private sector but now must be considered an integral part of community sport and PA.

In 1990, Thatcher was defeated by John Major in a contest over the leadership of the Conservative party, and, subsequently, Major went on to win the general election in 1992. In the context of this book, the key difference between these two prime ministers came in their views on sport. Major was a fanatical sportsman, with a particular passion for traditional team sports. It is perhaps unsurprising, therefore, that, in 1995, his government published 'Sport Raising the Game', which represented the first significant government policy statement on sport for around 20 years (Coalter, 2007). Interestingly, there was little reference to community sport in this policy and no acknowledgment whatsoever of the role of LAs; however, Major's government had, by this point, established the National Lottery (now called Lotto), and community sport continues to benefit from this today. As well as being a game for the general public, the National Lottery was designed to raise money for 'good causes', one of which was sport, and this is still the case today. It is not unusual, for example, for athletes to thank the National Lottery when being interviewed after a race or match, as this funding helps support them by allowing them to be full-time athletes. Likewise, at certain facilities or programmes, you may see the National Lottery branding, highlighting that Lottery monies have helped support that venue or scheme. But who is in charge of distributing this funding to community sport and PA? By this point in time, the GBSC had been rebranded into Sport England, Sport Wales, Sport Scotland and Sport Northern Ireland, and it fell to these organisations specifically to distribute funding (you will read more about the work of Sport England in Chapter 2).

2000 onwards

It is worth noting here that since the end of the 20th century, a number of changes in wider society have significantly impacted community sport and PA. For the first part of the 21st century, for example, the strength of the New Labour political party and, in particular, the popularity of the then Prime Minister Tony Blair had profound implications for community sport and PA. Coalter (2007, p. 14), for example, argues that 'the election of a New Labour government in the UK in 1997 placed sport more centrally on the broader social policy agenda, largely because of the presumed externalities, or benefits, associated with participation'. More specifically, starting in 1997, there was a particular emphasis on the use of sport to improve health, crime, employment and education, and, as a result, community sport and PA benefitted from funding that was designated for these areas. Within the UK, this approach saw community sport and PA gain record levels of funding with the establishment of Specialist Sports Colleges and County Sport Partnerships. In 2005, there was also the decision to bid for the 2012 Olympic Games, which was subsequently won. New Labour released more policies and strategies around sport than had ever been the case before, and, as King (2009) argues, one consequence of this was the modernisation of LA and voluntary sector sport bodies. This is a really important point. The modernisation King refers to was, and in many cases still is, characterised by new approaches to management such as enacting corporate planning, concentrating on managerial efficiencies, working under financial constraints and operating more closely with the corporate sector (King, 2009). This is one good example of how political changes have pushed the worlds of sport development and sport management closer together.

At the same time, although the roots of this can be traced much farther back in time, we cannot ignore the acceleration in the globalisation of sport that has occurred from the 1990s onwards. While the globalisation of sport (the spread of sport around the world) may seem like an odd topic to highlight in a book dedicated to communities, it is impossible to ignore the implications that this process has had for community sport and PA. For example, there are a growing number of programmes that use sport to aid the progress of so-called 'underdeveloped' countries. These programmes are largely funded by the developed world and work in communities in Africa, Brazil and India, among others. Professional sports teams have been central to this process, undertaking outreach work in communities, often under the banner of corporate social responsibility. Indeed, there is a lot of debate as to the strengths and weaknesses of this happening, and the work of Lindsey (2016) is a good place to start if you want to explore this work further.

Finally, at the time of writing, it would be obtuse not to make reference in some way to the role of elite sport within community sport and PA. Indeed, since the turn of the century, and in particular from the moment London was awarded the Olympics of 2012, there has been a growing emphasis placed on elite sport and the staging of elite sporting events as a mechanism for growing and sustaining participation within the community. Increasing amounts of funding have been directed into elite sport under a façade of role model creation and the subsequent 'trickle-down effect' that will, supposedly, help inspire people to participate. This is one topic that is worth keeping a close eye on over the coming years. There are some suggestions from UK Sport, the organisation responsible for distributing government funding to elite sport in UK, that the recent approach to funding, which placed greater emphasis on how likely NGBs were to succeed in winning medals or tournaments, may be changing. Similarly, the latest strategy from Sport England pays little attention to the legacy of mega events. All this has occurred against a backdrop of tightening financial spending in the public sector. Recent governments within the UK have prioritised an austerity agenda as a response to high national debt and periods of recession, and this has come to impact community sport and PA participation (Widdop, King, Parnell, Cutts, & Millward, 2017).

CURRENT ISSUES IN COMMUNITY SPORT AND PHYSICAL ACTIVITY

The current approach to using major sporting events as a way to help increase or sustain participation is not without its problems. First, there is little in the way of evidence that helps to support such a 'trickle-down effect' (Bauman, Bellew, & Craig, 2015; Reis, Frawley, Hodgetts, Thomson, & Hughes, 2017). Second, the lack of evidence has resulted in some questioning whether the pursuit of winning medals or tournaments is an effective use of public monies. As more countries adopt more professional approaches to success, the price of winning increases and, therefore, would it represent a better investment of public monies if this funding were targeted at specific communities? Third, investment in elite sport is ignoring the fact that the trend within wider society is to participate in more recreational, leisure-based forms of PA. Data shows that, over the course of our lives, we move away from competitive sport and more towards individual forms of PA. So, are role models from elite sport simply inspiring the next generation of elite athletes and nobody else? How does elite sport inspire those who are not interested in sport? What about those who are body conscious or struggling with ill health? What about those who are unable to play competitive sport? How does elite sport work for any of these groups?

The second topic that is worth considering here is the way in which the three sectors within the UK have changed over recent years and, more specifically, how this has come to impact the way community sport and PA is funded. Prior to the 1990s, there was a clear role for LAs with regard to community sport and PA provision. However, currently, the public sector, of which LAs are a part of, has been somewhat marginalised by central government and has, therefore, had to take a different approach towards its involvement in sport and PA in community settings. After all, as you will see in Chapter 2, sport and PA is not something LAs are required to deliver, and in recent years, LAs have been placed under increasing pressure to reduce its spending. As a result, we have seen less involvement from LAs in community sport and PA than in previous decades. What this has meant is that the third sector (sometimes called the voluntary sector, although not everybody working in this sector is a volunteer) has had to take a more active role in sport and PA in the community. In addition to this, organisations in the private sector have looked to move in on some areas of sport and PA in the community. This process has also given rise to some important questions. Can private companies deliver sport and PA in the community? Should community sport and PA be something that is used to create profit, or is sport and PA something we all should have access to?

If processes that occur within wider society have come to impact sport and PA in communities in the past, then it would be wise to take note of some of the current trends that are likely to impact the sector in the future. First among these within the UK is the ageing population. This trend is not confined to the UK, but what it does mean is that for those working within community sport and PA schemes in the future, there is a need to place greater emphasis on adults and older adults. This is in contrast to the majority of the work that has been conducted over the past 40 years or so where a particular emphasis has been placed on children and young people. In this scenario, how will programmes and schemes have to change in order for them to be appropriate for adults? While we are discussing demographics, it is an inescapable fact that in many countries around the world, the communities in which we live are becoming more ethnically and culturally diverse. This, of course, will have a knock-on effect for the way in which we manage and develop through community sport and PA. Indeed, one of the more popular rationales for the need for sport and PA in the community is its power to 'bring people together'. It is clear that those working in the sector in the future will be engaging with geographical communities made up of people from a range of backgrounds. At this juncture, it is also worth re-emphasising the growing number of online communities, which is something of a change in the way we interact with each other. Could this have implications for the way we think about and service communities with sport and PA?

Finally in this section, at different points in time, there are a number of issues that are occurring within society that those within community sport and PA need to be aware of. A good example of this is the urban riots of the 1980s and how, in the end, this came to shape sport development within a community setting. There are other examples from around the world such as the Midnight Basketball programme rolled out across the US following concern over disaffected young males in particular or work by numerous organisations in areas of Africa that were affected by the AIDS epidemic. With this in mind, one of the issues that appears to have come to the fore over recent years is that of mental health. While it may be hard, if not impossible, to explain whether this has become an issue because more people are struggling with their mental health or simply because we know more about it, what is clear is that it is something that community sport and PA practitioners will have to engage with over the coming years. We would also place the increase in inequality as a rather new phenomenon but something that has had, and will continue to have, profound implications for working within communities. The economic and social gap between those at the top of society and those at the bottom is increasing in a number of countries around the world (Wilkinson & Pickett, 2009), and these are, simultaneously, the countries that seem to experience a high number of social problems within all its communities. The list of issues that are currently seen as a problem is, of course, endless, and we would encourage you to spend some time exploring news outlets where you will be able to find a range of issues that are likely to have implications for communities and, as a consequence, those who are aiming to work within them.

CONCLUSION

Over the course of this chapter, I have attempted to outline a number of basic discussions that form the basis for this book. First of all, it is important to outline exactly what we mean by community and accept that, despite what we might think, everybody will have a different view of what their community is. I have also tried to briefly outline the way in which community sport and PA has developed from its roots in the 1960s. While this only outlines some of the developments that have occurred within the sector, there are a number of points for us to take away. The first is that one of the major players in shaping the landscape within community sport and PA has been central government, and we might, therefore, surmise that this will be the case moving forwards. That being said, there have been times in the past when government has not shown a great deal of interest in the sector, and, in that scenario, opportunities for other organisations and companies will arise. Finally within this chapter, I have sought to outline some of the issues that those who are looking to work in a community sport and PA setting are likely to come across and have used these issues as a basis for a number of challenging questions. As you move on to the remainder of this book, it is important that you are willing to grapple with some of these difficult questions. In doing so, we will expect you to question your own thoughts and feelings towards community sport and PA and be willing to change them. As you will see from the first half of this book in particular, the 'common-sense' assumptions we often make about community sport and PA regarding the power it has to 'do good' are often rather misguided. The key to successfully managing and developing sport and PA in the community is accepting this in the first instance and moving forwards from a more informed and realistic base.

REVIEW QUESTIONS

1. What factors might explain the developments and changes in the role of government in sport in recent decades?
2. What is the difference between the 'development of' and the 'management of' community sport and PA?
3. What is the difference between sport and PA, and what are the implications of both for community schemes?

NOTE

1 When talking about sport, we are referencing physically exertive, competitive, rule-based activities. When using the term physical activity, we are making reference to activities that also are physically challenging, however, are not rule based and have less of an element of competition.

FURTHER READING

Coalter, F. (2007). *A wider role for sport: Who's keeping the score?* London: Routledge.
Houlihan, B., & White, A. (2002). *The politics of sports development: Development of sport or development through sport?* New York: Psychology Press.

REFERENCES

Bauman, A., Bellew, B., & Craig, C. L. (2015). Did the 2000 Sydney Olympics increase physical activity among adult Australians? *British Journal of Sports Medicine 49*, 243–247.
Bloyce, D., & Smith, A. (2009). *Sport policy and development: An introduction.* London: Routledge.
Coalter, F. (2007). *A wider role for sport: Who's keeping the score?* London: Routledge.
Harris, S., & Houlihan, B. (2016). Implementing the community sport legacy: The limits of partnerships, contacts and performance management. *European Sport Management Quarterly, 4*, 433–458.
Houlihan, B. (2002). *Sport, policy and politics: A comparative analysis.* London: Routledge.
Houlihan, B., & White, A. (2002). *The politics of sports development: Development of sport or development through sport?* New York: Psychology Press.
King, N. (2009). *Sport policy and governance.* London: Routledge.
Lindsey, I. (2016). Governance in sport-for-development: Problems and possibilities of (not) learning from international development. *International Review for the Sociology of Sport*, 1–19.

Malcolm, D., & Scott, A. (2012). Suicide, sport and medicine. *British Journal of Sports Medicine, 46*(16), 1092–1093.

Reis, A. C., Frawley, S., Hodgetts, D., Thomson, A., & Hughes, K. (2017). Sport participation legacy and the Olympic Games: The case of Sydney 2000, London 2012, and Rio 2016. *Event Management, 21*(2), 139–158.

Roberts, K. (2009). *Key concepts in sociology.* Basingstoke: Palgrave.

Roderick, M. (2006). The sociology of pain and injury in sport: Main perspectives and problems. In S. Loland, B. Skirstad, & I. Waddington (Eds.), *Pain and injury in sport: Social and ethical analysis.* London: Routledge. 17–33.

Waddington, I. (2000). *Sport, health and drugs: A critical sociological perspective.* London: Taylor & Francis.

Waddington, I., & Smith, A. (2009). *An introduction to drugs in sport: Addicted to winning?* London: Routledge.

Walters, G., & Hamil, S. (2013). The contests for power and influence over the regulatory space within the English professional football industry, 1980–2012. *Business History, 55*(5), 740–767.

Weed, M. (2016). Should we privilege sport for health? The comparative effectiveness of UK Government investment in sport as a public health intervention. *International Journal of Sport Policy and Politics, 8*(4), 559–576.

Widdop, P., King, N., Parnell, D., Cutts, D., & Millward, P. (2017). Austerity, policy and sport participation in England. *International Journal of Sport Policy and Politics.*

Wilkinson, R. G., & Pickett, K. (2009). *The spirit level: Why more equal societies almost always do better* (Vol. 6). London: Allen Lane.

CHAPTER 2

Understanding the landscape of community sport

Chris Cutforth

SUMMARY

The aim of this chapter is to help you understand the roles of different organisations involved in the way sport is developed, managed and provided within communities. Primarily, this will be done by exploring community sport organisations in England; however, the reality is that some of these organisations operate across the United Kingdom or Great Britain and Northern Ireland as well. With this in mind, having read this chapter, we invite you to explore for yourselves how community sport is organised in other countries around the world.

AIMS

By engaging with this chapter, you will be able to

*   identify the roles and responsibilities of key organisations involved in community sport and physical activity,
*   describe the roles played by publically funded sport and physical activity programmes in local communities,
*   understand the current status and profile of sport and physical activity in local authorities and
*   explore the opportunities and challenges local authorities are currently facing in relation to their role in community sport and physical activity.

WHY IS GOVERNMENT INTERESTED AND INVOLVED IN SPORT?

In order to understand why any government might be interested in sport, there is first a need to define two interrelated terms – 'government' and 'the state'. Government refers to the political party, or more than one party in the case of a coalition, with a mandate to run the country for a specific period of time. This mandate is given to them by the general public who are eligible to vote in a general election. In contrast, Houlihan and Malcolm (2016) refer to the state as comprising not only the government, but also a range of publically funded organisations (sometimes referred to as 'institutions') such as the military, the courts system, the police, local councils and the education system. The state might be considered to be relatively more stable than government because we the people decide – normally every five years in the UK – who we wish to be 'in government'. Although in reality the relationships between government and the state are rather more complex, these definitions provide a useful starting point for the remainder of this chapter.

The government and sport

One of the fundamental rationales for any government taking an interest in community sport relates to the economic arguments referred to as 'public good' and 'market failure'. 'Public good' relates to anything that is deemed 'good' for society as a whole, and, as a result, governments do not want a high demand for that entity to drive its price up, thereby leaving it less accessible for certain groups (Hoye, Nicholson, Stewart & Smith, 2015). To prevent this from happening and to keep this entity accessible for a majority of society, the government or state-funded organisations may provide a subsidy to keep costs to the general public low. An example of this in community sport is the funding given for the construction and management of a public swimming pool or a municipal golf course, which enables the costs of using the facility to remain at an affordable level for the general public. The idea of 'public good' may extend beyond community sport. A good example of this is the continued support provided by successive governments for elite sport, which in part is justified on the basis of international sporting success boosting the country's international reputation and national pride or in providing role models to inspire young people. In trying to reap the 'good' elements of sport, any government may also choose to engage with the idea of 'market failure'. 'Market failure' materialises at two points, either when there is an undersupply of something that is highly desirable (often because there is little margin for profit) or when there is an oversupply of less desirable products (Hoye, Nicholson, Stewart & Smith, 2015). In community sport, we might look at the increase in budget gyms in the private sector as one area where, in the future, an oversupply might lead to 'market failure'. Similarly, the shortage of third-generation AstroTurf pitches is a good example of an undersupply of a desirable product. The final point to make on this is that 'public good' and 'market failure' can be viewed as part of the same process; the way government seeks to prioritise particular groups, such as women and disabled people, reflects the 'public good' that can come from this and some level of support missing from markets – for example, the empowerment and improved health and well-being that may be secured by these priority groups through participation in sport and physical activity.

Government roles in sport

If the rationale for government intervention is set, what do governments actually do as part of that intervention? The first function to explore is the important role governments play with regard to policy and strategy. *Sport: Raising the Game* (1995), *A Sporting Future for All* (2000), *Game Plan* (2002) and *A Sporting Future: A New Strategy for an Active Nation* (2015) are examples of government adopting this policy and strategy role. All of these publications have provided a clear indication of the government's priorities for a particular period of time. When the Labour Government under the leadership of Tony Blair published *Game Plan* in 2002, key strategy themes included an emphasis on creating a mass participation culture, an increased focus on elite sport including the staging of major international sporting events, structural reform of publically funded sports organisations and ensuring efficiency and value for money from public investment.

The final theme of *Game Plan* leads us nicely to the second function of government when it comes to sport, namely in determining where and how public money will be invested. Having developed the policies or strategies, there is then some level of expectation that state-funded organisations will follow these themes. To highlight how a change of government may impact the direction of strategy, the Conservative government's 2016 strategy placed less emphasis on increasing sports participation per se and more on the individual and societal benefits of sport. At the core of this strategy are five outcomes relating to physical and mental well-being; individual development; and social, community and economic development. Like its predecessor *Game Plan*, this strategy will continue to shape the priorities and expectations of government in relation to sport for the foreseeable future.

THE ROLES OF NATIONAL AND LOCAL SPORT ORGANISATIONS

Moving beyond the role of government, broadly speaking, community sport organisations can be grouped into two categories: direct provision and enabling organisations. Direct provision organisations operate at the 'front line' of community sport; that is to say, they are the closest to participants and provide sporting opportunities to local people by operating within and engaging with local communities. Community amateur sports clubs are a good example of direct provision organisations, but there are others such as youth organisations, charities and private coaching companies, all of which play important roles in the provision of community sport. In contrast, enabling organisations mostly operate one or more steps removed from the 'front line' of community sport by adopting strategy, planning and funding roles or by providing information and advice to direct provision organisations. Examples of enabling organisations include Sport England; Sport and Recreation Alliance (SRA); national governing bodies (NGBs) of sport such as the Football Association, England Hockey and England Athletics; local authorities; and county sports partnerships (CSPs). In reality, describing the function of an organisation as either one of direct provision or enabling is not always that simple; indeed, some organisations such as local authorities may combine both functions.

Let us now briefly examine the roles played by those organisations that fall predominantly within the enabling category.

Sport England

Sport England is a non-departmental public body, which means it is accountable to, but has a degree of independence from, government. The organisation plays a key role in co-ordinating the implementation of government sport policy. Sport England is accountable to government via the Department for Digital, Culture, Media and Sport from which it receives funding to discharge its responsibilities. The organisation uses its funds strategically to create opportunities for everyone, regardless of age, background or ability, to take part in sport and active recreation. Sport England's current focus is in the following areas.

> Increasing the number of people taking part in sport and activity and alleviating physical inactivity; encouraging young people to have a positive attitude to sport and being active; ensuring that public facilities are used fully and effectively to get maximum value for communities; increasing the physical literacy of children; increasing the use outdoor spaces, facilities and environments for exercise and wellbeing; supporting individuals with sporting talent; encouraging investment into sport from sources outside the public sector; increasing the number and diversity of people volunteering in sport.
>
> (Sport England, 2017)

Sport England, along with other home-country sports councils, Sport Scotland, Sport Wales and Sport Northern Ireland, also has Lottery funding distribution powers given to it by government via legislation. Lottery and government funds are used jointly to enable the organisations to achieve their objectives.

SRA

The SRA represents the interests of approximately 320 member organisations in the UK, including many NGBs as well as organisations responsible for a wide variety of active recreation and leisure pursuits. The SRA speaks on behalf of its members by making sure their views and common interests are heard and understood by policymakers. A key priority for the SRA is to influence the financial and regulatory environment within which community sport organisations operate. The SRA also provides wide-ranging information and advice to its members on issues such as integrity in sport, the contribution of sport to public health and by demonstrating the economic and social value of sport and recreation. The SRA has lobbied against cuts to public funding for grass roots community sport, works to help members improve their governance practices, monitors tax laws to highlight the impact of any changes and has helped develop safeguarding regulations for sport. More recently, the organisation has launched a mental health charter for sport and recreation as a positive response to growing public and political awareness and concern. In addition, the SRA undertakes research on topical issues that are of interest and concern to its members.

NGBs

NGBs are responsible for the governance and management of the sports given to them through a process of common consent. NGBs also play a key role in determining the strategic direction of its sport. At the time of writing, Sport England recognises and provides support to 136 individual NGBs representing 94 different sports. Some

NGBs receive government or Lottery funding in return, for which they are expected to contribute towards the achievement of government policy priorities. Some examples of NGBs you may have heard of include the Rugby Football Union, the British American Football Association, Badminton England, the Amateur Swimming Association and the British Judo Association. The typical governing body of sport workforce comprises both paid staff and volunteers, with the balance varying greatly between different sports.

NGBs, as the name suggests, mainly operate at a national level; however, many NGBs also have county and, in some cases, regional structures. County governing bodies (sometimes referred to as 'county associations') are responsible for the governance and development of their sport across the county area or equivalent. A good example of this is the Football Association, which operates through a network of county football associations covering the whole of England.

CSPs

CSPs provide the only consistent nationwide infrastructure for community sport in England. Established by Sport England in 2000, the roles of CSPs have evolved in line with changing national and local priorities. Today, CSPs are networks of local organisations (local authorities; governing bodies of sport, schools, colleges, universities; and others) working together to increase the number of people taking part in sport and physical activity. CSPs also play a key role in managing the implementation of Sport England policies and programmes in local areas. A network of 44 CSPs covers the whole of England, collectively employing in excess of 700 staff with a combined turnover of £60 million (CSP Network, 2017). CSPs provide a range of services including support for clubs, coaching and facility development; funding advice; research and insight; safeguarding; marketing; and communication.

Local authorities

According to Sport England, local authorities are the biggest investors in community sport, with a combined spending in excess of £1 billion per annum, which is substantially more than the contribution of Sport England and CSPs combined. Depending on where you are in England, local authorities (often referred to as councils) are organised and structured differently; for example, in some areas, there are city councils, such as Sheffield City Council, Birmingham City Council or Bristol City Council, sometimes referred to as unitary councils. In other areas – Derbyshire, Leicestershire and Surrey, for example – county and district councils operate alongside each other, albeit with different functions and providing different services. Some of these areas also include town and parish councils. You may want to investigate what local authority area you are currently living in and how local councils in the surrounding area are organised. Whatever structure the council is, they are largely free to decide how much they spend on community sport. However, just like the government, councils are elected and have to justify their spending to the voting public. So it is worth us briefly exploring the relationship between community sport and the local authority.

Sport is a non-statutory service for local authorities, meaning that they are not legally obligated to provide services for the public but can do so if they feel it important. Statutory services are the opposite of this, and every local authority has to provide these. Statutory services include things like education (mainly schools), refuse collection and social care. However, interestingly, since 2013, local authorities have had a statutory duty and responsibility for the health and well-being of their populations, and one of the ways they may decide to provide that duty is through the use of sport and physical activity. Partly for this reason, many local authorities continue to take an interest in community sport and physical activity; for example, councils engage in the provision and management of indoor and outdoor sport and recreation facilities, including parks, playing fields and open spaces. Many have established sport and physical activity outreach and development programmes, frequently aimed at specific population groups and targeted communities. They often engage in partnerships with other public, private and voluntary sector sport and recreation providers and have a role in developing local policy and strategy. Once again, we encourage you – having found your current local authority – to search for the work they are doing with respect to managing and developing sport and physical activity in the communities where you live.

Broadly speaking, there are four different approaches adopted by local authorities to the way they manage sport and physical activity facilities and services. These will be illustrated in more detail in some of the case studies later in the chapter. The first option is to manage all their provision *in-house*, and in this scenario, leisure facilities are operated and managed directly by the local authority. The second option is *outsourced management*, which involves the local authority inviting a third-party provider to undertake the day-to-day management of facilities. Through a process known as 'procurement', a specification is set by the local authority for how it wishes its facilities and services to operate, following which a range of possible providers are invited to bid to secure the right to run the contract. Once the contract has been awarded by the local authority, a legal agreement (contract) is negotiated between the two parties, and mechanisms are put in place to monitor and manage the arrangement in the interests of local people. The third option is for the local authority to *establish a new organisation*, such as a trust or social enterprise, to manage the facilities. These organisations can take different forms: non-profit, cooperative, charitable or a social enterprise. Finally, local authorities have the option to *asset transfer*, which, as the name suggests, involves transferring responsibility for the ownership and management of land or facilities to another group or organisation entirely.

The future role of local authorities

In recent years, local authorities have come under increasing financial pressure across many of their services, including statutory ones. So what might the future look like for sport and physical activity management and development from a local authority perspective, and what opportunities and challenges are they likely to face? The first point to make is that the financially driven agenda of recent years is likely to continue and requires local authorities to find new ways of working. Nick Boulter (2017, personal communication), Facilities and Planning Relationship Manager at Sport England, confirms this when he states

Local authority provision is certainly much more financially driven and business-like than it was in the past. Value for money is paramount and there is also much greater visibility and accountability for the sport and recreation service.

A key role for local authorities in the future is to establish and maintain new models of efficient, effective and affordable service provision that are aligned to local and national priorities. Achieving this in an environment of severe financial constraint and accountability remains a significant challenge. Boulter continues:

> Forward thinking authorities are adopting more of an outcomes-based approach, with outcomes determined locally and a strong emphasis on delivery through effective and efficient client-contractor partnerships as well as wider community based approaches to partnership working.

Another key challenge facing local authorities is preserving and enhancing their supply of sports and leisure facilities. Boulter explains:

> Many community sport facilities require expensive maintenance and major repairs whilst others may need to be replaced. Local authorities are having to rationalise their stock of facilities, which can involve some difficult choices. There are positives here too though with plenty of examples of local authorities managing to maintain and enhance their facility provision through effective planning, procurement and management practices.

Community amateur sports clubs

Some might argue that the final group of organisations we will examine are the 'lifeblood' of community sport. Indeed community amateur sports clubs are the oldest group of organisations we will examine and existed long before government started to take an active interest in sport – long before Sport England, CSPs and local authorities were on the scene, and it is the case that many of these clubs would remain in place if that funding and infrastructure support were ever to disappear or be reduced.

Community amateur sports clubs exist in many shapes and sizes ranging from large, multisport clubs at one end of the continuum to small single-sport clubs at the other. Some clubs own and operate their own facilities, and others may lease from local councils or other land owners or hire facilities from local authorities, schools or leisure trusts. A common feature between different clubs is their reliance on a primarily volunteer workforce. Volunteers can be seen in most clubs serving on club committees in various roles; coaching and managing teams; transporting participants to matches; organising events, fixtures and competitions; and, finally, organising fundraising events and sponsorship. In the most traditional of forms, clubs exist for the purpose of their members who pay a membership fee in order to be part of the club. In return, the committee at the club, who are normally elected by the members, administer and oversee the running of that club for the benefit of its members.

	EDUCATION	COMMUNITY SPORT	PERFORMANCE AND ELITE SPORT
NATIONAL	Department for Education (DoE) Association for Physical Education (AfPE) Youth Sport Trust (YST) British University and Colleges Sport (BUCS) Association of Colleges (AOC Sport) Governing bodies of sport	**Department of Culture Media and Sport Sport England (Sport Northern Ireland, Sport Scotland, Sport Wales) Sport and Recreation Alliance Governing bodies of sport StreetGames**	Department of Culture Media and Sport (DCMS) UK Sport English Institute of Sport British Olympic Association British Paralympic Association Sport England Governing bodies of sport British Universities and Colleges Sport
REGIONAL/ SUBREGIONAL COUNTY	Local education authorities County sports partnerships	**County Sports Partnerships County Councils Regional and county governing bodies of sport**	Regional and county governing bodies of sport County Sports Partnerships (talented athlete support)
CITY/DISTRICT	School Sport Partnerships (or equivalent)	**Local authorities Further Education Colleges Universities**	Local authorities Further Education Colleges Universities
LOCAL	Schools Further Education Colleges Universities Private coaching companies	**Parish Councils Community amateur sports clubs Schools Private coaching companies Charitable, not for profit, social enterprises**	
Cross cutting, sector wide organisations	<ul><li>UK Coaching</li><li>Sport and Recreation Alliance</li><li>English Federation of Disability Sport</li><li>Sporting Equals</li><li>Women in Sport</li><li>Pride Sports</li><li>Chartered Institute for the Management of Sport and Physical Activity</li></ul>		
Note: Some governing bodies of sport have a UK remit whilst others are focused just on England or one of the other home countries.			

FIGURE 2.1 The sporting landscape in the United Kingdom

Figure 2.1 provides a visual representation of the sporting landscape in the UK. The central focus is on community sport in England; however, the links to 'PE & school sport' and 'high performance and elite sport' in the home countries (mainly England) and UK contexts are also highlighted.

CASE STUDIES

Hopefully you now have a grasp of the national and local organisations with an interest in enabling and providing community sport. To build on this, three case studies are provided: the first case study is of Leeds City Council, a local authority that operates an *in-house* approach to its provision. The second case study focuses on the contrasting approaches of four local authorities in South Yorkshire to sport and recreation provision from the perspective of the CSP in that area. The third case study highlights the role of a CSP in working with community partners to plan and deliver a project that uses sport and physical activity to promote community cohesion and safety.

'Active Leeds' at Leeds City Council

Like many councils around England, Leeds City Council, under the banner of 'Active Leeds', aims to provide a range of services designed to encourage and support local residents to participate in sport and physical activity. Active Leeds adopts a 'whole-system approach', which means, where possible, they link sport and physical activity to wider planning, outdoor space provision, environmental considerations and asset management. For example, 'Active Leeds' contributes to the wider 'place-shaping role' of the City Council, which is designed to make Leeds an attractive place to live, visit, work, do business, relax and have fun. The City Council owns and manages 17 sports and leisure centres and swimming pools of varying sizes and provision, and this includes controlling pricing, programming, facility maintenance, upgrading and staff.

Community Sport team

The Community Sport team within Active Leeds provides opportunities for local residents to become active in sport and physical activity. The team caters to the whole city whilst also focussing its work in certain geographical areas of the city and with population groups where current levels of activity are proportionally lower. Three examples of the programmes they offer include 'Leeds Let's Get Active', 'Active Ageing' and 'Leeds Girls Can'.

- 'Leeds Let's Get Active' is designed to encourage people who do not do any physical activity at all to engage in at least 30 minutes of physical activity once a week. It does this by providing access to leisure centre and community activities within a supportive and welcoming environment.

- 'Active Ageing' targets the 45+ age group by offering enjoyable active recreation and socialising in an effort to prevent illness, maintain mobility and promote independent living and quality of life.
- 'Leeds Girls Can', a local version of Sport England's 'This Girl Can' campaign, aims to challenge traditional stereotypes regarding women's involvement in sport and physical activity and in so doing, encourage more women and girls to be more active in sport and physical activity.

With NGBs' support, and funding from Sport England, a 'Places Pilot' has been established by the Community Sport team, which has resulted in the appointment of eight multisport community activators whose role is to increase participation in specific sports in targeted communities across the city. The partnership with England Athletics has been particularly successful in involving the recruitment of a network of volunteer 'Run Leaders' to encourage previously inactive people (women in particular) to engage in recreational running in some of the more disadvantaged areas of the city. Key success factors have been the emphasis on fun and socialising with other women and the recruitment of female leaders with local knowledge, which gives them added credibility with local people. Learning from the 'Places Pilot' is informing how the City Council engages with NGBs, with particular priority being given to certain sports based on an assessment of the developmental potential of the sport linked to local priorities. The Community Sport team works with a variety of partners including the City Council's Active Schools Team, public health, asset management, transport, sport and leisure facilities, area committees and local sports clubs. Relationships with the Yorkshire Sport Foundation (the local CSP) and Sport England are also highly significant.

Sport Leeds

The work of the City Council in community sport is further supported and enhanced by having a strategic body that brings together the key organisations and individuals with leadership and management responsibilities for sport and physical activity in the City. Sport Leeds is a loose collaboration of people with no financial resources and no legal status, although its written constitution and annual general meeting provide an opportunity to regularly review its work and impact. Sport Leeds operates through a strong spirit of collaboration and trust built up over several years and now plays a key role in developing and coordinating the city's strategy for sport and physical activity. It aims to make a difference by pooling effort, resources, power and responsibility, as well as giving the city credibility with external partners and stakeholders. Membership of Sport Leeds includes the City Council, the three universities, health providers, the voluntary sport sector and the Yorkshire Sport Foundation. The key to its success is that it actively prioritises and focusses its work on issues where it feels it can make a positive difference rather than competing with or duplicating existing providers. By working together, the strategy for sport and physical activity sets Leeds' vision of being the most active city in England by the year 2018.

Sport Leeds has played a significant role in attracting some high-profile international sporting events to the city in recent years, including the start of the Tour de

France in 2014, Rugby World Cup pool games in 2015 and the World Triathlon Series in 2016. Not only have these events brought significant economic and social benefits to the city, the City Council's Active Schools and Community Sport teams have organised a series of linked events for children and young people to capitalise on the inspirational effect of having elite athletes and teams competing in the city on the world stage. The World Triathlon Series is returning to Leeds in 2017, and Leeds also stands to benefit from the decision to award Yorkshire the hosting rights for the Cycling Road World Championships in 2019. So clearly there is much to look forwards to for the people of Leeds.

Despite these many successes, the City Council in Leeds faces unprecedented financial challenges as they seek to maintain and enhance service provision in the city. Mark Allman (2014, p. 1), Head of Sport and Active Lifestyles for the City Council, explains:

> Working within the current local government environment has probably never been more challenging for sport and leisure-based services...We have to continue to do the things we do well and work more efficiently, differently and better in the areas where we need to improve.

The Active Schools service is under pressure to reduce its costs and become self-funding, whilst the Community Sport team is increasingly reliant on external funding from Sport England, Public Health, Police and Crime Commissioner and other local sources to continue its valuable work. A key challenge for both services is to become more enterprising and entrepreneurial in their approach whilst not losing sight of their core purpose.

Allman (2016, personal communication) offers some insights into the local authority's continued commitment to investing into the service:

> Inactivity is a major public health challenge in Leeds as it is elsewhere. Addressing this requires long-term investment and a strategic approach rather than quick fixes. In the current climate there may be a stronger justification for public investment into physical activity rather than sport, although context and settings are also important, so in some respects it is not quite that simple.

Clearly there are challenging times ahead for the City Council as it seeks to maintain and enhance its provision in a climate of severe budgetary constraint. Allman (2016) concludes:

> Our agenda around sport and physical activity isn't always high profile in the context of the Council's statutory functions, but nevertheless it does have a massive role to play. There are so many things we can do to contribute to some of those statutory functions whether it's children's services and obesity, adult social care, disability, mental health issues, transportation, the list goes on. Our biggest challenge is being able to hit all those agenda with limited resources, but I would argue that the value for money from the combined impact of all those things justifies what we do - it's just that sometimes it's really hard to articulate it.

Local authority sport and recreation provision in South Yorkshire

Sport and recreation provision varies substantially between different local authorities, a point illustrated by the four local authorities in South Yorkshire – Barnsley, Doncaster, Rotherham and Sheffield – where multiple influences determine local approaches. In Sheffield, most of the publically owned sport and leisure facilities are managed and operated by Sheffield International Venues, the operational arm of Sheffield City Trust, a charity whose primary role is to benefit the health and well-being of the people of Sheffield. Until recently, Sheffield City Council has also operated 'Activity Sheffield', a large team dedicated to promoting and supporting the health and physical activity of local communities. Recent financial constraints have prompted a major review of 'Activity Sheffield', leading to a change of emphasis away from direct provision of activities and towards more of an enabling and partnership approach.

By contrast, public leisure and sport facilities in Rotherham and Barnsley are operated under contract by two leisure management companies: Places for People Leisure and Barnsley Premier Leisure, respectively. Rotherham Council employs a sport development team to work with local schools, sports clubs, other sports and health providers, whereas Barnsley Council does not have such a bespoke service. Doncaster Culture and Leisure Trust, a registered charity, operates the 15 publically owned venues in Doncaster on behalf of the local authority and is supported by 'Active Doncaster', a City Council-funded service, which works to ensure that local residents have access to high quality sport, active recreation and physical activity opportunities.

Helen Marney (2016, personal communication), Director of Development at the Yorkshire Sport Foundation, suggests that two broad scenarios have emerged in recent years with regard to local authority sport and recreation provision in her area. One involves provision determined almost entirely based on an assessment of local needs with little consideration given to national policy; the other is characterised by provision that is mostly or exclusively determined by national priorities. A particular challenge for all four local authorities in South Yorkshire is the substantial reductions in financial support provided to leisure operators, which is having profound impacts on programming, charging policies and user profiles, arguably making them less accessible and affordable to low-income groups. On a more positive note, strong connections between sport and health in some areas have provided a lifeline and a renewed focus for sport development services, which otherwise may have been under threat due to financial constraints. An additional trend in South Yorkshire, which is also reflected nationally, is local authorities finding alternative asset transfer models of facility ownership and management, often as a way of reducing costs. Examples include Chapeltown Swimming Pool, Stocksbridge Leisure Centre, Woodburn Road Athletics Stadium and Wisewood Sports Centre. Potential advantages of these new management approaches include a greater responsiveness to local needs, more favourable financial arrangements and reductions in bureaucracy; disadvantages may include the reductions or removals of public subsidies, which can make financial sustainability more challenging, particularly in the medium to long term. An over-reliance on volunteers and limited facility management expertise may also be problematical. Furthermore, asset transfer models can also reduce strategic coordination and collaboration between facility providers, leading to unnecessary duplication and an inefficient use of resources.

Marney (2016) sums up the current situation in South Yorkshire when she states

> There are local authorities in South Yorkshire for whom sport in its most traditional form is still really important and they, therefore, invest in its provision and development. But, with dwindling resources in local authorities, this is becoming difficult for many. Interest is shifting to how investment in leisure centres or sport development can lead to stronger safer communities, reductions in crime and antisocial behaviour, reductions in hospital admissions, that sort of thing - a much more focused and tighter approach to how sport can add value to the things that local authorities cannot ignore.

Sport and community safety

A local initiative in South Yorkshire – Sport for Change – coordinated by the Yorkshire Sport Foundation in partnership with the South Yorkshire Police Crime Commissioner, focusses on engaging 11–18-year-olds in positive sporting activities. The vision of the programme is to use sport to reduce antisocial behaviour and crime across South Yorkshire involving young people aged 11–18. The programme uses sport to

- Act as a diversion from antisocial behaviour
- Help young people find future activities to sustain their interests
- Encourage young people to be more physically active
- Provide opportunities to break down barriers between groups of young people

Small grants of up to £1000 have been made available to support local projects and organisations working with young people wanting to make a difference in their communities. This funding has covered staffing costs and volunteer expenses, safeguarding checks, resources and materials, facility hire, transportation, marketing and publicity, training and coach education and small-scale equipment. Twenty-five per cent match funding has been required to demonstrate organisational capacity and commitment to the programme and its outcomes. Forty-nine projects were supported in the initial pilot phase covering a variety of public sector, voluntary and charitable organisations. The projects were delivered over the summer holiday period with independent research commissioned to evaluate the impact of the programme and to gain further insight into how it could be developed and improved for the future. An outcomes framework was developed that provided a key focus for the research by emphasising how and the extent to which the sport programmes can serve youth by

- Acting as diversion from taking part in antisocial or criminal behaviour
- Providing a 'hook' for follow-on or exit interventions
- Enabling behaviour modification
- Developing social inclusion

Quantitative data captured the number of participants, sessions and hours, as well as expenditure savings relating to crime, antisocial behaviour and substance misuse. Qualitative data provided further insights into participants' feelings regarding friendships, levels of trust, social connections, self-esteem, control over behaviour and skill acquisition linked to future employment. Quotes from staff involved with some of the project provide evidence of its impact and achievements included:

> We have several young men who have been in trouble with law enforcement and authority. When we offered the free multisport coaching courses in boxing, badminton and cricket they enrolled on the course and have started to help others through volunteering. Parents have been involved who have never participated in sport.
>
> These are children that struggle to find stimulating activities and have fully embraced the programme; their behaviour has improved considerably over the 6 week programme.
>
> Because of the regularity of the sessions we have seen some of the young people grow in responsibility; they take on helping setting up sessions and supporting the participation of others.
>
> We've had some really good outcomes; one of our volunteers has just started a Talent Match placement and the boys who have been coming have formed our under 16 football team, winning their first game 7-2!

The success of the pilot has enabled a case to be made for future investment. Particular aspects of the pilot that are of interest to the Office of the Police Crime Commissioner are the needs-led approach and being able to demonstrate genuine impact with a return on investment. Building on this evidence and success, The Yorkshire Sport Foundation is now working with local partners and commissioners of funding to build a longer term Sport for Change initiative designed to secure sustained behaviour change to continue addressing some of the local policing priorities.

Stuart Rogers (2017, personal communication), Development Manager at the Yorkshire Sport Foundation, reflects:

> The pilot project helped to provide a glimpse into the impact that a sports intervention could play in the engagement of young people in target communities and in reducing the incidents of antisocial behaviour. Showing the process that could be adopted to assess where activities should take place, using intelligence from a number of agencies, has demonstrated the added value that comes from a coordinated and needs-led approach.

CONCLUSION

This chapter identifies the key organisations involved in community sport and the roles they play as planners, funders, enablers or direct providers. The varied rationales and justifications for continued public investment into community sport are discussed along with some of the key opportunities and challenges currently facing these organisations.

REVIEW QUESTIONS

- Why do local authorities continue to invest in sport and recreation services?
- What partnerships are needed to ensure the provision of high-quality community sport opportunities?
- What is the justification for a nationwide network of publically funded CSPs when no such infrastructure exists for PE and school sport, elite sport or in the other home countries?
- Which management option or options are likely to deliver the best outcomes for community sport – and why?
- How can sport development professionals support community amateur sports clubs?

FURTHER READING

Bloyce, D., & Smith, A. (2010). *Sport policy and development*. London: Routledge.

Connect Sport - www.connectsport.co.uk/.

Hoye, R., Smith, A. C. T., Nicholson, M., & Stewart, B. (2015). *Sport management - Principles and applications* (4th ed.). London: Routledge.

Hylton, K. (2013). *Sports development: Policy, process and practice* (3rd ed.). London: Routledge.

King, N. (2009). *Sport policy and governance, local perspectives*. Oxford: Butterworth Heinemann.

REFERENCES

Allman, M. (2014). Leadership in sport: A local authority perspective. *The Leisure Review, 8*(7). Retrieved from www.theleisurereview.co.uk/articles14/articles14pdf/allmanleadership.pdf.

County Sports Partnership Network. (2017). *About the CSP network*. Retrieved from www.cspnetwork.org/about-csp-network.

Department for Culture, Media and Sport. (1995). *Sport: Raising the game*. London: Department of National Heritage.

Department for Culture, Media and Sport, Great Britain. (2000). *A sporting future for all*. London: DCMS.

Department for Culture, Media and Sport, Great Britain. (2002). *Game plan: A strategy for delivering government's sport and physical activity objectives*. London: Cabinet Office.

Department for Culture, Media and Sport, Great Britain. (2015). *A sporting future: A new strategy for an active nation*. London: Cabinet Office.

Houlihan, B., & Malcolm, D. (2016). *Sport and society: A student introduction* (3rd ed.). Los Angeles: SAGE.

Hoye, R., Nicholson, M., Stewart, B. & Smith, A.C.T. (2015). *Sport management: Principles and applications* (4th ed.). London: Routledge.

Sport England. (2017). *What we do*. Retrieved from www.sportengland.org/about-us/what-we-do/.

CHAPTER 3

Walking in the shoes of others

Critical reflection in community sport and physical activity

Donna Woodhouse and Jim Cherrington

SUMMARY

There are instances where, under the right circumstances, sport can be an extremely positive way to connect people from different backgrounds or to stimulate a range of senses that may be difficult to connect with in other contexts. But this isn't always the case. This chapter uses the sociological imagination as a tool for understanding the strengths and weaknesses of sport and physical activity in bringing about social good.

AIMS

By engaging with this chapter, you will

- Question the assumption that sport automatically does social good,
- Understand how community sport initiatives *can* address social issues when carried out by more reflective, open-minded practitioners and
- Develop your sociological imagination, a toolkit of skills and ideas that will help you plan and manage effective community sport initiatives.

INTRODUCTION

As a student studying sport, the chances are that sport is something you love. Typically, you will have been introduced to sport by a parent, or 'father figure', and, from a young age, you will have received a great deal of support, both financially and emotionally, so you could pursue your interests. If you are especially good at sport, you may have tasted success, having competed for your city, county or country. However, it is worth remembering that not everybody will recognise themselves in this story. If you are a woman, have a 'disability', are homeless or are seeking asylum, it is unlikely that your memories of sport are quite as positive. In fact, figures from Sport England (2016) suggest that the majority of people in the UK (57 per cent) would find it difficult to relate to your situation. Furthermore, as much as you may be loath to admit it, it is likely that even someone as sporty as yourself might be able to identify things about sport that are irritating or off-putting, with things such as excessive competition, public humiliation, anxieties about body image and confusion about rules cited as the biggest challenges to mass participation (Sport England, 2016).

This chapter is written by two people who love sport but who do not buy into the lazy idea that it is a miracle cure for social problems. With the above considerations in mind, we will encourage you to challenge 'common sense' assumptions about sport and its ability to act as a vehicle for social good. In order to help you do that, we will present three case studies. The first case study is around football; the second relates to multisports, leisure and the arts; and the final study explores 'alternative' sport and leisure activities. We will use these case studies to demonstrate what is needed to address social issues using sport and physical activity. In exploring community sport in this way, we are promoting a critical approach to community sport management and development that encourages you to exercise your sociological imaginations, to question the relationship between sport and society and to consider its value within the contexts that you may be working in now and in your future careers. In order to do this, we will challenge assumptions about 'community', 'sport' and 'management', whilst highlighting the advantages of using your sociological imagination to tackle contemporary social problems such as discrimination, ill health, crime and poverty. To conclude the chapter, we suggest that sport *can* have positive impacts, but only if we move away from traditional sport development and management approaches and deliver sport as part of projects that offer opportunities for wider personal and social development, with a focus on the local context delivered by staff using their sociological imagination, displaying skills more valuable than just the sporting.

WHAT IS THE SOCIOLOGICAL IMAGINATION?

We all have imaginations. We can drift off in class and imagine ourselves in a hammock on a tropical island where robot butlers bring us cold drinks. We can picture ourselves running out of the tunnel onto a pitch and lifting the trophy at the end of the game. That's base-level imagining; the sociological imagination is much more sophisticated and will provide you with the ability to think, and act, differently and to stand out from the crowd.

Sociology provides students, of all sport disciplines, with a different way of thinking about the world, and our sociological imaginations help us understand that our personal experiences are connected to broader public issues. After 9/11, the author Ian McEwan said 'Imagining what it is like to be someone other than yourself is at the core of our humanity. It is the essence of compassion, and it is the beginning of morality' (McEwan, 2001). The sociological imagination allows us not just to *describe* sport, but also to *understand and change* it because it gets us to examine ourselves, others and the institutions that manage and deliver sport.

Mills (1999) tells us that the sociological imagination allows people to understand their 'private troubles' in terms of 'public issues'. To give a concrete example, our private trouble may be that we are worried about losing an important sporting competition; this is influenced by the public issue of having a performance-orientated culture, which organises sport around leagues and tables, which removes much of the enjoyment from physical activity and means that only those with 'winning' bodies/mentalities can take part and succeed. It is sometimes difficult to make connections between public and private, to make links the way sociologists do between different components of society. We lead relatively privileged lives, and, as we revel in our sporting success, we forget that whilst our life is good, others are excluded. We may say to ourselves that we're successful because we work hard and that if others worked hard they could be just as successful. However, it's only when we look at the wider societal picture that we develop our socio-logical imagination – the ability to place yourself in someone else's shoes and understand their behaviours – which gives us the chance to bring about change.

As you will have noted from what was written in Chapter 1 and 2 of this book, various governments invested heavily in sport for decades, yet, as we have seen before, the majority of people still do not engage with it, and our levels of physical and mental health continue to decline. We have to rethink how we deliver sport in a society that has changed significantly and will continue to do so with, for example, new forms of media and technology competing for our attention and creating a more sedentary population. We would argue that to keep on doing what we've been doing shows a lack of a sociolog-ical imagination. This chapter will help you to think and act differently.

THE CONTEXT

Let us now take the idea of the sociological imagination, and the ability to place yourself in someone else's shoes, and place it into a more familiar context for those interested in sport in the community. When it comes to sport provision, Torkildsen (2010) outlines two approaches. The first, which is most common in the UK, he calls social planning. This approach is 'top down', meaning projects are developed by those in positions of power, such as the government, Sport England or national governing bodies, who empha-sise the importance of management and administration. This rigidly organised delivery of sport can exclude many who require sport and physical activity provisions to fit with the kind of lives we live today by offering flexible delivery in terms of venues, times of day and variety of sports, for example. The short-term nature of some projects, often caused by funding that is time-bound, exacerbates the shortcomings of this approach. Anxious not to 'fail', as funding might be cut, and keen to be portrayed as having made an impact quickly, this style of working is also risk averse, with organisations and staff loathing to experiment with new activities, as positive results may take longer to demon-strate. There are also issues around staff skills and attitudes, which lock people into par-ticular ways of working. Sennett (2004) highlights the lack of mutual respect between staff and participants, which is present in much of this type of provision. The deep-rooted tradition means that much delivery is still, as Haywood and Kew pointed out as long ago as 1989, 'trapped behind a mask of outdated, out of touch values' (p. 188).

The key to addressing this is the cultural intermediary, someone who acts as a bridge between those who are excluded from sport and physical activity and those in positions of power such as the police or local authorities. They are involved in Torkildsen's second approach, community development, which recognises the knowledge and skills of local people and promotes self-help rather than the 'top down' approach noted previously. The role of the community sport manager or development officer here is not to dictate what should be provided but rather to act as an animateur (Baldry, 1976) energising local people, developing their capacity and encouraging social cohesion. This model examines peoples' lives and responds to the increasingly diverse needs of the population in terms of, for example, ethnicity and age. In short, it uses the sociological imagination to help individuals address their private troubles, e.g., gain skills to become more employable in the context of the public issue of a struggling economy. This community sport approach recognises the failure of sport to reach significant numbers of people, despite decades of policy efforts. Crucially, it acknowledges that sport reflects wider social inequalities and works with local people to identify needs rather than assuming what problems and solutions are.

This way of working acknowledges the persistence of social exclusion, which is about more than poverty. It is 'a combination of linked problems such as unemployment, poor skills, low incomes, poor housing, high crime, bad health and family breakdown' (Batty, 2001) and impacts people's ability to participate in sport. Those who are excluded lack the social capital, described as follows by Collins, as well as the money, to participate 'in sport and leisure, and also the confidence to seek out opportunities, and the ability to organise one's time, friends and companions, childcare and transport to make participation real' (2014, p. 24). Changing patterns of work, the economic crisis, increased geographical mobility and the rise of electronic entertainment, amongst other factors, have affected our ability to meet others – to create the networks that allow us to participate in new activities. Despite the fact that sport can generate fierce rivalries and can exclude those who are not like 'us', two of the projects we focus on as follows aim to help people create social capital (Putnam, 2001), an asset that helps us make connections with people.

Working in partnership is seen as a way of responding to change and addressing social issues, with the government still urging us to 'marshal the contributions of the public, private and voluntary sectors, and of communities' (Department for Transport, Local Government and the Regions, 2001). Partnership working neatly demonstrates the idea of the sociological imagination, with local organisations and individuals working to address broad social issues such as crime, obesity and the rise in those experiencing mental health issues. Partnerships vary from informal groupings of agencies and community representatives to the very formal and legally binding.

From the 1990s, it has been *the* way of working in terms of boosting sustainability and improving services, with one of its main objectives being dealing with major social issues, such as crime and physical inactivity. Partnerships are made up of stakeholders, each of which should play an active role. Some councils have found sharing control and resources – letting go of power – difficult. Sometimes, communities struggle to embrace partnership working, as they see agencies such as councils as the problem rather than as the solution. Community involvement can also develop social capital but requires good communication and investing time to create respect. We'll illustrate the value of partnership later with our case studies.

TABLE 3.1 A taxonomy of projects

Category	Approach	Characteristics
Dominant (the most common in the UK)	Sports development	• Sport for sport's sake • Activity-driven • Mass participation • Structured/standardised • 'Expert'-driven • Fixed-term national/regional programmes • Institutional
Residual (now less common)	Social control	• Sport to deliver social outcomes • Targeted • Focused on control/management • Disciplinarian
Emergent, e.g., Positive Futures, discussed later (most in line with using the sociological imagination)	Social inclusion	• Addressing disadvantage • Personal and social development • Flexible outreach • Broader, non-sports activities • Long-term participant focussed • Community-based and -led

In terms of the delivery of sport projects, within a community setting, we identify three styles, which we have broken down in Table 3.1.

The emergent form outlined in the table above is called community sport practice, and it recognises the failure of organisations to get more people playing sport. In this approach, sport might be viewed as almost incidental, an initial hook to engage individuals. Again, we can view this in terms of the sociological imagination, with an individual's private troubles, such as disengagement with school, located against a social backdrop of a pressured education system. Those adopting this style possess a wider range of skills than those involved in facility management and traditional sport development. The approach acknowledges the limitations of sport and draws on research, rather than using 'common sense' or tradition as justification for working in certain ways. Indeed, the claim that sport can solve social problems by encouraging self-discipline, adherence to rules and responsibility for self and others is common, yet research provides little evidence to support claims that sport reduces 'deviant' behaviour (Coakley, 2002).

In community management settings, the sociological imagination allows us to understand the multitude of ways in which local, national and international issues intertwine to prevent peoples' participation in any given activity. In outlining what she calls a pedagogy of difference, Ledwith (1997) uses a three-dimensional model represented in Figure 3.1.

On the top face of the cube are the markers of identity used by individuals and groups to differentiate one person from another, often described as social formations. These are the factors that emerge through social interaction and in the context of sport, for better or worse, are used to make judgements about people who participate. On the right side are the contextual or environmental factors, such as family influence, school and workplace, that structure our daily experience and give meaning

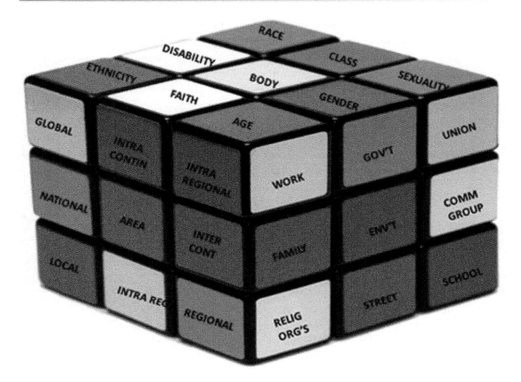

FIGURE 3.1 Ledwith's (2005) 3D model of difference
Source: Adapted from Crabbe et al. (2006)

to our sporting activities. Finally, on the left side are the levels of influence, through local and national to international, that show the various ways in which our participation in a particular activity is conditioned by various levels of social interaction, from seemingly mundane conversations with a neighbour in the street (private) to the international trends that influence how we participate and think about a particular activity (public).

The potential of this model is that it helps those responsible for managing and developing community sport to question things in a more complex and interrelated way. For example, research has shown that gendered attitudes (top face) towards sport often begin in physical education (right face), as girls are taught to behave in 'feminine' ways that exclude their participation from physically demanding, competitive, contact sports in favour of those that are more 'graceful' and cognitive. Such attitudes become normalised and are reinforced by everyday conversations and interactions in sport, such as patronising comments about women 'not understanding the offside rule' or wolf whistling and unsolicited sexual comments when women go swimming. As we grow older, these attitudes are also present in other environments (right face) such as the workplace, which further cement their acceptance. However, we know that attitudes towards women in the Western world can be different from those in parts of Asia and Africa, so it is important to consider the needs and motivations of different 'types' of women when developing and managing sports in different communities (left face).

It is clear that changes in society, such as having to move to find work and the increase of technology-based leisure pursuits such as gaming, have led us to lead more individualised existences, which can negatively impact the way we engage with sport and reduce our awareness of the ways our lives are linked to others. We must be alert to the complexities of the lives of the people we are working with and trying to work with, as well as really understanding the places where they live. We must be critical thinkers, people who always question how things are done, being conscious of our personal biases and how the traditions of sport might please and favour us but work to the detriment of others.

FOOTBALL UNITES, RACISM DIVIDES: HELPING PEOPLE TO BELONG

Football Unites, Racism Divides (FURD) is a Sheffield, third-sector organisation that aims to tackle racism within football and wider society. Established in 1995, FURD is based in an electoral ward that is the third most populous of 28 in terms of Black Minority Ethnic (BME) residents in a city where 19.2 per cent of the population is BME, rising from 10.8 per cent in the previous census (Sheffield City Council, 2011). The organisation works to increase BME participation in football in terms of players, spectators and employees. As with many third-sector organisations, it has sought funding from places such as the local authority, Football Foundation and European Union. Using the sociological imagination to connect issues, FURD builds partnerships and creates networks, linking the local and private to the international and public. FURD's partners include professional sports clubs, the County Football Association, local schools, the local authority and Sheffield Hallam University.

At a practical level, FURD works with local football clubs, helping them implement anti-racist strategies and become more involved in the community. It delivers anti-racist education and youth work as well as coaching, organising tournaments and helping participants set up their own leagues, bringing together members of isolated communities, such as refuges and asylum seekers.

Its 'Belonging Together' activity groups, for instance, offer opportunities to play football, try different kinds of dance, access computers and take English classes to people who are referred by agencies or who simply turn up. Engaging with changes in society, it also carries out research, such as the Football and Connected Communities project, which examines things like the role of football in the lives of young people and the increasing cost of watching live football. FURD has hosted a Positive Futures (PF) project and takes Streetkick, a portable football game, to neighbourhoods to engage hard-to-reach young people – the kind of flexible delivery we mentioned earlier that brings sport to people rather than expecting people to go to sport. Demonstrating yet more flexibility, as well as football, the organisation uses music via its Soundkickers project and has recording and dance studios, a gym and IT facilities.

FURD, then, is about more than simply football coaching. Sport and non-sport activities are used as hooks in an attempt to bring together socially excluded individuals and groups to try and generate a sense of community – a sense of belonging. Some activities are delivered at their purpose-built venue, but there is also outreach, and FURD operates seven days a week, delivering at times that best fit with local people. Regular programmes, activities and events are delivered by responding to immediate need, such as redoubling of outreach and cohesion work at times of local or national racial tension. In doing this, they encourage volunteering so that participants can gain skills and then, hopefully, move into paid work, addressing the private trouble of low skills and unemployment experienced against the public backdrop of a global economic crisis. Volunteers also bring with them high levels of local knowledge, know people in the community and are often highly respected. The idea of 'community' is key to the organisation's work. Bauman (2001), though, talks about our nostalgia for community – of our continuing need to experience warmth and togetherness – something that can be difficult in our fast-paced society. Projects like FURD can help disparate isolated people and groups to find common ground through the activities it runs – to feel welcomed.

For this to happen, it is important that projects encourage interaction between the local white and BME communities, and we also need to listen to authors such as Spracklen, Long and Hylton (2015) who suggest that sport can reinforce difference, with many clubs, projects or organisations made up of like-minded people not seen as welcoming by those on the outside. However, there is evidence that sport creates a sense of belonging for some people, promoting social inclusion, the process by which people are able to participate fully economically, socially and culturally in society. Woodhouse and Conricode (2016) carried out research with FURD and talk of how football offers escapism to refugee and asylum seekers and can help to build relationships with other local people. Football then, because of its accessibility and familiarity, is something that offers those at the project common ground with others – the opportunity to feel part of something.

POSITIVE FUTURES: BUILDING SOCIAL CAPITAL

Launched in 2000, PF is a national sports-based social inclusion programme for people aged 10–19. Rather than aiming to merely 'divert' participants from crime by providing large doses of sport, PF attempts to address the many interconnected private issues participants have by equipping them with skills. Despite being a national programme, PF is locally designed, delivered and managed. Projects reject the hierarchical 'top-down' approach discussed earlier, in favour of a more organic 'bottom-up' one where members of staff consult local people to build lasting relationships, allowing them to deliver bespoke activities. Interestingly, PF has identified the importance of its staff having trust, empathy and respect – that is to say, drawing on their sociological imaginations – as the crucial factor in ensuring the development of sustainable, successful projects and not staff possession of sport skills.

PF is an example of targeted provision and works with those considered at risk of offending, aiming to reduce crime and drug and alcohol misuse, as well as preventing serious youth violence. Recognising that education is key to developing social capital, projects aim to steer participants into education, training or employment. PF, now run by Catch 22, has approximately 100 projects in total, utilising the arts, sport, physical activity, social enterprise and education. PF ended as a national programme in 2013, but handing control to local partners was always part of the plan, an attempt to move from centralised provision to projects that were locally responsive and funded in a sustained fashion.

PF draws heavily on Hellison's (2010) social responsibility model in which young people are seen not as a problem but as resources with strengths that can be developed. Projects influenced by this model provide significant, sustained, local contact with caring adults in what for many participants may be their only physically and psychologically safe environment. Whilst many traditional diversionary sport projects set targets and are only available for a short time, the number of participants in PF is purposefully low, and participation over a long period is encouraged to promote belonging and sustained development.

In terms of measuring success, personal development is mapped through the idea of a journey – of the distance travelled by participants. Typically, an agency refers a young person to the local project, or they self-refer, having spoken to a friend who attends. As well as having a positive impact on the young person's behaviour or improving their school attendance, for example, the improved sense of belonging created can have a positive impact on the local area by, among other things, reducing fear of crime. Participants gain qualifications, making them more employable or helping them back into education, and rather than a focus on the acquisition of sporting skills, the aim is to build 'soft skills', such as better sociability and communication, and to instil ambition. While we do not have the room to explore this in detail, it is key to note that PF employs a sophisticated monitoring and evaluation system, which allows for a personalised mapping of a person's journey and provides evidence that organisations can use for future funding bids and demonstrating that projects are value for money.

Its effectiveness is, in large part, down to this focus on the local, in terms of identifying need, staffing, recruiting volunteers and providing appropriate activities and venues. One worker talks of providing realistic aspirations and helping participants to achieve these and claims 'my background definitely helps: *I show them where I'm coming from and they're like "wow, I can do this too"*' (Woodhouse, 2005). This demonstrates the value of the sociological imagination, of being able to see life through the eyes of participants and to share with them the experience of what you need to do to succeed in wider society. This can be contrasted with staff brought in from other agencies, using more traditional delivery styles, as evidenced by a health workshop with one young person saying '*I asked the posh one if she'd ever taken drugs and she said she hadn't. How can she tell us about drugs when she knows jack shit?*' (Woodhouse, 2005).

In a similar way to FURD, those who work with PF are cultural intermediaries. Importantly, staff are seen by young people as different to adult authority figures, such as teachers or police officers, and are seen as providing guidance and support rather than asserting their power. They use their sociological imaginations to address issues that participants face and, in demonstrating that they know the area and are aware of the complex issues facing young people who live there, mutual respect and trust is built. Project workers have credibility. If this is not the case, and staff do not have the skills of a cultural intermediary, not only are they not able to help young people reach their potential, in fact, their approach can have a detrimental effect. As one Project Manager put it:

> They have got to have respect for the staff... but likewise the staff have got to have respect for the young people: We had a session on Tuesday [and] the member of staff had no respect for the kids and it was just chaos...very negative towards the kids, didn't want to be there and the kids pick up on it straight away...She has probably taken them back about three steps.
>
> (Woodhouse, 2005)

While projects often have core activities, these are adapted to respond to local issues, whether increased violence in a particular postcode area, a specific health issue or the arrival of drug dealers on an estate. Although initial funding from the Football Foundation meant many projects offered a diet solely or heavily focussed on football, what is delivered has developed projects using a range of activities to 'make a real difference to health, crime, employment and education in deprived communities' (DCMS, 1999, p. 8). Workers try to capture the enthusiasm of participants, and draw in new ones, by offering music, dance, art and nontraditional sports, such as parkour. Activities are delivered at local authority and private leisure venues, in parks, in schools, at professional sports clubs, theatres, dance studios and climbing centres; residential locations are also used. PF is an example of using local knowledge and skills to encourage long-term involvement and the progression of participants. Activities are delivered by credible staff, some of which started out as participants so are able to demonstrate to young people attending that *their* lives can change too.

THE MENTRO ALLAN/VENTURE OUT INITIATIVE: ENCOURAGING PEOPLE TO THINK (AND FEEL) DIFFERENTLY

Based in Wales between 2005 and 2010, The Mentro Allan programme used outdoor environments to engage a range of under-represented groups in physical activity, including the over-50s, single mothers, people with mental health problems, carers and BME communities. From the outset, groups were targeted as they demonstrated higher-than-average levels of inactivity (World Health Statistics, 2015) nationally, which in the case of the over-50s was over twice as high (48 per cent) as those between 16 and 21 (21 per cent). However, perhaps more worrying is that many of the groups listed, particularly those from BME backgrounds, were much more likely to experience other social problems such as crime, ill health (both physical and mental), substance abuse and suicide (ONS, 2012). As such, the Mentro Allan programme was funded to help address some of these issues and was supported in doing so by a range of local and national partners, including Sport Wales, Countryside Council for Wales, National Public Health Service, Wales Council for Voluntary Action and the Welsh Local Government Association.

The uniqueness of Mentro Allan's approach to community sport management was evidenced in both its relationship with its participants and its overall philosophy towards 'sport'. For example, write Ledwith and Springett (2010, p. 16), this programme puts participants at the heart of the issue in ways that 'give more local people voice and the confidence to take autonomous control of their lives'. Like those case studies we have already identified, they encourage facilitators and participants to see their work as going beyond the physiological benefits of physical activity to consider its social (i.e., friendships), cultural (i.e., closer families, less racial discrimination), spiritual (i.e., enhanced feelings of confidence and self-worth) and political (i.e., lower levels of crime/obesity) contributions. The sociological imagination was, therefore, a key part of this process.

This approach was adopted at every stage of the project, from the design and implementation of individual activities to the analysis of its success. In the first instance, the decision was made to avoid those activities that were traditionally classed as 'sport', as many of the target groups had turned their backs on more traditional, organised forms of sport. Instead, a range of informal, outdoor activities such as walking and woodland activities, treasure hunts, cycling, rock climbing and orienteering were developed to include a wider range of people, many of which were conveniently located within Wales' surrounding natural landscapes. These activities, often called 'lifestyle sports' or 'alternative physical activities', have a range of benefits when it comes to engaging groups who have struggled to 'fit in' with mainstream sport and society (see Cherrington and Gregory, 2017). They also work well with the approach to community sport development that we have talked about throughout this chapter. For instance, they are much more informal, containing few of the rules and limitations that are placed upon participants in traditional sporting environments. This may work well when trying to engage under-18s or over-50s, many of whom, because of the way they are treated elsewhere, are reluctant to be told what to do. They can be risky, often involving a battle against the 'elements', which can be great when you are trying to empower somebody, such as a young, single mother, to try something new and discover her personal potential. Finally, they can relieve much of the psychological stress that comes with living in a city, which has obvious potential regarding the treatment of certain mental illnesses. In fact, research has shown that 'green exercise' can reduce feelings of anxiety and depression by as much as 71 per cent (Mind, 2015).

Such thoughts were shared by many of the beneficiaries who took part in the Mentro Allan project. Individuals talked about the sensory pleasures of the natural environments, such as the smell of flowers and the sound of running water, and often expressed a preference for natural rather than man[sic]-made environments: *'I like seeing the world. I want to see it [world] as nature intended it, not as people in the world muck it up'* (Allen-Collinson and Leledaki, 2015, p. 463). This was particularly important for participants with physical disabilities, such as those with limited vision. Equally, participants also commented on the 'freedom' available in the outdoors and the therapeutic effect of being away from technology such as computers and televisions: *'Well it's where we're all one isn't it? Regardless of the fact that we've got all this technology … but we're still part of nature, aren't we?'* (Allen-Collinson and Leledaki, 2015, p. 463). This suggests that physical activity cannot be promoted as an end in itself and must be offered alongside wider social benefits such as those outlined before.

However, the activities chosen were not the only reason why the Mentro Allan initiative was so successful. The methods of promoting each project and the attitudes, behaviour and philosophy of staff were also significant. Staff members were patient in their approach to the recruitment of beneficiaries – they took the time to know certain communities, and individuals within those communities, so that they could understand the best ways to motivate people. As one staff member noted,

> I could go there and speak to the kids themselves, just mingle with them and play pool with them etc. and then try to get them to talk to you, rather than go as an appearance of an official.

An important element of this approach was the development of mutual respect between the participants and the project workers in that both parties understood that they had something to learn from one another, which is an important element of the sociological imagination. This was especially significant when we consider the backgrounds of many of Mentro Allan's target groups who may not have had positive experiences with institutional and familial authority figures such as teachers, police officers and parents. Where barriers were in place that prevented beneficiaries from attending certain activities, every effort was made by the staff to ensure that those barriers were overcome. For instance, those with mental health conditions were encouraged to attend 'mixed sessions' to avoid exposing their condition, car shares were organised for those who struggled with transport and, where possible, interpreters were arranged for those individuals for whom English was not their first language.

Doing things in this way is not easy, and the methods adopted by Mentro Allan presented numerous challenges at every stage of the community-management process. For example, the economic climate of the time meant care workers were being asked to work longer hours for less money, which made it difficult for them to build positive relationships. The lack of available time and poor wages also made care workers reluctant to undertake the relevant training and take many of the 'risks' often associated with outdoor activity. Young people were often reluctant to wear appropriate outdoor clothing for fear of appearing 'unfashionable', BME women refused to travel alone due to cultural values regarding gender and individuals on welfare benefits, particularly those with a mental health conditions, were anxious about engaging in public physical activity for fear of being accused of benefit 'scrounging' (i.e., you are on a mountain bike; why are you claiming benefits?). However, by engaging with their sociological imaginations, planners were able to come up with a range of simple, yet effective, solutions to these problems, including staff training, the use of 'doorstep' locations and adopting a 'graduated approach' to ensure that people developed their confidence and fitness over time.

CONCLUSION

One of the questions we're often asked by first-year students is 'what's the point of thinking sociologically?' Often, when we dig a little deeper, we realise that what students are really asking is 'what's in it for me?' Many students would much rather focus on the more practical or fact-based elements of their course, as they see these aspects as being more beneficial to their skills development and feel that thinking sociologically is something they can do later in their degree. We do not blame students for asking the question. Trying to get someone to understand how privileged they are – and you really are privileged – will cause you discomfort. Thinking sociologically is not easy; some people will see you as awkward, and the solutions you come up with will rarely offer quick fixes. A scientist can establish pretty quickly how to improve someone's performance on the running track, but we are not going to find a solution to social exclusion overnight. There are few millionaire sociologists, but you are not going to become full-time sociologists; you're going to use your sociological imagination in whatever your role is.

When you use your sociological imagination, you consider your life and the lives of others in social context and see how all of our lives are connected, which should encourage you to consider the consequences of your own actions. In addition, thinking sociologically about sport will undoubtedly make you more employable. As we highlighted earlier, society, and with it, the sport industry, is becoming increasingly complex. Sport and leisure providers have to cater for a much larger variety of interests and tastes, and being able to understand these nuances and deliver meaningful sporting experiences is a valuable employability skill. You will be able to communicate with people from a range of different backgrounds, will develop the emotional intelligence to understand and empathise with the experiences of people very different from yourself and, most importantly, will be able to facilitate change in a way that is beneficial to those you are trying to empower. Ultimately, this will impact your sense self as you become more at home with difference and more confident about your ability to continue developing.

In recent years, those responsible for sport and physical activity provision in the UK have begun to appreciate the social value of sport, as well as the importance of delivering such activities in an inclusive and accessible environment. The most significant change happened at the national level where, in 2016, the government changed sport funding so that it is no longer was merely about how many people take part but rather how sport can have a meaningful and measurable impact on improving people's lives. As part of this, they have redirected funding towards those groups, such as women, or BME communities, that have traditionally had lower participation rates. Perhaps more significantly for you, however, is that within this strategy document, much emphasis is placed on the importance of developing a new generation of sport-industry workers who have the appropriate skills to implement and deliver this philosophy. As such, it is not difficult to see why those with an understanding of social inequalities and how to address these through sport can do well in this new political climate.

Finally, and perhaps most importantly, you will be able to make one of the most difficult admissions that anyone who is deeply passionate about sport (as a supporter or participant) will ever have to make. You will be able to admit that sport is flawed, and with any luck, you will think twice before you prescribe sport as a solution to societal problems. Indeed, as we hope to have shown throughout this chapter, there are instances where, under the right circumstances, sport can be an extremely positive way to connect people from different backgrounds or to stimulate a range of senses that may be difficult to connect with in other contexts. However, for every success story, there is another example of how sport was adopted when other activities, such as writing, music production or gardening, may have been more appropriate. Hopefully, having engaged with this chapter, this is something that you will now have the humility to consider.

REVIEW QUESTIONS

- Did one of your schoolmates dread PE? Could you now use your sociological imagination to understand why they hated it? Perhaps they were embarrassed because they were overweight or couldn't afford the 'right' kit.
- Think of a time when you felt a teammate wasn't trying hard enough. Could you now use your sociological imagination to realise that their performance may have been affected by problems at home? Perhaps a parent had lost their job.
- In both of these examples, can you see the public issues? Obesity and pressure to buy brands because of the commercialisation of sport is the issue in the first example and the economic crisis leading to job losses is the issue in the second.
- Could you turn your understanding into actions to improve their lives? If so, how would you go about doing this?

FURTHER READING

Hylton, K. (2013). *Sport development: Policy, process and practice* (3rd ed.). London: Routledge.
Spracklen, K. (2014). *Exploring sports and society: A critical introduction for students.* London: Palgrave.

REFERENCES

Allen-Collinson, J., & Leledaki, A. (2015). Sensing the outdoors: A visual and haptic phenomenology of outdoor exercise embodiment. *Leisure Studies, 34*(4), 457–470.
Baldry, H. (1976). *Leisure and the community: Conference proceedings.* Birmingham University, December 10–11, for the LSA.
Batty, D. (2001). *Social exclusion: The issue explained.* Retrieved from www.theguardian.com/society/2002/jan/15/socialexclusion1.
Bauman, Z. (2001). *Community: Seeking safety in an insecure world,* Cambridge: Polity.
Cherrington, J., & Gregory, M. (2017). Where nature and culture coalesce: The social, cultural and political impact of outdoor recreation in Sheffield. In D. Turner & S. Carnicelli (Eds.), *Lifestyle sport and public policy* (pp. 100–117). London: Routledge.

Coakley, J. (2002). Using sports to control deviance and violence among youths: Let's be critical and cautious. In M. Gatz, M. Messner, & S. Ball-Rokeach (Eds.), *Paradoxes of youth and sport* (pp. 13–30). New York: SUNY Press.

Collins, M. (2014). *Sport and social exclusion.* London: Routledge.

Crabbe, T., Bailey, G., Blackshaw, T., Brown, A., Choak, C., Gidley, B., … Woodhouse, D. (2005). *Getting to know you: First interim national positive futures case study research report.* London: Home Office.

Crabbe, T., Bailey, G., Blackshaw, T., Brown, A., Choak, C., Gidley, B., … Woodhouse, D. (2006). *Knowing the score. Positive futures case study research: Final report for the Home Office.* London: Home Office.

Department of Transport, Local Government and the Regions. (2001). *Strong leadership – Quality public services.* London: HMSO.

Gramsci, A. (1971). In Q. Hoare & G. Nowell Smith (Ed. & Trans.), *Selections form the prison notebook.* London: Lawrence and Wishart.

Haywood, L., & Kew, F. (1989). *Community recreation: New wine in old bottles.* In P. Bramham, I. Henry, H. Mommaas, & H. van der Poel, (Eds.), *Leisure and urban processes. Critical studies of leisure policy in western European cities175–191.* London: Routledge.

Hellison, D. (2010). *Teaching responsibility through physical activity.* Leeds: Human Kinetics.

Ledwith, M. (2005). *Community development: A critical approach.* Bristol: The Policy Press.

Ledwith, M., & Springett, J. (2010). *Participatory practice. Community-based action for transformative change.* Bristol: The Policy Press.

McEwan, I. (2001). *Only love and then oblivion. Love was all they had to set against their murderers.* Retrieved from www.theguardian.com/world/2001/sep/15/september11.politicsphilosophyandsociety2.

Mills, C. W. (1999). *The sociological imagination.* Oxford: Oxford University Press.

Mind. (2013). *Ecotherapy.* London: Mind.

ONS. (2012). *Mental health of children, adolescents and adults.* London: Office for National Statistics.

Putnam, R. D. (2001). *Bowling alone: The collapse and revival of American community.* New York: Simon and Schuster.

Sennett, R. (2004). *Respect: The formation of character in a world of inequality.* London, Penguin.

Sheffield City Council. (2011). *2011 Census for Sheffield.* Retrieved from www.sheffield.gov.uk/home/your-city-council/census-2011.

Sport England. (2016). *Active lives survey 2015–2016: Year one report.* Retrieved from www.sportengland.org/media/11498/active-lives-survey-yr-1-report.pdf.

Spracklen, K., Long, J., & Hylton, K. (2015). Leisure opportunities and new migrant communities: Challenging the contribution of sport. *Leisure Studies, 34,* 114–129.

Torkildsen, G. (2010). *Leisure & recreation management.* London: Routledge.

Woodhouse, D. (2005). Unpublished field notes. Retrieved from www.theguardian.com/society/2002/jan/15/socialexclusion1.

Woodhouse, D., & Conricode, D. (2016). In-ger-land, In-ger-land, In-ger-land! Exploring the impact of soccer on the sense of belonging of those seeking asylum in the UK. *International Review for the Sociology of Sport,* March.

World Health Statistics. (2015). *Global health indicators.* Copenhagen: World Health Organisation.

PART II

Contemporary issues in community sport and physical activity

CHAPTER 4

Physical activity interventions impacting health in the community

David Broom and Stuart Flint

SUMMARY

This chapter will introduce you to and define physical activity and sedentary behaviour. It will highlight the low levels of the population meeting the recommendations of physical activity in the UK. Thus, interventions are needed to increase physical activity levels. Using a lifespan approach, we will introduce you to key interventions. Case studies will highlight the key components of these interventions as well as what community sports managers need to consider when developing their own approaches through the highlighting of good practice.

AIMS

By engaging with this chapter, you will be able to

- Define physical activity and sedentary behaviour,
- Highlight the physical activity recommendations and the percentage of children and young people, adults and older adults meeting those recommendations,
- Identify good practice from previous physical activity interventions and
- Provide key considerations for community sports managers when developing physical activity initiatives.

INTRODUCTION

Physical Activity is defined as 'any bodily movement produced by skeletal muscles that results in energy expenditure' (Caspersen et al. 1985). It is a broad term that describes bodily movement, posture and balance all requiring energy. It includes different types of sports, physical education and dance activities, as well as indoor and outdoor play and work-related activity. It also includes outdoor and adventurous activities, active travel (e.g., walking, cycling, rollerblading and scooting) and routine, habitual activities such as using the stairs, doing housework and gardening. Exercise was initially defined by Caspersen et al. (1985) as 'a subset of physical activity that is planned, structured, and repetitive and has as a final or an intermediate objective the improvement or mainte- nance of physical fitness'. A new definition is offered by Winter and Fowler (2009) as 'a potential disruption to homeostasis by muscle activity that is either exclusively, or in combination, concentric, eccentric or isometric' (p. 447). This definition applies to exer- cise and physical activity that encompasses elite-standard competitive sport, activities of daily living and clinical applications in rehabilitation and public health.

On the opposite end of the activity continuum is sedentary behaviour, which is de- fined as 'any waking behaviour characterized by an energy expenditure ≤1.5 metabolic equivalents while in a sitting, reclining or lying posture' (Tremblay et al. 2017). Seden- tary behaviour is not the same as being 'inactive', which is an insufficient physical activ- ity level to meet present physical activity recommendations. In the UK, according to the Chief Medical Officers (2011), adults (aged 19–64 years) should aim to be active daily. Over a week, activity should add up to at least 150 minutes of moderate-intensity activ- ity in bouts of 10 minutes or more. One way to approach this is to do 30 minutes at least five days a week. Alternatively, comparable benefits can be achieved through 75 minutes of vigorous-intensity activity spread across the week or a combination of moderate and vigorous-intensity activity. In addition, adults should also undertake physical activity to improve muscle strength at least two days a week as well as minimise the amount of time spent being sedentary such as sitting for extended periods.

In 1994, the epidemiologist Jeremy Morris described physical activity as the "best buy" in public health (Morris 1994) because undertaking moderate-intensity physi- cal activity has numerous health benefits. This includes the prevention and treatment of non-communicable diseases (i.e., chronic diseases that cannot be passed from per- son to person) including cardiovascular disease, obesity, Type 2 diabetes and some cancers and can reduce the risk of premature death, improving mental health and quality of life (Lancet Physical Activity Series 2016). Despite numerous organisa- tions promoting the health benefits of physical activity and encouraging more people to be active, over the last 60 years, there has been a large shift towards less physically demanding work, which has been accompanied by an increasing use of mechanised transportation, a greater prevalence of labour-saving technology in the home and fewer people participating in active hobbies. Using historical data on time spent on occupational and domestic work, travel and leisure activities, Ng and Popkin (2012) estimated that between 1961 and 2005, physical activity levels dropped by around 20 per cent in the UK. The greatest reduction in physical activity was observed in occu- pational and domestic activity, and although voluntary active leisure or recreational activities have increased slightly, this was insufficient to account for the shortfall. Ng and Popkin (2012) also predict that by 2030, time spent in sedentary behaviour will exceed 50 hours per week.

The Health Survey for England reports 67 per cent of adult men and 55 per cent of adult women met the Chief Medical Officers (2011) physical activity recommendations in 2012 (Joint Health Surveys Unit 2013). However, due to the introduction of these new recommendations, there are no long-term trends. Health Survey for England (2008) data has been reanalysed to measure physical activity against the 2011 recommendations, which shows that there was no overall change between 2008 and 2012. However, these statistics should be interpreted with caution since they measured physical activity using self-report, which is prone to over reporting, as this is a subjective measure. It should be noted that an objective measure of physical activity was used in a subsample of adults who wore an accelerometer for a week in the Health Survey for England in 2008 (Health and Social Care Information Centre 2009). Only 6 per cent of adult men and 4 per cent of adult women met the Department of Health (2004) recommendations, which is alarming, as this demonstrates that a large proportion of the population is not achieving the recommended levels of physical activity to benefit health.

In England, a higher proportion of boys (21 per cent) than girls (16 per cent) reported meeting recommendations aged between 5 and 15 years in 2012 (Joint Health Surveys Unit 2013). In boys, the most activity was reported between the ages of 8 and 10 years (26 per cent), whilst for girls, most activity was reported in 5–7 years (23 per cent). In both boys and girls in England, the proportion of children aged 5–15 years meeting recommendations fell between 2008 and 2012. The largest declines were aged 13–15 years for both sexes. Globally, physical activity levels decline with age, and men are more active than women in 137 of the 146 countries for which data are available (Sallis et al. 2016). There is a large decrease in activity, particularly in sport participation once young people leave school (Telama et al. 2005). Due to the prevalence of health inequalities associated with physical inactivity and increasing sedentary behaviour, there is a clear need to develop effective interventions that will lead to population level increases in physical activity.

A physical activity intervention encourages participants to make their own choices about how to increase their physical activity (Foster et al. 2005). Laboratory-based research and experiments reporting increased physical activity are largely ineffective in real-world settings. The concern of many health and physical activity promotion specialists is which interventions are effective for getting people to change their behaviour in the community. Thousands of physical activity interventions exist, but the remainder of the chapter will focus on a case study approach to introduce the reader to some that have been successfully implemented in the community. These successful approaches can be considered by sport-development coaches when designing and implementing new strategies to engage people across the life course in physical activity.

Case study: young people – Sheffield Let's Change4Life

In November 2008, Sheffield City Council and NHS Sheffield were awarded £5 million from the Department of Health's obesity unit, which they match funded to develop the Sheffield Let's Change4Life programme. The £9.6 million programme, which commenced in April 2009, aimed to prevent obesity in children, young people and families by modifying attitudes and culture in Sheffield by delivering a range of universal and targeted interventions on all levels and, thus, a Whole Systems Approach: individual, families, children's centres, schools and communities within the city (See Figure 4.1).

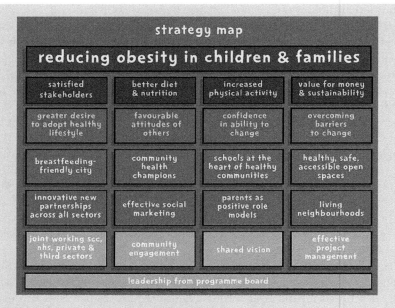

FIGURE 4.1 Sheffield Let's Change4Life strategy map
Source: From Copeland et al. (2011)

Specifically, Sheffield Let's Change4Life programme aimed to increase support for breastfeeding across communities, public places and workplaces; support parents to be positive role models; and support schools to empower children and families to live healthier lives. It was also essential to remove barriers to healthy living within communities, create well-being promoting environments as well as increasing opportunities for children and families to enjoy safe, active recreation in parks and green spaces. Finally, they developed effective marketing campaigns using the Change for Life brand (see Figure 4.2) to achieve positive behaviour change as well as establish networks of local volunteers to support their local community. The programme benefitted from using the Theory of Planned Behaviour (Ajzen 1991), which states that attitude towards behaviour, subjective norms and perceived behavioural control, together, shape an individual's behavioural intentions and behaviours. This programme has been recognised as a model of good practice across the region and nationally.

Sheffield Let's Change4Life programme has provided a platform in Sheffield for tackling obesity that, over time, the effectiveness and buy-in of the city's communities, organisations and stakeholders can be assessed against. The aim of Sheffield Let's Change4Life programme was to reduce childhood obesity in Sheffield by 2012. The programme did report a slight decrease in childhood obesity prevalence for those aged 4–5 years and 10–11 years (Copeland et al. 2011); specifically, halting the rise in the prevalence of obesity and observing a reduction in childhood and longer-term adult obesity. Importantly, the families reported that participating in the programme was enjoyable and easy to participate in, which is likely to lead to sustained engagement with the programme.

FIGURE 4.2 Sheffield Let's Change4Life marketing materials
Source: From Copeland et al. (2011)

The programme had an impact on many people across the city, engaging a diverse community and partnership approaches. It was reported that the programme led to an increase in children walking to school from 56 per cent to 57 per cent and cycling from 16 per cent to 24 per cent, with a drop in children driven to school between 2008 and 2011 (from 22.9 per cent to 20.7 per cent). The largest reduction in sedentary travel was in the use of school buses, which reduced by 5.7 per cent, compared with 1.6 per cent for car use. This is likely to have contributed to the increased physical fitness and increased steps per day (typically 12,000–15,000 steps) of children that was observed. Copeland et al. (2011) also reported that there was an improvement in attitudes towards physical activity in children accessing targeted, physical activity, growing clubs and those receiving a bike. The impacts on children as part of the programme were influenced by the role of parents who engaged and supported the children, acting as positive role models. Healthcare professionals attending training and awareness programmes reported improved confidence and intention to influence the management of obesity – a group that is clearly needed for the Sheffield Let's Change4Life programme to be effective. In schools, the stay-on-site policies and modifications to the dining environment led to several beneficial changes; more children dined in school, social interaction was enhanced and children's behaviour improved. These improvements were attributed to promoting effective communication between kitchen staff and children.

The programme initiatives led to improvements in breastfeeding attitudes and behaviours. Mothers who received peer support reported favourable attitudes towards breastfeeding and were more confident of breastfeeding in public; the breastfeeding initiation rates and breastfeeding prevalence six to eight weeks post-birth increased between 2008 and 2010 (from 76.43 per cent to 79.2 per cent and from 44 per cent to 54.7 per cent, respectively). There was also an increase in free school meal uptake between 2009 and 2011. An important element of this programme was the buy-in from stakeholders across the city and ensuring that stakeholders remained satisfied and retained the programme's vision. It was reported that 93 per cent of the programmes strand positively rated their engagement in the programme, and 97 per cent of those attending the Sheffield Let's Change4Life conference reported a belief that the programme would have a beneficial impact on reducing obesity in line with the targets and priorities of the city.

The Sheffield Let's Change4Life programme developed a Whole Systems Approach to childhood obesity that brought together a range of partners across the city to contribute to eight domains key to children's health. The longer-term effectiveness of the programme will continue to be realised as the prevalence of childhood obesity is monitored over time and data is collected on engagement in healthy behaviours that foster physical activity, healthy food and drink choices and social and mental well-being.

Implications for community sports mangers

What community sport managers should consider from this case study is that there are key barriers that need to be addressed in physical activity-related programmes including enjoyment, cost and access. It is also evident that marketing materials from an already-established heath campaign were effective and contributed to the local buy-in of a community group.

Case study: adults – Football Fans in Training

In response to the UK obesity epidemic, the Football Fans in Training (FFIT) project was developed as an innovative weight loss intervention aimed at males attending Scottish Premiership clubs. The FFIT project was a collaboration between The Scottish Premier League Trust; Scottish Premiership football clubs; and academics from the University of Glasgow, Leeds Beckett University, University of Strathclyde, University of Edinburgh, University of Aberdeen, University of Dundee and the Medical Research Council. The FFIT project used scientific evidence related to weight loss, physical activity and diet that is delivered to attendees at their favourite club by community coaches, with over 3,000 men participating in the programme by 2013 (FFIT 2013, see Figure 4.3). The initial pilot of the FFIT project was delivered during the 2010/2011 season and was funded by the Scottish Government's Chief Scientist Office and the Scottish Premier League Trust.

Delivery of the project at each Scottish Premier League club between 2010 and 2013 was funded by the Scottish Government and the Football Pools, covering the cost of the community club coaches' training, materials, equipment and staff time. In 2011, the FFIT project also received funding from the National Institute for Health Research Public Health Research programme to evaluate a Randomised Controlled Trial (RCT) of the project. In an RCT, the people participating in the trial are randomly allocated to either the intervention group or to a standard treatment group (or placebo treatment) as the control. The intervention was gender-specific, meaning that the programme was developed incorporating the values of masculinity; content was designed to be attractive to men, and camaraderie, team bonding and banter was encouraged to facilitate discussion of sensitive topics (Wyke et al. 2015).

The dietary component of the programme aimed to deliver a 600-kcal deficit by adopting nutrient-based foods, reduced portion sizes in particular energy-dense food and reduced snack and sugary and alcoholic drinks. The physical activity element had two components; a pedometer-based walking programme and pitch-side physical activity sessions. Men were encouraged to set daily walking goals, recording their weekly progress in step-count diaries. As the programme progressed, the participants were encouraged to engage in more vigorous physical activity to supplement the walking. FITT was based on 37 behaviour-change taxonomy strategies, with particular use of self-monitoring, implementation intentions, goal setting and review. Social support and relapse prevention was built into the programme (Wyke et al. 2015).

The RCT attracted 747 men aged 35–65 years with a body mass index (BMI) of ≥ 28 kg/m^2 (90 per cent with a BMI ≥ 30 kg/m^2) who were classed as high risk of ill health such as Type 2 diabetes, hypertension and cardiovascular disease (Hunt et al. 2014a). FFIT led to clinically significant weight loss, with Hunt et al. (2014b) reporting a significant difference between the control and intervention group, where the intervention group lost on average 4.94 kg, which was 4.36 per cent more than the control group. It was also reported that the intervention group achieved significantly greater reductions of objectively measured waist circumference, percentage body fat and systolic and diastolic blood pressure than the control group. They also improved self-reported physical activity, diet and indicators of well-being and physical aspects of quality of life compared to the control group.

Interviews with the coaches offered support for the participants' perceptions, where coaches reported that use of pedometers; self-monitoring; and novel, tangible and visible approaches to demonstrate weight loss (e.g., use of sandbags and replica lumps of fat to represent weight lost) was key to the success of the programme. Coaches also reported that they were concerned about the perceived responsibility of leading a men's health improvement programme, difficulty of fitting FITT into their current coaching schedule and the need to diversify approaches to goal setting. They also felt that greater training for how to respond to exercise-related medical emergencies was warranted. Despite these concerns, the beneficial impact of FITT relative to the cost delivery led to the conclusion that FITT represents a cost-effective weight loss intervention for overweight males (Wyke et al. 2015).

The FITT project has been immensely successful not only in terms of the project that was delivered in Scotland, but also in the emergence and sustainability of FITT projects across the UK. Indeed, the creative methods used to measure weight loss are used in other FITT and weight-management programmes. Thus, the project has led to development of other initiatives aimed at improving health and well-being of sports fans using elite sport clubs as the draw for fans, addressing drop-out rates that are consistently high in weight management intervention programmes/services.

FIGURE 4.3 Football Fans in Training
Source: From FFIT (2013)

Implications for community sports mangers

What community sport managers can consider is the importance of the environment created, as in this case study, the sport setting was a huge draw for fans. Community sport managers should also consider the benefits of developing a team spirit, which, in the case study, was developed early in the intervention and where the group commonality of attendees (i.e., similar-aged males attending for weight loss) was evident. This impacted their engagement in the project and, thus, can be beneficial to include in new approaches by community sports managers.

Case study: older adults – walking sports

Walking sport teams are being established across the UK to get older and less physically able individuals together to enjoy competitive team sport at a slower pace without the high impact, risk of injury or strenuous level of activity that standard versions of the same games require. Most of the sports have the same rules as the standard versions, except you walk to get to the ball, position or next base instead of running. This means that one foot must be on the ground at all times with a 'fine' or 'sin bin' for participants who run instead of walk. The great thing about this type of sport is that it's open to all, so women and men can compete alongside each other and less physically abled individuals can participate. The manner in which these sports are played allows participants to maintain an active lifestyle and promotes cardiovascular fitness whilst producing less stress on the body with the added benefit of being in a social setting.

Walking football was arguably the first walking sport, devised in 2011 by Chesterfield Football Club (FC) Community Trust. It can be played both indoors and outdoors, and though based on association football, if a player runs, they concede a free kick. This restriction, together with a ban on slide tackles, is aimed at avoiding injuries and facilitating the playing of the sport by those who are physically disadvantaged. The game was originally played without goalkeepers (though goalkeepers now play in some variations), and, crucially, the ball must never be kicked above hip height. Different footballs are used in the indoor and the outdoor variations of the sport. When played indoors, a size-4 futsal ball is used, whilst outdoor games use a traditional size 5. The size of the pitch can vary to suit different locations but should be between 20 and 40 yards in length and between 15 and 30 yards in width.

Arnold et al. (2015) examined anthropometrical and fitness changes following a 12-week walking football programme in adults 50 years and older. Ten male participants (mean age 66 years), with a range of health conditions, completed a 12-week walking football programme consisting of a single two-hour training session each week. Walking football significantly reduced body fat mass and percentage body fat measured before and after the intervention. There was a significant increase in time to volitional exhaustion during an incremental exercise test without any change in peak blood lactate. There was also an effect seen for a reduction in whole body mass, increase in lean body mass and a reduction in BMI, although these changes were not significant. This study highlights that walking football can be an effective public health intervention.

Despite evidence that walking football improves health, actual evidence of participation is limited. The sport came to wider public attention in July 2014, when Barclays Bank aired a television advertisement featuring walking football to promote their services. In 2016, there were 800 walking football clubs registered in the UK, twice the number that existed in 2015. Due to the surge in popularity, the Football Association issued standardised rules in 2017.

Walking netball is another sport that has evolved from a growing demand for walking sports. Women and men play the game for the fun and camaraderie the social session brings, as much as for the health benefits. It can give those who feel isolated an outlet, provide an activity for those who don't deem themselves fit enough to run anymore and can attract those who have retired from playing the standardised game. Rules have been adapted to ensure that the game is played appropriately, and England Netball has recommended that a player must have at least part of one foot in contact with the court at all times. During the game, an extra step maybe taken once a player has received the ball, which reduces the impact on landing. It also improves the momentum of the game, so a player may receive the ball with one foot grounded and then take two steps while in possession of the ball before it must be thrown or shot. An extra second has been allowed to increase the decision-making time whilst in possession of the ball, which encourages improved ball placements so a player may throw the ball within four seconds of receiving the ball.

Whilst launching walking netball was not originally in England Netball's plans, research undertaken between July and October 2015 highlighted that there was enough demand for the game. The game was launched nationally in 2016 and is going to be a key part of England Netball's strategy in the future. Other walking sports have been implemented including basketball and rounders, but there is limited evidence on their impact.

Implications for community sport mangers

What community sport managers can learn is that regardless of the walking sport played, it's important to deliver a fun and flexible session. Despite the limited evidence to date on the benefits of walking basketball and other sports, community sport managers should have confidence that these activities can be beneficial in improving physical activity levels of older people in their communities. Walking sports should be a prominent feature of any local authority's plans to increase population levels of physical activity, particularly for older adults. Adhering to rule adaptations should depend on the demands of the players so that it is the taking part that counts.

Case study: community lifespan approach – Sheffield Move More

Move More is a community lifestyle strategy based in Sheffield that is delivered across the city. Move More was developed after the establishment of the National Centre for Sport and Exercise Medicine (an Olympic Legacy programme) in Sheffield, which aims to create a culture of physical activity that leads to an improvement in the population's health, well-being and quality of life. The five-year Move More Plan provides a rationale for increasing opportunities and stimulating demand for physical activity across a number of sectors: planning, transport, health, sport, education and workplaces (Copeland 2015). Within the plan are six priority areas for action: (1) empowered communities, (2) active environments, (3) active people and families, (4) physical activity as medicine, (5) active schools and active pupils and (6) active workplaces and an active workforce (Copeland 2015, see Figure 4.4). To achieve the citywide project aims, Move More is comprised of the city's major partners including the voluntary sector, NHS Sheffield, Sheffield City Council, Sheffield Hallam University, University of Sheffield, Sheffield Chamber of Commerce and Sheffield International Venues.

The Move More Sheffield website (www.movemoresheffield.com/) hosts an array of content including information about the project, details of physical activity opportunities

FIGURE 4.4 Move More plan
Source: From Copeland (2015, p. 8)

within the community and current initiatives. For instance, in 2016, Move More developed a range of workplace and school interventions focussed on increasing physical activity. Overall, over 50,000 people in the city are engaged in physical activity using the Move More App, 5,000 of whom were previously inactive. Postcodes of the app users have informed the areas of the city where people are more active, which is being used to direct future efforts to increase participation.

The Move More Workplace Challenge is a web-based activity competition for organisations and their employees. The challenge is based on data retrieved using the Move More App, pedometers and other devices that record movement in and around the workplace. Data for each organisation is displayed on a website where organisations can view their participation, compare their efforts to other organisations on the Move More League table and receive participation medals. In July 2016, Move More ran a 'Go for Gold' Olympics-themed challenge with 374 teams from 23 workplaces, comprised of 3,000 participants across Sheffield. Move More reported that the challenge resulted in 4.4 million minutes of activity.

A school-based intervention was the Move More Schoolyard Challenge, which was piloted in 2016. The challenge aimed to motivate primary school children to be more active at lunch and playtime and, where possible, during elements of the curriculum. Using wristbands worn by pupils and timing gates, children's activity across the schoolyard was recorded. In total, amongst six primary schools, children have made over 100,000 journeys, and within a two-week period, children have travelled 2,500 miles. The project has recorded data from 1,941 children, reporting that some of the

FIGURE 4.5 The Move More Sheffield Schoolyard Challenge
Source: From Move More Sheffield (2016)

least active children were motivated by Move More, with schools creatively devising curricular activities to engage children in physical activity (see Figure 4.5; Move More Sheffield 2016).

The Move More month takes place every July. A key element of the Move More month in 2016 was the development of a competition between the two professional football clubs in the city: Sheffield Wednesday FC and Sheffield United FC. The 'Steel City' (as Sheffield is known) Derby allowed fans to identify their allegiance on the app, where overall scores for both clubs could be viewed. In total, 689 fans participated, with 1.2 million minutes of activity recorded. The competitiveness between the two football clubs was the key motive to participants' activity, where an individual's activity contributed to their team's score. Thus, team identity and desire to support their team encouraged physical activity and suggests that identity may be an important driver that can be considered in future interventions where individuals can contribute to a team or organisation's participation. Indeed, this supports the aforementioned FITT project, where participants' identity with their football club was a crucial motivation and adherence factor that saw lower dropout than commonly reported dropout from weight management programmes. Figure 4.6 shows participation in the Move More Steel City Derby, workplace and school challenges.

Whilst Move More is still in its infancy, the impact that the project has had across the city leading to increased physical activity is clearly evident, and the longer-term impact on physical activity and associated health risks such as cardiovascular disease and obesity needs evaluation over time. The Move More model can inform future citywide efforts to increase physical activity or engagement in other health-related behaviours.

FIGURE 4.6 Move More participation

Source: From Move More Sheffield (2016)

Implications for community sports mangers

Community sport managers should be aware that a successful citywide initiative can lead to increased physical activity in children and adults through education, workplace and sport settings and organisations. In addition, the success of the Move More campaign was underpinned by media engagement with appearances on BBC Breakfast, BBC Radio Sheffield, an array of local newspapers and social media sites including Facebook and Twitter. Thus, community sports managers should not overlook the importance of engaging with the media and social media outlets.

INTERVENTIONS IN THE DIGITAL AGE

The Couch to 5K app is a nine-week running programme for beginners to running. It was developed by a novice runner, Josh Clark, who wanted to help his 50-something mum get off the couch and start running as well. Over the nine-week duration, the app guides users through a mix of running and walking three days per week. This progresses until the participant can comfortably run continuously for 30 minutes or complete a 5-km distance. You can download the app as well as podcasts at www.nhs.uk/Livewell/c25k/Pages/couch-to-5k.aspx. It continues to be promoted through NHS Choices, and the app has been downloaded thousands of times, but to the authors' knowledge, there has been no official evaluation or published research to show whether it is effective. Pickering and Colleagues (2016) at Leeds Beckett University are currently determining the feasibility of the app. Qualitative data gathered so far from over 900 Couch to 5K users (aged 18 years or over) indicates that those who use the app are surprised by the level of physical activity they are capable of achieving upon completion of the programme, compared to their level of activity and fitness before using the app (Pickering et al. 2016). Users report that they like the flexibility of being in charge of when and how often they use the programme and can repeat sessions or full weeks as many times as they feel necessary before progressing. Thus, while running apps may not be suitable for everyone (e.g., younger people are generally more comfortable using technology and smartphones), they may be an effective way to engage those people not currently participating in physical activity.

Pokémon GO is a free-to-play, location-based, augmented-reality game that was released globally in July 2016. The media has anecdotally reported increased physical activity with one study estimating that Pokémon GO has added a total of 144 billion steps to physical activity in the US (Althoff et al. 2016). Since no study has examined the differences in walking and sitting time between Pokémon GO users and non-users, Broom and Flint (2017) developed the 'Physical Activity and Pokémon Go' questionnaire. The questionnaire was distributed using social media from 22 July 2016 onwards. After four weeks, 461 participants ($n = 193$ male, $n = 265$ female, $n = 3$ transgender) who were predominantly white ($n = 420$) and did not self-report a disability ($n = 443$) completed the questionnaire. Their mean $\pm$ SD age, body mass and BMI was 29 ± 10 years, 73.2 ± 16.6 kg and 24.6 ± 5.1 kg/m^2, respectively. When analysing differences between Pokémon GO users ($n = 236$) and non-users ($n = 225$) during the last seven days, Pokémon GO users walked on more days and spent more time walking on one of those days than non-users. Whilst there was no difference in sitting time during weekdays, Pokémon GO users reported greater sitting time at weekends than non-users. Pokémon GO users usually spent 90 ± 101 minutes walking on one of those days when using the app. Therefore, Pokémon GO users reported greater walking time and sitting time during weekends than non-users. Greater weekend sitting time could be due to increased walking, and whilst health benefits are likely, these need to be substantiated. Also, the effect of Pokémon GO on physical activity might be different in children, who were not included in the study.

Implications for community sports mangers

Despite Pokémon GO potentially being a short-term fad, both this and Couch to 5K show that interventions in the digital age can lead to population increases in physical activity. Community sports managers should keep up to date and be aware of the latest apps and monitoring tools to embed them in their sports and physical activity programmes.

EMERGING INTERVENTIONS IN DEVELOPMENT

Supporting Young People to Move More, Improve Lifestyle and Eat Well

Childhood obesity is a major public health concern, particularly in Lancashire where 23.5 per cent of reception-aged children are overweight or obese, with this figure rising to 32.4 per cent in Year 6. Evidence-based interventions that promote successful and sustained weight loss are needed. Consequently, Supporting Young People to Move More, Improve Lifestyle and Eat Well (SMILE) has been commissioned for pilot in three areas across Lancashire by Preston City Council (Coulton et al. 2014). The intervention design was informed by a review of literature and an extensive consultation using semi-structured interviews with local professionals, children and families, including those attending and seeking treatment. The programme runs weekly for the first six weeks, followed by a two-week home programme where families implement changes within their 'normal' environment. This is followed by a further four weekly sessions. Additional group sessions are provided at Week 14, 18, 33, 34 and 35. The participants are being followed over 12 months, with data collected at baseline, immediately post-intervention (12 weeks) and six months, nine months and 12 months from baseline. The primary outcomes include weight, height, BMI centile and waist circumference, and the secondary measures include quality of life, eating and activity behaviours and self-esteem of the child. Whilst the intervention and sessions are continually being reviewed and evaluated, a research student at Sheffield Hallam University is monitoring and evaluating the intervention. If successful, and after further review and development, it is the intention to disseminate the programme further afield.

WHOLE SYSTEMS APPROACHES

Whole Systems Approaches have become a focus of public health action, with emerging efforts that aim to develop community-wide interventions and work in partnerships across sectors. Systems thinking aims to understand how objects at different levels within a given system operate (i.e., cell, organ, individual, group, organisation, community, earth) whilst appreciating that any system is dynamic. The dynamic nature of a given system, therefore, means that the properties of a system are consistently changing, which can have an impact on different levels, and that the ever-changing landscape of a system highlights the complexity and multifaceted nature of systems thinking. The premise of systems thinking is that by working collaboratively and appreciating that the system continually changes over time, new ways of working can emerge to create a healthier system. In 2015, Public Health England, the Local Government Association and Association of Directors of Public Health commissioned Leeds Beckett University to explore Whole Systems Approaches to obesity that act at a local authority level. Working with four local authorities across England, Leeds Beckett University is examining local system understanding of causal loops across sectors where the causes and consequences of obesity are highlighted for each local authority (Leeds Beckett University, 2017, see Figure 4.7). To date, the project has highlighted the need to work with authorities to understand their systems, the role that partners within a given system play to develop new ways of thinking and working that pull in the same direction rather than disparate efforts that may lead to counterproductive outcomes. Thus, if a system is set up to cause obesity, it is pertinent to understand why that is the case and what the key leavers are so that these can be disrupted and the system can work towards achieving the desired outcome (i.e., healthy lifestyle behaviours).

FIGURE 4.7 Whole Systems Approach to Tackle Obesity (2015)

In October 2016, the Whole Systems Approach to Tackle Obesity project hosted a national conference at Leeds Town Hall attracting over 300 attendees. The importance of strong partnerships and senior management engagement was emphasised, as well as the need for commitment and action from a range of stakeholders. As part of the conference, workshops on the key themes that have emerged from the project were delivered. The topics were weight stigma covering how people talk about obesity, the need for planning and public health to work collaboratively, making use of community assets, the influence of the food environment and encouraging local authorities using the wide range of available data and information to inform future strategies.

Integrated health services have received a lot of attention and in 2015/2016 saw several local UK authorities release Integrated Healthy Lifestyle Service tenders. However, it is recognised that there is little evidence base on how they function or what outcomes they achieve in isolation or in comparison to other service models. In April 2016, an integrated public health service commissioned by Suffolk County Council delivering prevention and targeted interventions around healthy lifestyle training and awareness, NHS health checks, weight management, physical activity and smoking cessation programmes to adults and children across the county commenced. The service (OneLife Suffolk, see Figure 4.8) is a collaborative project delivered by Leeds Beckett University, MoreLife Ltd and Quit51. The service is free for all attendees who are both referred and self-referred. The service uses a Whole Systems Approach to recruit, deliver and support adults and children in making healthy decisions about their lifestyle behaviours. Thus, based on systems thinking, the service uses a variety of techniques to engage several sectors and settings approaches to foster collaborative efforts across the county. In doing so, OneLife Suffolk aims to reduce the risk of early death and reduced quality of life that is associated

FIGURE 4.8 OneLife Suffolk service (2016)

with unhealthy food and drink behaviour, providing targeted programmes that have a focus on health inequalities to reduce health risks associated with obesity, smoking, high blood pressure and physical inactivity. The service is research informed, and over time, the programme of research will examine the effectiveness of the service in supporting attendees' behaviour change, its cost-effectiveness and its sustainability. Attendees are recruited from across the county through awareness raising, health checks, stakeholder engagement or general practitioner or professional referrals to the service, where they are registered through a triage system. Once registered, they attend the programme in nearby locations, making use of local facilities, community assets and green and blue spaces.

Implications for community sports mangers

The Whole Systems Approach to Tackle Obesity and the OneLife Suffolk service represent novel programmes of work that over time can be assessed for their effectiveness in improving the health of communities across England. Community sport managers should follow these programmes as well as interventions such as SMILE, as they will provide much needed evidence regarding the most effective ways to tackle complex lifestyle behaviours that are impactful on individuals as well as wider society health and well-being.

SUMMARY

In summary, physical activity and sedentary behaviour have been defined because the two are different. Despite the Chief Medical Officers recommending specific amounts of physical activity to benefit health, levels are low and are predicted to fall alongside an increase in sedentary behaviour in years to come. Interventions are implemented to increase physical activity, and thousands have been developed and implemented, many with little evidence of success. The chapter has adopted a case study approach to introduce the reader to interventions the authors feel are models of good practice and/ or are currently being developed. It is hoped the content will stimulate the reader to seek further information about these interventions and provide ideas for developing and implementing community sports managers' own interventions. All have a role to play in increasing the nation's physical activity and reducing sedentary behaviour, including the community sports managers of the present and future.

Key take-home messages

- Physical activity benefits health, but levels are decreasing
- Interventions are needed to increase physical activity
- Citywide interventions can increase levels of physical activity
- Use of sport and sport facilities can increase the effectiveness of physical activity initiatives
- Walking sports can increase activity of all ages and abilities
- Physical activity and health initiatives can be delivered successfully through education, workplace and sport settings and organisations
- Technological advances and new ways of thinking means that there are novel approaches to increase physical activity that are emerging

REVIEW QUESTIONS

1. Describe physical activity trends in the last 60 years.
2. State what the Chief Medical Officer's (2011) physical activity guidelines are.
3. Define what a physical activity intervention is.
4. Discuss why FFIT was such a successful physical activity intervention for the target population group.
5. Identify a sport in your community where there is no walking sport provision. What key stakeholders might you need to engage to realise this into an offer for local people?
6. Using the Move More case study example, how might you develop an intervention to increase physical activity in your community?
7. Why might using a Whole Systems Approach be beneficial to improving the health of a city?

FURTHER READING

Crone, D. & Barker C. (2009). Physical activity interventions in the community. In Dugdill, L., Crone, D. and Murphy, R. (Eds). *Physical Activity and Health Promotion: Evidence-based approaches to practice.* Chichester: Wiley-Blackwell.

   Evidence-based practice from the UK. Dated now, but provides a sound introduction to the area of physical activity interventions in the community.

Public Health England (2015). *Identifying What Works for Local Physical Activity Interventions.* London: Public Health England.

This project aimed to take a rigorous, objective look at local physical activity interventions across England to identify 'what works'. This is the first time such a large-scale and academic approach has been taken to analysing and categorising the extent of physical activity interventions across the country.

Cavill, N., Roberts, K. & Rutter, H. (2012). *Standard Evaluation Framework for Physical Activity Interventions*. Oxford: National Obesity Observatory.

The Standard Evaluation Framework aims to describe and explain the information that should be collected in any evaluation of an intervention that aims to increase participation in physical activity. It contains a list of 'essential' and 'desirable' criteria for data required for a comprehensive and robust evaluation.

REFERENCES

Ajzen, I. (1991). The theory of planned behavior. *Organizational Behavior and Human Decision Processes*, 50, 179–211.

Althoff, T., White, R.W. & Horvitz, E. (2016). Influence of Pokémon Go on physical activity: study and implications. *Journal of Medical Internet Research*, 18(12), e315.

Arnold, J.T., Bruce-Low, S. & Sammut, L. (2015). The impact of 12 weeks walking football on health and fitness in males over 50 years of age. *British Medical Journal Open Sport and Exercise Medicine*, 1.

Broom, D., & Flint, S. W. (2017). Gotta Catch'em all: Increased walking time and sitting time at weekends in Pokémon Go users compared to non-users. In International Society of Behavior, Nutrition and Physical Activity Annual Conference, Victoria, Canada, June 2017.

Caspersen, C.J., Powell, K.E. & Christenson, G.M. (1985). Physical activity, exercise and physical fitness: definitions and distinctions for health-related research. *Public Health Reports*, 100, 126–131.

Chief Medical Officers. (2011). *Start Active, Stay Active: A Report on Physical Activity for Health from the Four Home Countries' Chief Medical Officers*. London: Department of Health.

Copeland, R.J. (2015). *Creating a Culture of Physical Activity. The Move More Plan: A Framework for Increasing Physical Activity in Sheffield 2015–2020*. http://movemoresheffield.com/Media/Default/Documents/move-more-plan.pdf [Last accessed 30 January 2017].

Copeland, R.J., Moullin, M., Reece, L., Gibson, D. & Barrett, D. (2011). Sheffield-let's change4life: A whole systems approach to tackling overweight and obesity in children, young people and families. A Local Evaluation Report. Sheffield Hallam University, UK.

Coulton, V., Reece, L., Copeland, R.J., Crank, H., Cross, K. & Broom, D.R. (2014). Development of a family, community-based intervention to reduce obesity in children aged 8–12 years. Abstract presented at Association for the Study of Obesity, Annual conference.

Department of Health. (2004). *At Least Five a Week. Evidence on the Impact of Physical Activity and Its Relationship to Health*. London: Department of Health.

FFIT. (2013). *Football Fans in Training*. www.ffit.org.uk [Last accessed 30 January 2017].

Foster, C., Hillsdon, M., Thorogood, M., Kaur, A., & Wedatilake, T. (2005). Interventions for promoting physical activity. The Cochrane Library.

Health and Social Care Information Centre. (2009). *Health Survey for England 2008: Physical Activity and Fitness*. Leeds: The Information Centre.

Hunt, K., Gray, C.M., Maclean, A., Smillie, S., Bunn, C. & Wyke, S. (2014a). Do weight management interventions delivered at professional football clubs attract and engage high risk men? A mixed methods study. *BMC Public Health*, 14, 50.

Hunt, K., Wyke, S., Gray, C.M., Anderson, A.S., Brady, A., Bunn, C., Donnan, P.T., Fenwick, E., Grieve, E., Leishman, J., Miller, E., Mutrie, N., Rauchhaus, P., White, A. & Trewick, S. (2014b). A gender-sensitive weight loss and healthy living programme for overweight and obese men delivered at Scottish Premier League football clubs (FFIT): a pragmatic randomised controlled trial. *The Lancet,* 383, 1211–1221.

Joint Health Surveys Unit. (2013). *Health Survey for England 2012: Health, Social Care and Lifestyles.* Leeds: The Information Centre.

Lancet Physical Activity Series. (2016). Physical activity 2016: Progress and challenges. www.thelancet. com/series/physical-activity-2016 [Last accessed 06 August 2017].

Leeds Beckett University. (2017). Whole systems approach to tackle obesity. www.leedsbeckett.ac.uk/ wholesystemsobesity/ [Last accessed 06 August 2017].

Morris, J.N. (1994). Exercise in the prevention of coronary heart disease: today's best buy in public health. *Medicine and Science in Sports and Exercise,* 26(7), 807–814.

Move More Sheffield. (2017). Get ready for move more month… your city needs you. www.movemore-sheffield.com [Last accessed 06 August 2017].

Ng, S.W. & Popkin, B.M. (2012). Time use and physical activity: a shift away from movement across the globe. *Obesity Reviews,* 13(8), 659–680.

NHS UK. (2014). Couch to 5K. www.nhs.uk/Livewell/c25k/Pages/couch-to-5k.aspx [Last accessed 06 August 2017].

OneLife Suffolk Service. (2016). Helping local people live healthier lives. http://onelifesuffolk.co.uk/ [Last accessed 06 August 2017].

Pickering, K., Pringle, A. & McKenna, J. (2016). Does Facebook offer social support during app based physical activity behaviour change programmes? *ISBNPA Conference: Cape Town,* June 8–11 2016. Cape Town, South Africa.

Sallis, J.F., Bull, F., Guthold, R., Heath, G.W., Inoue, S., et al. (2016). Progress in physical activity over the Olympic quadrennium. *Lancet,* 388(10051), 1325–1336.

Telama, R., Yang, X., Viikari, J., Valimaki, I., Wanne, O. & Raitakari, O. (2005). Physical activity from childhood to adulthood: a 21-year tracking study. *American Journal of Preventive Medicine,* 28(3), 267–273.

Tremblay, M.S., Aubert, S., Barnes, J.D., Saunders, T.J., Carson, V., Latimer-Cheung, A.E., Chastin, S.F., Altenburg, T.M. & Chinapaw, M.J. (2017). Sedentary behavior research network (SBRN)–terminology consensus project process and outcome. *International Journal of Behavioral Nutrition and Physical Activity,* 14(1), 75.

Winter, E. & Fowler, N. (2009). Exercise defined and quantified according to the Systeme International d'Unites. *Journal of Sports Sciences,* 25(7), 447–460.

Wyke, S., Hunt, K., Gray, C.M., Fenwick, E., Bunn, C., et al. (2015). Football fans in training (FFIT): a randomised controlled trial of a gender-sensitised weight loss and healthy living programme for men – end of study report. *Public Health Research,* 3(2).

CHAPTER 5

Including the excluded

Community cohesion through sport and physical activity

Chris Platts

SUMMARY

This chapter is designed to give you critical insight into the way sport and physical activity is used to improve community cohesion. 'Bringing communities together' is advocated as a key advantage of sport and physical activity schemes, however, this is often accepted uncritically. The aim of this chapter is to offer a balanced view of the possibilities and limitations of sport and physical activity being used for social inclusion purposes.

AIMS

By engaging with this chapter, you will

- Have a better understanding of the term social inclusion,
- Be introduced to the key debates that aim to explore whether sport and physical activity can help improve social inclusion,
- Explore a range of issues that those working in programmes aimed at improving social inclusion need to consider and
- Outline the different approaches used by StreetGames as a way of including socially excluded groups.

INTRODUCTION: UNDERSTANDING THE TERM SOCIAL INCLUSION

As has been noted in other areas of this book, such as Chapter 3, over the past thirty years or so, an increasing number of programmes have attempted to use sport and physical activity to deal with some of the issues that exist within our communities. One of those issues can be framed as 'social inclusion'. But what is social inclusion? And why do we need to study it?

In their work on the subject, Waring and Mason (2010) argue that in order for any person or group to be defined as socially included within a community, two areas need considering. First, does the group or individual people feel able and empowered to participate in that community? And, second, in engaging with the community around them, are those people, as a group or individually, able to improve their social experiences? If the answer to either of these questions is no, then there is reason to categorise those individuals or groups as being – or at the very least at risk of becoming – 'socially excluded'. Notwithstanding the difficulty in identifying when someone should be categorised as 'socially excluded' (Coalter, 2007; Bloyce and Smith, 2009; Collins & Kay, 2014), what is important for those with an interest in developing and managing sport within a community setting is how 'particular concern has been expressed about what can happen when people and local communities become "socially excluded" by experiencing a combination of linked "problems"' (Bloyce & Smith, 2009, pp. 79–80). Although this list is not exhaustive, and the 'problems' to which Bloyce and Smith (2009) refer do not impact everybody in the same way, common issues for those people who feel socially excluded may include health problems, such as those who are stigmatised as obese, those with severe mental health problems and people with long-term illnesses; mental and physical impairments, including extreme learning difficulties, significant visual and hearing impairments or physical disablement; substance abusers; those who are economically deprived, from people who are employed but are low earners through to the unemployed or underemployed and those who are homeless; single parent families and those who are living on their own; those who have offended or reoffended; immigrants and refugees; and those who are socially isolated due to a lack of family or friendship groups. A good example of an organisation that has, over recent years, shown a growing concern for those people who are socially excluded because of their exposure to any of the above problems is the European Union (2017) that argues that 'programmes should be developed to improve social inclusion out of the "respect for the fundamental rights of people experiencing poverty and social exclusion, and enabling them to live in dignity and take an active part in society"'. Indeed, in its latest strategy, the European Union estimates that 120 million people across Europe are at risk of poverty or social exclusion and, as a result, urges that 'Member States and the Union should … aim to build a cohesive society in which people are empowered to anticipate and manage change, and can actively participate in society and the economy' (European Union, 2015). It is worth noting, at this point, the interrelated nature of the problems faced by those who are at risk of, or already feeling, socially excluded (Bloyce & Smith, 2009). That is to say, when an individual or group encounters one challenge, it is likely to increase the chances of them encountering another. As an example, in dealing with long-term illness, a person is also likely to have to deal with a change in economic status as a consequence of that illness. While some may be well equipped to deal with this, through health insurance or employment that supports them through their illness, others may not. Similarly, if someone encounters mental health issues, there are potential further consequences for their social or family life.

SPORT, PHYSICAL ACTIVITY AND SOCIAL INCLUSION

On some level, it would be easy to view social exclusion as an issue for those people who find themselves feeling excluded and having to manage the consequences. However, increasingly, it has been recognised that higher levels of social exclusion within a community gives rise to other, more widespread, issues. For example, communities that have higher levels of social exclusion are more likely to face higher crime rates, lower life expectancy and so on (Putnam, 2001; Wilkinson & Pickett, 2009). The collective consequences of poor social inclusion – alongside the more individual ones – have forced local and national governments to take a greater interest in addressing exclusion, and, in doing that, sport and physical activity has offered an opportunity to help bridge the exclusion gap. Particularly since the 1980s, successive governments in the UK have identified that sport and physical activity could be one medium through which greater social inclusion could be developed. Although with varying levels of commitment, Margaret Thatcher in the 1980s, John Major in the 1990s and Tony Blair in the late 1990s and early 2000s all developed programmes and policies that focussed on sport as a tool for developing or restoring community cohesion (Coalter, 2007). Following on from this, in 2015, the Conservative government developed its latest strategy on sport and highlighted five key outcomes, two of which were focussed on 'social and community development' and 'individual development', which reflected the role they believed sport could play in the individual who was socially excluded as well as a wider role within communities. In doing so, the strategy placed specific emphasis on the role of volunteering in helping people become socially included. The government claim is that

> Volunteering in the sport and leisure industry is the most common form of volunteering and is a good opportunity to build social inclusion and community cohesion, particularly for socially isolated individuals.
>
> (Cabinet Office, 2015, p. 38)

Taking their lead from the government strategy, Sport England was quick to follow by outlining the ways in which they can help deliver on the government outcomes. Of notable inclusion in their own strategy was a reference to increased support for charities that aim to support those at risk of social exclusion. They claim that

> In the past we have invested in a small number of charities who use sport for wider development purposes. For example we have recently invested in Fight for Peace, a charity working with young people at risk of exclusion, offending or becoming involved in gangs, working with local schools and youth offending teams, to offer sport sessions such as boxing, taekwondo and judo late at night. This type of investment will be a much stronger theme of our new approach.
>
> (Sport England, 2016, p. 32)

As Coalter (2015) has noted, the shift towards using sport for wider social goals such as social inclusion has, in particular from the 1990s onwards, opened up a number of new funding streams to traditional sport development organisations that have sought to exploit the benefits of these new avenues for income. However, Coalter (2015) also notes that the increasing level of funding available has, simultaneously, meant more challenges. One such challenge relates to the increasing focus on making sure that the money invested by local and national governments in sport for social inclusion projects is, in fact, having an effect. There is a greater need now more than ever for managers to monitor and evaluate their community sport projects. As Weiss (1993) contends, inflated promises are most likely to occur in marginal policy areas that are seeking to gain legitimacy and funding from mainstream agencies, which is where sport and physical activity often finds itself. So, having established what social exclusion is, and how national government interest in reducing it has led to the growing involvement of sort and physical activity programmes, we will now turn our attention to debating whether sport and physical activity can, *in fact*, have a positive impact on social exclusion. Or are these all, as Weiss suggests, overinflated promises in order to gain funding?

CAN SPORT AND PHYSICAL ACTIVITY BE USED TO IMPROVE SOCIAL INCLUSION WITHIN COMMUNITIES?

In order to try and further develop our understanding of whether sport and physical activity can be used as a tool for improving social inclusion within communities, the next section of this chapter will explore four key debates that sit at the heart of answering this question. To that end, the foundations of each debate are set out within this chapter, after which, further reading at the end of the chapter points you to academics who have developed these debates in much more detail than is possible here. The first of these debates concerns itself with evidence and whether there is any to support the use of sport and physical activity as a tool for reducing social exclusion.

Where is the evidence?

As was noted earlier in the chapter, recent decades have seen a greater emphasis on the need to gather evidence to monitor and evaluate programmes that have attempted to use sport and physical activity to reduce social exclusion (Lindsay & Bacon, 2016). Indeed, under such circumstances, we might, therefore, expect an increase in evidence linking increased sport and physical activity in communities with greater social inclusion. However, this picture is far from clear. For example, writing in 2006 about the role that physical activity can play in the lives of young people who are at risk of social exclusion, Sandford, Armour and Warmington (2006) note that 'although there is a popular belief that sport "builds character" in some way, the evidence to support such a belief is inconclusive' (Sandford et al., 2006, p. 252). Also writing of the potential impact physical activity can have on young people, but this time in relation to Physical Education, Lindsay and Bacon (2016, pp. 68–69) claim that even if we could link participation to wider social benefits such as 'character building', 'systematic reviews have … identified that there remain gaps in knowledge on effective approaches to increasing young people's participation in sport and physical activity'. Likewise, when it comes to preventing young people from engaging in activities that can lead to social exclusion,

> despite the vast numbers of such schemes currently in operation in the UK and elsewhere, there is a widespread lack of robust research on, and hence very little evidence for, their effectiveness in reducing and preventing crime and drug use among young people.
>
> (Bloyce & Smith, 2009, p. 98)

Away from participation in the activity itself, it is also suggested that engaging in sport and physical activity in other ways, such as through volunteering, may reduce the likelihood of social exclusion. However, in a similar way to participation, there appears to be a gap in the evidence to reinforce these claims. For example, when exploring whether sports coaching as a volunteer activity has benefits for the individual and the society within which it takes place, Griffiths and Armour (2014) note that 'a number of recent studies have suggested that participation in community sport has the potential to deliver a wide range of individual and social benefits' such as social inclusion; however, by their own admission, their work is

> the first review of its kind, and is important because both the workforce (volunteers) and the context (community sport) are expansive with increasing government expectations placed upon them. Yet, both areas are under-researched and poorly understood.
>
> (Griffiths & Armour, 2014, p. 308)

In emphasising this point, when assessing the role that involvement in sport can have on those with learning disabilities, Southby (2013) emphasised that while policymakers have been keen to stress the positives of participation in football as a player, referee, administrator, coach or spectator,

> as yet there is little evidence to substantiate all the claims of such football-based inclusion policies. Whilst some health and social benefits have been recognized for learning-disabled people playing football, there is currently no empirical evidence as to the social benefits of being a fan for learning-disabled people.
>
> (Southby, 2013, p. 1387)

It is worth noting at this point that the lack of evidence for the usefulness of sport and physical activity in reducing social exclusion is not limited to the UK, and a number of writers have documented similar issues in other countries around the world. For example, it seems that 'evidence linking social inclusion outcomes to community sports participation is limited in the Australian context' (Maxwell, Foley, Taylor, & Burton, 2013, p. 467), and when referring to the work done in this area across North America, Jones, Edwards, Boccaro, Bunds and Smith (2017, p. 162) claim that 'many youth sport programmes ... have a clear vision of the youth development outcomes they should be targeting, yet only vague conceptualizations of how that development is achieved'. In other words, in some areas where there is evidence of a positive relationship between sport, physical activity and social inclusion, there is little known about how that change was brought about. What was good about those programmes that helped to reduce social exclusion?

Is sport and physical activity an inclusionary activity?

On one level, a lack of evidence to suggest that sport and physical activity can help increase social inclusion does not necessarily mean that it does not work; it could just mean we do not have the evidence to support it working. Therefore, notwithstanding the lack of evidence we have to hand, the remaining three debates relate to whether sport and physical activity ever can work as a tool for social inclusion. First among these debates is the argument that sport and physical activity, by its very nature, excludes people and, therefore, may not be useful as a tool for increasing social inclusion. In short, while we might be tempted to look at the positive attributes of sport and physical activity programmes when considering their role in 'bringing the community together', it is equally important to understand the 'countervailing view [that] stresses the tendency of sport to maintain, reproduce or deepen social divisions' (Brown, Hoye, & Nicholson, 2014, p. 438).

In the UK, a number of surveys have been used to measure levels of participation including the Active People Survey from Sport England and the Taking Part Survey conducted on behalf of the Department of Culture Media and Sport. However, when it comes to social inclusion, one key point is worth noting about the findings from these surveys. Certain groups within society have lower participation rates in sport and physical activity when compared to other groups. Over time, those who find themselves in low socio-economic groups, those who are unemployed, those from black and minority ethnic groups, females, groups in certain geographical areas and those with low or poor levels of health have consistently participated in sport and physical activity less than their counterparts who are in more affluent and socially included groups. That is to say, rather than being seen as an arena in which people 'come together', sport and physical activity has, historically, been a place that reinforces social exclusion. If those groups who are socially excluded from society are excluded from sport and physical activity, how can we use sport and physical activity to include them? As Coalter puts it, 'the limited inclusivity of sport, especially among women in socially and economically deprived areas, raises significant questions for the nature and extent of sport's supposed role in strategies of social regeneration' (Coalter, 2007, p. 49). As you will see from the case study in this chapter, in order to use sport for social inclusion, we first must question the more traditional approaches to sport and how discriminatory they can be. It appears that organizations and clubs who have been the most successful in being inclusive are those that have sought to distance themselves from 'mainstream sport' (Watson, Tucker, & Drury, 2013).

Does sport and physical activity reinforce good behaviours?

The third key debate regarding whether sport and physical activity can be used to reduce social exclusion comes from the fact that, in many programmes or schemes that use sport and physical activity for this end, there is an inherent belief that sport teaches values, morals or behaviours that are not only good but, at the same time, can be transferred into other aspects of life. Consider the following statement from David Cameron, prime minister when the latest strategy for sport was released in 2015, and note the reference to claims that sport is good for us because of its ability to challenge us, build character, nurture discipline and help develop skills for life and work:

> Sport is also good for us. It teaches our children how to rise to a challenge, nurturing the character and discipline that will help them get on in life. It

encourages us all to lead healthier and more active lives ... it is good for our society too, with governing bodies and charities alike delivering many brilliant programmes that already use sport to strengthen community cohesion and give our young people new skills for life and work.

(Cameron 2015, cited in Cabinet Office, 2015, p. 6)

Let us set aside, for one moment, the first two debates we have covered. Let us suppose that participation in sport and physical activity does not differ between groups in society. That is to say, there is equal access to sport and physical activity whatever social, cultural and economic background. In this situation, the reason often cited for the use of sport for social inclusion purposes – as in the quote by David Cameron – is the supplementary benefits that are associated with participation. These often include, among other things, that sport helps us to deal with defeat, teaches us to be part of a team, helps cultivate leadership skills or introduces us to rules and regulations. More importantly, these benefits associated with participation are said to mirror the life skills we need to remain included in society. However, for this to play out in reality, arguments of this kind focus on the extent to which sport and physical activity is viewed as inherently good and ignores the negative aspects of participation; this is regarded as something of a paradox by those who research this area. While an absolute belief in what is often described as the 'positive power' of sport and physical activity is often at the core of any decision to use it for reducing social exclusion, *paradoxically*, a failure to appreciate the limitations or negative sides of sport and physical activity can serve to undermine the success of any programme aimed at doing so. Can you think of some negative aspects of sport and physical activity that may actually increase the chances of social exclusion? One of the reasons behind such a one-sided view of the power of sport is perhaps the background of those who design, manage and deliver programmes in this area. These are often people who have a positive view of sport and physical activity, perhaps because it has played a positive role in their life and they are eager to pass on those supposed benefits to others. This argument led to Bloyce and Smith (2009, p. 82) concluding that

> it is not uncommon in policy areas of this kind for the contribution that sport, and those working in sports development, can make to the development of people and their communities to be based on a one-sided perception of sport that amounts almost to a statement of faith in its effectiveness to achieve desired social outcomes associated with the social inclusion agenda.

While we would be foolish to suggest that there are no benefits for anyone who decides to participate in sport and physical activity, especially for social inclusion, this debate highlights the need to understand that those benefits must be understood alongside the detrimental consequences of sport and physical activity participation. For an individual, these can include issues around injury, mental health problems or negative feelings around self-worth. Likewise, there are negative consequences for society, including increased cost of injury treatment, feelings of exclusion for those uncomfortable with sport and physical activity or issues with abuse that have come to characterise competitive sports.

Structure, agency and social exclusion

The final debate worth exploring relates to processes that may be considered outside of sport and physical activity but, nevertheless, play an important role in whether we can use sport and physical activity as a tool for reducing social exclusion. When debating why social exclusion exists and how to reduce it, we can consider two opposing arguments. First, we can assume that everybody has some 'agency' in life, which is defined as the 'ability to think, to reflect, to interpret, to exercise choice and to act accordingly' (Roberts, 2009, p. 5). For those who believe in the power of 'agency', the argument follows that if someone finds themselves socially excluded, they can choose to undertake activities that will assist them in becoming more included. However, there is another school of thought that emphasises the 'structure' within which people live and, in particular, the ways that structure has an impact on the choices people can make. As an example, those who subscribe to this view would argue that, while we may think everybody has a choice, that choice, and the ability of a person to make the correct choice, is dependent upon the education they received from their parents and their schooling. This is the 'structure' within which they have been living.

In order to make more sense of this debate in relation to social inclusion and sport and physical activity, consider Figure 5.1. Along the x-axis, the population of the UK is split into 100 different percentiles with the wealthiest at the right-hand end of the axis and those who are poorest economically at the left-hand end of the axis. The y-axis shows the change in household income after housing costs (AHC). What the graph shows is how the AHC of the different groups within the UK population will change between 2014 and 2015 and 2021 and 2022 in two different scenarios. The first scenario, which is represented by the dark line, is the projected change in AHC if the government in the UK does not change the tax and benefit rules. On this line, you can see that the wealthiest (the right-hand end of the x-axis) will see their AHC rise by roughly 10 per cent between 2014 and 2015 and 2021 and 2022, while the poorest 10 per cent (the left-hand end of the x-axis) will see their AHC reduce. Now, turn your attention to the lighter line, which also shows changes in AHC, however, this time it shows the projected change if the government changes the rules on tax and benefits. In this scenario, the poorest 15 per cent will now see a reduction in AHC, with the poorest 35 per cent being worse off than if no change was made. At the other end of the spectrum, the highest 65 per cent of society will see an increase in AHC with a rise of around 12 per cent for the wealthiest.

The data presented in Figure 5.1 are a good illustration of how the structure within which people live may come to impact their exclusion from society and, at the same time, reduce the ability of sport and physical activity to be used to improve social inclusion. Within this example, government changes to tax and benefit laws may have the effect of increasing the financial pressure on some and put them more at risk of being socially excluded while reducing the pressure on others. Likewise, the 35 per cent who find they're economically worse off now have less 'choice' in the activities they may undertake, not least because they are in a weaker position to pay for them. The government within every country around the world is a good example of a structure within which people operate.

These structures are, however, not fixed and can change over time as different governments take different approaches to the issues within society. Note in Figure 5.2 how, over time, the percentage of pensioners living in low-income households has, since the

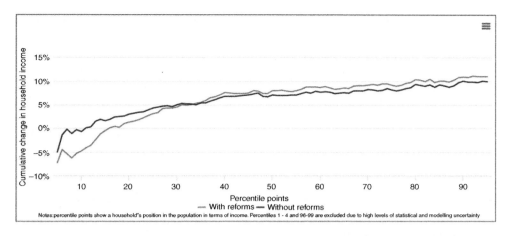

FIGURE 5.1 Change in real household AHC income between 2014 and 2015 and 2021 and 2022 by percentile point, with and without direct tax and benefit reforms during this parliament

Source: Authors calculation using Family Resources Survey – various years – and projections for 2015–2016 to 2021–2022 using methodology and assumptions specified in the full report

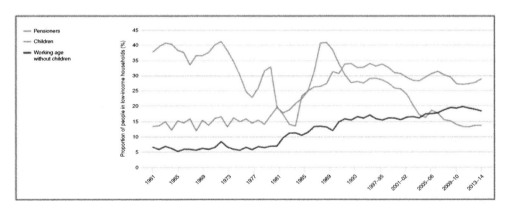

FIGURE 5.2 Percentage of people in low-income households over time

Source: Living standards, inequality and poverty dataset, IFS; the data is for Great Britain to 2001/2002 and for the UK thereafter

1960s, fluctuated at different points but, on the whole, reduced. Over the same period, the number of children living in low-income households has risen to around 30 per cent. We might ask ourselves: how much 'agency' these children will have currently or in later life to remain socially included if they are already at risk during childhood?

In relation to sport and physical activity and its role in reducing social exclusion, there are a number of things we can take away from this debate. First, as a general rule, social inclusion programmes within communities have placed emphasis 'on personal responsibility – to work or seek to work, to provide for family, to behave responsibly, to take responsibility for personal health, to contribute to the solution of community problems and so on' (Coalter, 2007, p. 47). If sport and physical activity programmes do the same and underplay the importance of the structure within which people live, those programmes are likely to prove unsuccessful in bringing about change. Second, by understanding the structure within which people live, we open up the possibility that 'major aspects of "social inclusion" come before and not as a result of participation in a single activity, such as sport' (Coalter, 2007, p. 48). That is to say, those people already feeling included in their community are likely to be afforded more opportunities to become involved in sport and physical activity and feel like they are better able to take advantage of those opportunities. This argument is nothing new, as noted earlier in the chapter.

STREETGAMES AND REDUCING SOCIAL EXCLUSION

Who are StreetGames and what do they do?

When it comes to using sport for social inclusion, there are a variety of different approaches that are employed; however, at a very basic level, it is possible to break the approaches into three different groups. First, there are programmes where sport is used as a hook to entice people to participate in a programme, and then support in other areas of life is offered, such as in relation to employment or mental health. Second, some programmes use sport as the key component for introducing participants to more socially acceptable behaviours. As we have already discussed, sport and physical activity is used in these programmes because it is thought to have important characteristics that help to highlight the importance of rules, teamwork, fair play and respect. All the behaviours that participants are introduced to in these programmes are seen as vital for being socially included in everyday life. Finally, there are programmes that simply serve to deliver sport to groups that are traditionally low in terms of their participation in sport. The philosophy underpinning this is that every person should have access to sport and physical activity, however, as we have noted earlier in the chapter, that is not always the case. These approaches serve to improve this situation. Dividing programmes that use sport and physical activity into these three groups is useful, as it highlights the differentiation in approaches used, however, it is also worth highlighting that different programmes may take more than one of these approaches. For example, delivering sport to underprivileged groups while also subscribing to the belief that sport and physical activity can help to introduce people to behaviours and ways of living that will help them to remain, or become more, included within society. One such organisation that would fall into this category is StreetGames.

StreetGames is a charitable organisation, established officially in 2007, with a vision to change lives, change sport and change communities (StreetGames, 2017). This organisation, and the programmes it offers, provides an excellent case study through which we can begin to further understand the debates we have explored in the first half of this chapter because of the focus StreetGames places on those at risk of social exclusion. Of particular interest is the fact that StreetGames highlight women and girls, black and minority ethnic communities and people with disabilities as 'target groups' as well as a general approach that looks to use sport as an instrument of social change in disadvantaged communities. In short, StreetGames targets those who are at risk of becoming, or are already defined as, socially excluded and attempts 'to make sport more widely available for disadvantaged young people and to maximize the power of sport to change young lives and to change disadvantaged communities' (StreetGames, 2017). In this regard, we might suggest that StreetGames looks to improve social inclusion on two fronts: first by delivering sport to people who are under-represented in terms of their participation, but also to introduce participants to the characteristics of sport that are able to help people in their lives. But how successful are StreetGames? And how do they approach this?

Doorstep Sport Clubs

The first piece of work undertaken by StreetGames that we shall explore is the establishment of 'Doorstep Sport Clubs' (DSC). The concept behind these clubs is to develop clubs that are not traditional sports clubs but rather clubs that 'are fun, informal sports clubs that operate at the right time, for the right price, in the right place and in the right style' (StreetGames, 2017). On their website, StreetGames (2017) claim that

> at their core, they provide young people aged 14-25 years living in areas of high deprivation with accessible and affordable opportunities to take part in sport within their local community. Providing vibrant, varied, fun and sociable sessions, with a strong emphasis on youth leadership.

But how is this different to any other community sports club? The first point to note is that, as the name suggests, DSC are delivered on the 'doorsteps' of the communities they are designed to serve. That is to say, sport and physical activity is provided at the location of the participants rather than expecting participants to travel to the club. It is also worthy of note that the delivery of doorstep sport takes place at the 'right time' for the participants. Again, in a change from more traditional sports clubs where specific sessions, training or games may be scheduled at certain times and if participants want to be a part of that club then they must conform, StreetGames take their lead from the desires of the participants when it comes to scheduling activities. One of the core principles of DSC, which is vital to the chances of them being successful, is that the design is from the 'bottom up' and not from the 'top down'. What this means is that the characteristics of the clubs are driven by the views and desires of participants who StreetGames are trying to engage. This runs opposed to more traditional clubs, the characteristics of which are often determined by tradition and an elected committee. In their vision for DSC, for example, StreetGames note that they must be designed to address 'the needs and interests of the young people in the local community', clubs 'must reflect the demographic of the local community' and it is vital that those developing clubs 'consult with young people on any current or future activity provision to ensure it is meeting their needs'.

A further way that DSC are different to more traditional style sports clubs and, at the same time, are attempting to grapple with some of the issues we have discussed at the start of this chapter is through the use of youth leaders. There is a real emphasis within DSC to use '"home-grown" volunteers/promoters and older or more experienced participants to act as promoters, positive role models and inspiration' (StreetGames, 2016, p. 10). This is a further example of how a more 'bottom-up' approach to delivery may be viewed in a practical sense. The use of 'home-grown' volunteers distances the scheme from certain problems that occur when the groups of people who coach, lead, manage and assist on such schemes are people unknown to members of the community. While people from outside a community have a role to play, the work of StreetGames highlights that knowing the people in the community is a distinguishing feature of the more successful schemes, and volunteers and workforce members drawn from the community itself is key in this regard.

The final area to explore with regard to DSC is to look at some of the practical lessons that StreetGames have uncovered in their own evaluations. In that regard, there are both positive and negative lessons to be learnt here, and, for anyone who is studying or thinking of a career in social inclusion, these are valuable snapshots of the day-to-day lives of managers and development workers in this field. StreetGames (2011, p. 2) have noted that if not used properly, in particular, sport, 'can reinforce existing divisions based on social class, faith, area and ethnicity' and 'can encourage people to compete against each other, to be rivals and not to integrate and get to know each other'. Designing programmes that constrain people to mix with people from other backgrounds is important. Getting individuals to 'bridge' the divide between themselves and others who have different characteristics is, in short, at the heart of improving social inclusion. In that regard, StreetGames note that while we must acknowledge the ability of sport and physical activity to provide 'contact opportunities', it is vital that the positive benefits that are possible from these contacts are not left to happen by chance. Making sure that programmes are seen as 'safe and neutral', helping newcomers integrate and developing a 'code of conduct' that is owned by participants are all examples of things that will not happen simply by the power of sport, but by skilled development officers and managers.

CONCLUSION

Hopefully this chapter has highlighted that the use of sport and physical activity as a way of increasing social inclusion is a rather complex issue. In that regard, notwithstanding that many different governments around the world, National and International Governing Bodies and more local-based organisations extol the virtues of sport and physical activity for 'bringing people together', for those working in the sector, a more measured and realistic approach enlightens us to the fact that greater integration within communities does not just happen, it is a topic that requires careful consideration.

REVIEW QUESTIONS

1. What issues might be caused for sport in the community schemes if it is hard to define social exclusion?
2. Who is responsible for social exclusion? Is it the individuals who have become socially excluded or is it those who run our society who have allowed people to become socially excluded?
3. How can Putnam's concepts of Bridging and Bonding help us to understand both the strengths and limitations of using sport and physical activity for social inclusion?

4. What opportunities and challenges may present themselves when government policy focus moves from developing sport in communities to developing communities through sport?
5. Why might some people or groups of people not feel able to participate in their local community?

FURTHER READING

Coalter, F. (2007). Sport and social regeneration: A capital prospect. In *A wider social role for sport: Who's keeping the score?* Abingdon: Routledge.
Collins, M., & Kay, T. (2014). *Sport and social exclusion.* London: Routledge.

REFERENCES

Brown, K. M., Hoye, R., & Nicholson, M. (2014). Generating trust? Sport and community participation. *Journal of Sociology, 50*(4), 437–457.
Bloyce, D., & Smith, A. (2009). *Sport policy and development: An introduction.* London: Routledge.
Cabinet Office. (2015). Sporting future: A new strategy for an active nation. London: Cabinet Office.
Coalter, F. (2007). A wider social role for sport: Who's keeping the score? Abingdon: Routledge.
Coalter, F. (2015). Sport-for-change: Some thoughts from a sceptic. *Social Inclusion, 3*(3), 19–23.
Collins, M., & Kay, T. (2014). *Sport and social exclusion* (2nd ed.). Oxon: Routledge.
European Union. (2015). *Europe 2020: Europe's growth strategy.* Brussels: European Union.
European Union. (2017). *Inclusive growth – A high-employment economy delivering economic, social and territorial cohesion.* Available at http://ec.europa.eu/europe2020/europe-2020-in-a-nutshell/priorities/inclusive-growth/index_en.htm.
Griffiths, M., & Armour, K. (2014). Volunteer sports coaches as community assets? A realist review of the research evidence. *International Journal of Sport Policy and Politics, 6*(3), 307–326. doi:10.1080/19406940.2013.824496.
Jones, G. J., Edwards, M. B., Bocarro, J. N., Bunds, K. S., & Smith, J. W. (2017). An integrative review of sport-based youth development literature. *Sport in Society, 20*(1), 161–179. doi:10.1080/17430437.2015.1124569.
Lindsey, I., & Bacon, D. (2016). In pursuit of evidence-based policy and practice: A realist synthesis-inspired examination of youth sport and physical activity initiatives in England (2002–2010). *International Journal of Sport Policy and Politics, 8*(1), 67–90.
Maxwell, H., Foley, C., Taylor, T., & Burton, C. (2013). Social inclusion in community sport: A case study of Muslim women in Australia. *Journal of Sport Management, 27,* 467–481.
Putnam, R. D. (2001). *Bowling alone: The collapse and revival of American community.* New York: Simon and Schuster.
Roberts, K. (2009). *Key concepts in sociology.* Basingstoke: Palgrave Macmillan.
Sandford, R. A., Armour, K. M., & Warmington, P. C. (2006). Re-engaging disaffected youth through physical activity programmes. *British Educational Research Journal, 32*(2), 251–271.
Southby, K. (2013). Social inclusion through football fandom: Opportunities for learning-disabled people. *Sport in Society, 16*(10), 1386–1403. doi:10.1080/17430437.2013.790899.
Sport England. (2016). *Towards an active nation strategy 2016–2021.* London: Sport England.

StreetGames. (2011). *Community cohesion and sport: Information and guidance for delivery staff.* www. streetgames.org.uk.

StreetGames. (2016). Doorstep Sport Club Year 3 Report. www.streetgames.org.uk.

Waring, A., & Mason, C. (2010). Opening doors: Promoting social inclusion through increased sports opportunities. *Sport in Society, 13*(3), 517–529.

Watson, R., Tucker, L., & Drury, S. (2013). Can we make a difference? Examining the transformative potential of sport and active recreation. *Sport in Society, 16*(10), 1233–1247. doi:10.1080/1743043 7.2013.821258.

Weiss, C. H. (1993). Where politics and evaluation research meet. *Evaluation Practice, 14*(1), 93–106.

Wilkinson, R. G., & Pickett, K. (2009). *The Spirit Level: Why More Equal Societies Almost Always Do Better* (Vol. 6). London: Allen Lane.

CHAPTER 6

Corporate social responsibility in community sport management

Daniel Plumley and Rob Wilson

SUMMARY

This chapter provides an overview of the concept of Corporate Social Responsibility (CSR) and its application to sport and community sport management. The chapter presents and reviews the main dimensions of CSR in sports organisations and discusses how such organisations leverage CSR activities to showcase the organisation in a positive light. CSR is an important concept for all community sport managers to consider, as it can have profound effects on the perception of the organisation in the eyes of the general public.

AIMS

By engaging with this chapter, you will be able to

- Understand the concept of CSR and its importance to sports organisations,
- Understand the different dimensions of CSR in sports organisations,
- Appreciate the importance of CSR to sports organisations,
- Consider the uniqueness of CSR in a sporting context and outline the advantages that sports organisations have/hold (compared to other sectors) in relation to CSR and
- Identify and discuss key management issues arising through CSR and how sports organisations can implement effective CSR.

INTRODUCTION

This chapter introduces you to the concept of CSR and its role within community sport management. Managing sport organisations, as you will be aware from reading this book, is no easy task. This is because the essence of sporting competition forces Sport organisations to balance multiple objectives in order to satisfy a variety of different stakeholders. Professional and community Sport teams operate under a concept of 'multiple institutional logics', which simply means that they have to satisfy a number of different groups of people who all have a vested interest in the operations of the team. By way of an example, consider a professional football team in the UK. There will be a number of people who are interested in how the football club is operating, including (but not limited to) the Chairman/owner, investors, the manager, the players, the fans, the media, the governing body of the sport and the general public itself. Keeping all of these people happy is a difficult task. Furthermore, sport organisations exist and operate in a competitive and changing environment, which in today's modern world extends much further than just winning at sport.

The concept of CSR has, today, become significant for modern sport organisations because sport has a profound social impact. Therefore, the aim of this chapter is to provide you with an introduction to CSR and how CSR is managed and implemented within the sport industry. It is particularly relevant given that the focus of this text is on community sport management, as CSR initiatives in sport organisations form an integral part of their community operations.

This chapter will highlight practical examples of sport organisations implementing CSR from a global perspective. To begin with, however, we need to understand why sports organisations are keen to engage in CSR-related activities. A list of reasons why sport organisations should deploy CSR is listed below:

- The popularity and global reach of sport can ensure that these practices have mass media distribution and communication power.
- Sport has youth appeal, thus, children's engagement in programmes designed to tackle or contribute towards the above-mentioned issues becomes easier if such programmes are associated with a sports organisation or a well-known athlete.
- Sport offers the perfect platform to encourage activity, including health awareness and anti-obesity campaigns, as well as disease prevention.
- Linked with the previous reason, social interaction can be, thus, facilitated by group participation in sports activities.
- Environmental and sustainability awareness and consciousness can be further reinforced, especially with the hosting of mega-sporting events (e.g., the Olympic Games, the Football [Soccer] World Cup).
- Sport may also lead to enhanced cultural understanding and integration.
- Both active and passive participation in sport offer immediate satisfaction benefits with unclear social advantages, albeit scarcely unimportant.

(Smith & Westerbeek, 2007)

Considering the above list, we will now walk through the main components of CSR (both in general industries and in sport) before discussing the different dimensions of CSR in sport and how sport organisations are in a privileged position to implement CSR initiatives. We will then conclude with the goal of assisting you to identify and discuss the key managerial issues associated with CSR in sport and why effective CSR is so important to sport organisations.

WHAT IS CORPORATE SOCIAL RESPONSIBILITY?

CSR is currently of growing societal interest and is seen as one of the key areas of modern corporate sustainability on the business, public and research agenda. However, it is not necessarily classed as a new phenomenon, and discussions on the topic can be traced back to the early 1950s. CSR, as we know it today, has evolved significantly, although the basic components of it remain relatively similar. Essentially, there are four key areas that CSR in businesses covers:

- Economic (the basic responsibility to make a profit and, thus, be viable)
- Legal (the duty to obey the law)
- Ethical (responsibility to act in a manner consistent with societal expectations)
- Discretionary (activities that go beyond societal expectations)

These areas are also found in the CSR pyramid in Figure 6.1.

Interest in CSR from organisations of any type and size has accelerated rapidly in recent years, particularly in the field of community sport management. Despite its success, however, it is arguable that CSR is still challenging to measure and consists of many different variables, particularly when applied to the sport industry. What is clear is that sport plays an important role as a vehicle for deploying CSR, as it exposes the social responsibilities implicit in sport as well as those found in the corporate world. However, the world of sport is a little more complex than the corporate world, and this is why it is important that we take a look at CSR explicitly in relation to sport. For example, consider the emotional attachment that fans have to a sport team that is not found in any other industry. Think of a team that you support. Would you swap that team for another one? Possibly not, but would you swap from your choice of supermarket if the price is cheaper and can save you money? In this case, you might choose to swap, but it is very rare that fans of sports teams will swap to support a different team. In fact, this is one of the key differences between sport and other sectors that put sports organisations in a privileged position when deploying CSR.

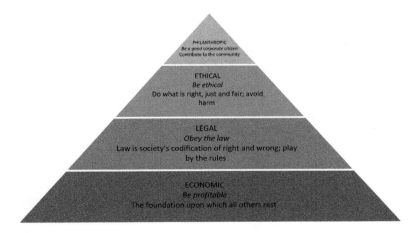

FIGURE 6.1 The Corporate Social Responsibility Pyramid

WHAT IS CORPORATE SOCIAL RESPONSIBILITY IN SPORT?

CSR in sport is also a relatively new concept, and professional sport organisations are now entering into socially responsible initiatives at a rapid pace. As a result of this, many teams have set up charitable foundations as part of their business operations during the last 20 years or so. Indeed, the philanthropic activity of these foundations is an area regularly cited in CSR sport literature (Inoue, Kent, & Lee, 2011). There is little doubt that during the last two decades, sport has extended its reach into the global marketplace. Professional sports are followed the world over, and the media coverage of sport entertainment assures a disproportionally high degree of visibility of small- and medium-sized enterprises as well as larger ones. Subsequently, sport has a virtuous potential from promoting various forms of development. However, on the other hand, the product of professional sport is heavily tarnished and has throughout history been associated with cheating, corruption and exclusionary practices. There are, undoubtedly, positive and negative values attached to sport, and controversy in sport is nothing new. For example, it could be argued that corrupt dealings might equally be viewed as human nature and the understandable quest for power and influence rather than something that is just confined within sport. Society does not evolve in a totally benign manner, and sport (as an element of society) is no exception, and the values inherent in sport also change. Despite this, sport also has positive values: the education of children, the health of the public and the identity and morality of the nation. Ethical values are largely related to sport in general, and by extension to sports clubs. In the next section, we will cover the different dimensions of CSR in sport organisations and highlight relevant examples from a variety of different sports in a variety of different countries.

DIMENSIONS OF CORPORATE SOCIAL RESPONSIBILITY IN SPORT ORGANISATIONS

Philanthropic activities, community involvement and environmental initiatives

These three areas are discussed under one heading, as there is a certain degree of similarity and connection between them. Furthermore, many of the examples outlined are taken from the four major sports present in the North American model of team sports: the National Football League (NFL), National Hockey League (NHL), National Basketball Association (NBA) and Major League Baseball (MLB). There are two specific CSR practices adopted by teams in these sports, and these practices evidence the connections between philanthropic, community and environmental activities. First, teams engage in CSR by implementing community outreach programmes, such as athlete volunteerism, community development, youth educational initiatives and environmental programmes, through their community outreach or community affairs department. For example, The Florida Marlins (a baseball team since renamed as the Miami Marlins) launched a free online educational programme in 2007 designed to teach children in Grades Four–Six about subject areas such as science, mathematics and language arts. Similarly, The Philadelphia

Eagles (an American football team) have designed an environmental programme labelled 'Go Green', which is designed to reduce their environmental impacts through recycling, the use of renewable energy resources and the reduction of greenhouse gas emissions. Leagues such as the NFL, MLB, and the NHL have also begun to address environmental concerns with programmes to offset carbon emissions, as well as recycling efforts during games and major events being implemented in recent years.

The second practice that teams adopt to engage in CSR is to establish independent charitable foundations to enact their philanthropic activities. At present, nearly 90 per cent of American sports teams currently have their own charitable foundations. The primary activity of these foundations is to provide charitable contributions to local organisations operating programmes in the areas of education, youth development, community development and health-related issues. Examples of this include the NHL's 'Hockey Fights Cancer', wherein funds are raised to support cancer research, and the Pacers Foundation, the charitable foundation of the Indiana Pacers (an NBA team), which has provided more than $6 million in donations over the last decade to support issues related to youth health education. There is also evidence of such charitable foundations in European football. The English Premier League (EPL), for example, set up a new charitable fund in 2010 that supports the league's existing 'Creating Chances' scheme. This scheme uses the power of football to authorise clubs to create social intervention opportunities at the heart of their communities that can positively change lives for the better. The EPL states that this scheme has benefited 14 million people worldwide at the time of writing this textbook. The vast majority of football clubs that compete in the top two tiers of English football (the English Premier League and the Championship) now have their own charitable arms through which they engage in CSR-related activities. Everton Football Club (FC), for example, runs a scheme called 'Everton Free School', which is an alternative learning programme for disenfranchised youth.

Youth educational initiatives

One of the most important areas that CSR in sport organisations addresses is issues that are centred on youth education including grassroots sports, the training of young players, social inclusion, gender and racial equality and athletes as role models for young people. An example of an initiative aimed at covering a number a number of these factors is the NBA Cares programme that was launched in 2005 following a string of incidents that led to negative publicity for the sport and its players. The league's global community outreach initiative addresses social issues with an emphasis on programmes that support education, youth and family development, as well as health-related causes. Perhaps one of the most interesting elements of the initiative though was a well-publicised change concerning a newly established dress code for players not in uniform at NBA and team-related functions. The idea behind this was twofold. First, to highlight that in business, image is everything, and a smart dress code makes perfect sense for fostering corporate interest, sponsorship and increased revenue. Second, this policy also constituted an effort to strengthen and enhance a positive player image.

In modern day sport, we are all aware that athletes are role models, whether they like it or not. They are essentially thrust into the role of prominent public figures the moment they become professionals. Subsequently, they are left with a choice regarding their role in the lives of their supporters; however, that choice is not whether to be a role model, it is whether to be a *positive* role model. Undoubtedly, athletes will have an influence on teenagers, which means that CSR activities that engage with youth education initiatives are becoming increasingly important to professional sport organisations. A positive sporting role model can do wonders for an organisation's CSR, but a sporting role model that gets embroiled in a scandal can have an equally negative effect. By way of an example, consider a number of sport stars that do outstanding work for charities and foundations and raise money and awareness on their behalf. David Beckham, for example, has supported 16 different charities and foundations to date throughout the course of his playing career and beyond and would be considered a positive sporting role model by some. Contrast this to a sport star that has been embroiled in a controversial case such as the recent drug scandal in tennis (e.g., Maria Sharapova) or the widespread blood-doping cases in professional cycling (e.g., Lance Armstrong). Does their sporting behaviour make you think differently about them? Having sporting role models promote youth initiatives through CSR is a good idea in principle, but there are risks attached.

Health initiatives

Health initiatives have often been bookended into philanthropic and community activities in relation to CSR. However, we would argue that there is a clear distinction between health initiatives and philanthropic activity and that such initiatives warrant discussion as a separate topic, particularly as sport offers the perfect platform to encourage activity, including health awareness and anti-obesity campaigns as well as disease prevention. One of the main initiatives linked to this area is the Football Fans in Training (FFIT) programme launched by professional football clubs (first piloted in Scotland) in 2010. FFIT uses professional football clubs as a setting for a weight-management group. However, the key difference in this programme compared to other general weight-management programmes is that FFIT is predominantly aimed at the male population. The rationale behind this is that commercial and NHS weight-management programmes are still predominantly attended by women, and this is reflected in the growing evidence base on what works in weight-management interventions. Subsequently, in an attempt to provide a programme more attractive to the male population, FFIT was implemented. The FFIT research team hoped that men's loyalty to their football teams would encourage them to sign up. Men taking part in FFIT are 'trained' by club community coaches for 12 weeks at their team's home stadium. They receive a programme of advice on how to eat more healthily and become more active, grounded in current science. Men are also given a pedometer to count the number of steps they walk each day. The scheme has proved to be extremely popular so far, to such an extent that FFIT programme is now also currently being applied in other European countries such as Norway, England, Portugal and the Netherlands – where it is also seeing similar signs of success.

Financial responsibility

Even though this book is primarily aimed at community sport management – a subject not historically known for its links with finance – we cannot ignore that fact that sport is now a business in its own right and that financial responsibility is important to all sport organisations. One of the main reasons that sport is now considered a business is because of its increased commercialisation in recent years. However, a side effect of this commercialisation has been mounting criticism for various business practices (e.g., poor governance, financial problems, corruption and controversial players' behaviour). As sport becomes more commercial and sport organisations become more visible, there is a greater need for them to be transparent and accountable. The caveat to this is that a number of sport organisations and clubs (across all sectors) have faced financial difficulties in recent years, and many organisations appear financially unsustainable. Issues of governance in terms of transparency and recruitment processes, or mechanisms to ensure financial sustainability and eschew money laundering, have risen up on the corporate agenda. This is evidenced by the introduction of Financial Fair Play regulations by the Union of European Football Associations in 2010, which aimed to limit losses and debt levels at individual clubs and promote financial sustainability amongst the European leagues.

One of the primary reasons financial responsibility is an important component of CSR, particularly in English professional football, is the increasing revenue available to clubs through the broadcasting deals signed to show the games live on television. The latest deal, due to run from 2016 to 2019, is worth £5.1 billion in the UK, with a further £3 billion anticipated from the sale of overseas broadcasting rights. Upon the announcement of the deal, an article in *The Guardian* newspaper summarised the importance of the deal in the context of CSR, stating that it would be better for everyone – for fans, for clubs, for the communities they serve and for the broadcasters pouring billions into their pockets – if the huge allure that currently attracts ever-larger commercial deals could also power so-called 'community projects' on a more ambitious scale. Clubs are more than just businesses and fans more than mere consumers, but even the corporate world recognises the value of significant CSR investment.

Stakeholder management

Success in the sport industry necessitates the ability to work within a complex set of stakeholder relationships; a team cannot operate effectively without cooperation. As such, relations with stakeholders such as the media, players, various levels of government, sponsors, fans and local communities can benefit from CSR activities. All organisations in the sport industry have to interact with the different stakeholders listed before, and there are two primary reasons as to why CSR activities benefit from these relationships. Some organisations believe that doing good is the right thing to do and are involved in such initiatives for noble reasons. Some organisations, on the other hand, believe that doing good is good for business and are motivated by pragmatic matters.

Many of these pragmatic reasons have been noted in this chapter and are concerned with projecting a positive image, generating goodwill among various stakeholders (e.g., employees, extant and potential customers and the local community), countering negative media scrutiny and/or receiving tax breaks and subsidies from governing bodies. A third potential viewpoint is to propose a bridge between the 'right thing to do' and 'good business rationales for CSR in organisations'. Porter and Kramer (2002) propose such a scenario, suggesting that corporations can use their charitable efforts to improve their competitive context - the quality of the business environment in the ... locations where they operate. Using philanthropy to enhance context brings social and economic goals into alignment and improves the company's long term business prospects.

(p. 6)

Recognising the importance of various stakeholder groups in the implementation of CSR is vital. In order for sport organisations and teams to enjoy the best possible benefits that CSR implementation can offer, a multiple stakeholder perspective – that is, an outside-in approach – should be more seriously considered. The practical problem with this exercise is that it primarily requires the identification of the most significant stakeholders in such considerations. This is tricky, as different people in the organisation will have different views on who is the most important/significant stakeholder(s). In sport, we argue that one of the most important stakeholders is the fan. Fans hold the ultimate key to success for sport teams in relation to CSR activities, as they interact with all the different dimensions noted by this chapter. Not only this, but through interacting with these dimensions, fans have the power to build up the brand equity of the team, an important management concept in relation to CSR.

WHY DO SPORT TEAMS ACTIVELY ENGAGE IN CORPORATE SOCIAL RESPONSIBILITY ACTIVITIES?

This section focuses specifically on sport teams rather than organisations because of the strong influence that fans can have on the teams that they support. Some examples here might have some bearing on more general community sport organisations, but it is easier to discuss this concept in relation to team sports to help us understand the context. There are many complex relationships between a club and its fans and 'non-fans'. However, this complexity also helps us to explain, in part, the reason why CSR activities work so well in professional team sports and individual clubs. First, let us consider the relationship between a club and it's 'non-fans' using the principles of CSR outlined in the stakeholder management section. Under the context of deploying CSR because 'doing good is the right thing to do', sport teams can be portrayed in a positive light (from a 'non-fan' perspective), as engaging with the local community and certain disadvantaged groups is seen as a positive act on a societal level. As we know, sport has its dark side and receives plenty of negative press on a daily basis. Thus, being seen to engage with the local community in general is good for changing perceptions amongst 'non-fans'.

The second relationship, between a club and its fans is much easier to clarify under the context of CSR activities; it is also a much more reciprocal relationship than that which is shared with 'non-fans'. It is also, we argue, more aligned with the second concept of CSR, that 'doing good is good for business'. CSR activities are deemed to be good in general, but they can have an even more profound effect on fans of the club due to the psychological relationship they share with fans. No other sector really aligns with themes of identity, image and reputation as much as sport does. Furthermore, the sport industry appears immune to traditional expectations. This is further enhanced by the fact that sport teams benefit from a product-consumer (fan) relationship that would be the envy of many mainstream businesses (e.g., it is highly likely that the CSR activities of Manchester United FC would always be positively viewed than the CSR activities of Tesco). It is highly unlikely, for the majority of fans, that they would 'substitute' the team they support for another team in the same way that a consumer may do when deciding whether to purchase a product (as we mentioned earlier in the chapter). The emotional attachment that fans have to their sport teams is a powerful tool that can be converted into positive behaviour from fans towards their clubs if the right relationships are formed through CSR activities. Put simply, if a club manages to secure a positive image with its fans through CSR activities, then the direct result may be a conversion to equity through the purchase of merchandise, tickets, etc. That said, there is a counterargument that fans will always be favourable of their club irrespective of CSR activities, but you can never have too much of a good thing, particularly in business!

Sport organisations and teams will always be heavily indebted to fans and, as such, have a responsibility to those fans. Indeed, previous sections in this chapter on *financial responsibility* and *stakeholder management* cited the need for transparency and the importance of fans in a stakeholder context, whilst this section has discussed the unique relationship that sports teams share with their fans. This unique relationship is what puts sport organisations in a privileged position when deploying CSR and is reflected in the fact that over the last 20 years or so, a large number of professional sport teams across a multitude of different sports have adopted CSR practices and charitable arms and foundations.

Case study: Sheffield Wednesday Football Club in the community

Sheffield Wednesday FC is an English football club currently competing in the second tier of English professional football (The Championship). They have a large fan base both inside and outside of the city of Sheffield. In January 2015, a Thai businessman called Dejphon Chansiri purchased the club in a takeover deal believed to be in the region of £30 million. Following this takeover, the new owner stated that the aim over the coming years was to achieve promotion to the English Premier League (EPL), the top tier in English football. The club has also attracted interest on a more global scale, particularly in the Far East, as a result of the takeover.

Given this context and the standing of the club in the city and the English football system, it is perhaps of no surprise that the club places a strong emphasis on its CSR operations and that it has its own scheme entitled 'The Sheffield Wednesday Community Programme'. This case study provides a brief overview of this programme and the CSR activities that it engages with (the majority of which link back to the dimensions of CSR as described in this chapter).

In 2015, Sheffield Wednesday FC stated that CSR-related activities and the community programme continue to go from strength to strength. As of 2015, the club estimated that through their programme, they have been able to reach around 100,000 young people and that the range of activities provided has also expanded, creating one of the most wide-ranging community programmes not only in football, but also throughout the world of sport. Below is an extract from the club's 'statement on social responsibility' that outlines the main aim of the programme:

The Sheffield Wednesday Community Programme is the Football Club's charitable arm, established to support the development of cohesive communities around South Yorkshire and to seek to increase engagement, training provision and support amongst its residents working across four key themes:

- Participation
- Social inclusion
- Health and well-being
- Education

We endeavour to encourage confidence, active lifestyle and participation of sport regardless of gender, ethnicity and disability. The Sheffield Wednesday Community Programme enjoys major success in connecting the local community to our club and is widely recognised as an exciting market leader.

The Sheffield Wednesday Community Programme fits under five key aims:

- Raising educational achievement
- Creating pathways to employment
- Building healthier lifestyles
- Bringing communities together
- Reducing crime

The programme provides a wide variety of opportunities across a large range of different socio-economic groups and across all ability levels, with a particular focus on young people. Different groups include Early Years Programme and Mini Owls (ages 3–5); Holiday Programme (ages 4–14); Overseas Programme (ages 7–18); Healthy School Programme (Year 6 school children); Education Programme (ages 16–18); as well as a Special Needs and Disability Programme, Social Inclusion Programme (aimed at deprived areas of Sheffield) and new initiatives to link the programme to other funded projects such as running a community partnership with table tennis clubs in the local area in conjunction with Sport England. The programme has links with local and national parties (including the Premier League and other football clubs) and supports local charities such as Bluebell Wood Children's Hospice, The Children's Hospital Charity (Sheffield) and Western Park Hospital Cancer Charity. The programme also has its own sustainability policy with a focus on reducing the environmental impact of its activities.

The football club firmly believes in investing in its community programme, and they are currently building a new community facility on Penistone Road (near the football club's home stadium of Hillsborough), which, when complete, will hold the proud status as the biggest and best of its kind in the country. The building is a unique, family-friendly facility based on the fundamental foundation of social inclusion, participation, education, job creation, sport, health, leisure and well-being. The extensive site projection also houses a healthcare centre and pharmacy, up-skills centre, classrooms, kids' zone, indoor and outdoor pitches and ancillary accommodation. The facility will place CSR at the very heart of Sheffield Wednesday and allow work to expand into new areas, firmly underlining that the concept of CSR activities is an important management consideration for a professional sports team in the modern-day sport industry.

CONCLUSION

This chapter has introduced you to the concept of CSR and the different dimensions of CSR activities that affect sport organisations. Against the objectives of the chapter, you should now understand and appreciate the importance of CSR in sport and the uniqueness of CSR in sport compared to other mainstream businesses.

CSR in sport is still very much, and will continue to be, an ongoing matter for community sport managers and researchers. It should continue to consider the economic, legal, social and ethical issues sport organisations need to address and strategically incorporate into their business operations. Furthermore, the social nature of sport lends itself to social initiatives and outreach programmes. More and more sport organisations are beginning to realise the power sport holds to deploy CSR, and whilst the nature of the industry will always be dominated in some way by commercial aspects, a shift towards formulating charitable foundations is apparent. This is particularly relevant for organisations operating at a community level.

Such power is not exclusively confined to the sport industry either. There is currently an ever-increasing number of corporations who now see sport organisations, events or athletes as an appropriate vehicle to achieve their own social and commercial ends. As such, sport organisations are in a privileged position that is the envy of other business sectors in respect to CSR and deploying CSR practices for maximising positive impact within the community. Since the concept of CSR was first introduced in the 1950s, there has been a proactive shift within the sport industry to deploy CSR as a strategic tool. The nature of sporting competition is to obtain a competitive advantage over rivals, and the multitude of CSR practices creates a perfect opportunity for strategic gains for sport organisations amongst their competitors in the industry.

REVIEW QUESTIONS

1. What are the main types of CSR activities that are deployed by professional sport clubs?
2. Do these types of activities vary depending on the country, size, level or culture?
3. Why do sport clubs engage in CSR-related activities?
4. Describe the unique relationship that sport clubs share with their fans and how this might impact their CSR-related activities.

5. Read the case study on Sheffield Wednesday FC Community Programme. Find another professional sport club's community programme (in the UK or overseas) and list the main similarities and differences between your chosen club and the Sheffield Wednesday FC Community Programme.
6. Who do you think are the most important stakeholders in an organisation? And should CSR be pursued for noble or business reasons?

FURTHER READING

Bradish, C. L., & Cronin, J. J. (2009). Special issue: Corporate social responsibility in sport. *Journal of Sport Management, 23*(6), 691–794.

This special issue (consisting of four papers, in addition to an introduction) addresses a number of topics and contexts relevant to CSR in sport, including the determinants of CSR in professional sport, the influence of CSR on consumer attitudes in the sport industry and community development and sporting events.

Djaballah, M. (2017). Corporate social responsibility in sport. In U. Wagner, R. K. Storm, & Nielson, K. (Eds.), *When sport meets business: Capabilities, challenges, critiques* (pp. 137–150). London: SAGE.

A chapter that focusses more on CSR in bigger commercial team sports with more of a business management focus. Good international case studies.

Paramio-Salcines, J. L., Babiak, K., & Walters, G. (Eds.). (2013). *The Routledge handbook of sport and corporate social responsibility.* London: Routledge.

A comprehensive text that covers a wide range of CSR concepts and functions in sport such as how to implement and measure CSR activities.

REFERENCES

Inoue, Y., Kent, A., & Lee, S. (2011). CSR and the bottom line: Analyzing the link between CSR and financial performance for professional teams. *Journal of Sport Management, 25*(6), 531–549.

Porter, M. E., & Kramer, M. R. (2002). The competitive advantage of corporate philanthropy. *Harvard Business Review, 80*(12), 56–68.

Smith, A., & Westerbeek, H. (2007). Sport as a vehicle for deploying corporate social responsibility. *Journal of Corporate Citizenship, 25,* 43–54.

CHAPTER 7

Community engagement through elite sport

Chris Stone

SUMMARY

In the 1980s, problems surrounding one of Britain's most popular elite sports alongside changes in society more widely encouraged the development of a more instrumental engagement between football clubs and particular communities. One way in which this was attempted was through Football in the Community (FitC) schemes. Since then, community football departments, which often operate as independent not-for-profit organisations but remain linked to their professional clubs, have become important parts of local service delivery. This chapter takes a critical look at these organisations to help shed light on the strengths and weaknesses they bring to community sport and physical activity.

AIMS

By engaging with this chapter, you will be able to

- Understand the historical context of football clubs' formal and informal relationships with various 'communities of need',
- Begin to be able to critically examine football as a community engagement and development tool,
- Differentiate between various aspects of the football industry's communal responsibilities, and
- Locate community sport engagement approaches and football within wider social, economic and political debates.

INTRODUCTION

We've probably all seen the excerpts on Football Focus, Sky Sports News or on Social Media of football players visiting a local hospital or joining in with a local event. Many of you may have been involved yourselves in a community event or programme organised by a professional sport club. So, what is the purpose of such engagement, and why do clubs, many of which are multimillion-pound companies and global brands, undertake such work? What moral obligation do professional athletes, many of whom are also major celebrities and global brands in their own right, have in engaging with their local communities? The aim of this chapter is to explore the community responsibilities of professional football clubs and football's governing bodies.

In order to do this, the chapter will start by considering the development of football club community organisations and, in particular, the ways in which those who govern the game have sought to maintain ethical relationships between the sport's structures and their various constituents. For example, those who organise the football leagues and cup competitions may have different views on the values of sport to those who participate or spectate; a football club's owner may have a very different perspective on the purpose of the club to that of the supporters; the importance of a football club to local residents may not be as football club staff expect and vice versa; commercial imperatives may impact upon certain groups and individuals to the point where they become excluded from engaging with the sport as they would want; the mass media may be interested in telling a story that differs considerably to the version a player's agent or club's marketing department want to convey or that fans want to hear.

The chapter discusses the relationship between a football club and its key stakeholders – the supporters – who historically have had a strong connection to the club's locality. The question I ask in this part of the chapter is to what extent are different professional football clubs businesses like any other or conveyors of civic identity and part of local heritage? How do clubs reconcile themselves as both a 'profit maximiser' and 'utility maximiser' (Hamil & Morrow, 2011)? In other words, to what extent do football clubs operate in a similar way to conventional businesses in trying to maximise their profits compared with maximising playing success whilst remaining solvent and operational as a local provision?

As one of the most popular spectator sports and recreational leisure activities, the development of modern football as an elite sport in the UK is linked with local social history and community involvement.[1] In recent years, professional football clubs' community sport departments have been increasing in size, stature and responsibilities, often leading in the delivery of local services. Consequently, for those interested in the development and management of community sport, understanding how and why this has come about is vital, whether looking for a career in the ever-increasing community football industry or in other sports that are beginning to use similar models.

FOOTBALL AND ITS COMMUNITIES: A HISTORICAL UNDERSTANDING

Organic relationships

Professional football clubs have historically had a significant connection with their local communities (Holt, 1989; Russell, 1997). During the sport's early years, many of the pioneering professional clubs were borne out of local entities such as Working Men's Clubs, church organisations or prominent industries. As clubs developed through the 19th century, despite some questions over their motivations, they provided a solid local identity during a period of great expansion that resulted from mass urban migration and the industrial revolution. Clubs were also a distraction from the toil and underdeveloped living and working conditions, which many people had to tolerate. For their owners, they were used to signify local status and possibly a source of income that exploited local people's need for recreational distraction.

Nonetheless, clubs became linked to cities, towns or districts and have developed long-standing relationships with local communities, both positively and negatively. For example, while some may see football clubs as a symbol of civic pride or personal identity, others see them as an inconvenience or aggravation (Bale, 1993).

Instrumental engagement

The 1970s and 1980s was a turbulent time in Britain with regard to football culture and, indeed, society more widely. Years of relative prosperity changes in politics and society resulted in deep class divisions, as the government of the time chased economic progress at the expense of unity within society and industry (Ling, 1998; Mankiw & Taylor, 2017). In this context, working-class communities suffered as long-standing local industries declined, resulting in mass unemployment. There was tension in inner-city areas as increasing numbers of ethnic minorities challenged the prejudice that had held them at the bottom of the socio-economic scale and demonised them for attempting to maintain their cultural distinctiveness.

Over the same period of time, football clubs had neglected the core of their support with, for example, little in the way of improvements to stadia and a lack of investment in infrastructure. This period also saw a rise in football disorder in and around stadia, as 'hooliganism' became synonymous with British football culture. Indeed, following more than a decade of football-related violence dominating the headlines, the need for a solution left the authorities turning to clubs themselves as a possible panacea to the problem that was perceived to be dominating the sport. Clubs were also seen as having potential practical influence in supporting people within the local community who were suffering from the consequences of deindustrialisation.

In 1986, a pilot scheme, FitC, was initially started by the Football League and Professional Footballers' Association (PFA) at six clubs in the north-west of England: Bolton Wanderers, Bury, Manchester City, Manchester United, Oldham Athletic and Preston North End, with funding from the Manpower Services Commission.[2] The programme was initially promoted as aiming to

- Provide employment and training for unemployed people,
- Promote close links between professional football clubs and the community,
- Involve minority ethnic groups in social and recreational activities,
- Attempt to prevent acts of hooliganism and vandalism and
- Maximise the use of the facilities of the football clubs.

As part of the PFA Footballers' Further Education and Vocational Training scheme, it also provided a crucial role for the PFA's members once their playing careers came to an end.

Despite this range of aims, the core business activities of FitC were school-based programmes, holiday courses and soccer schools, which all centred on coaching activities for young people, fitting the sport development model of encouraging participation and promoting progression towards elite performance. This allowed clubs to benefit from potential talent if spotted through the activities, but predominantly helped maintain the club's brand with new generations of potential supporters. It also brought in a small income and provided a role for former players within the club. There is little in the way of evidence showing the achievements of this pilot, but it was clearly perceived a success and led to FitC being rolled out to all football-league clubs. This was perhaps because, as has been mentioned in Chapter 1 of this book, at that time, there was a perceived need to address so-called 'problematic' categories in society, and, as a result, 'community development' work had emerged as an increasingly common part of public policy and local authority delivery.

Expansion, diversification and the politics of engagement

During the 1990s, the work in which FitC departments engaged began to expand to include other activities with a wider social agenda. Classroom-based activities within football stadia often supplemented the FitC activities through schemes such as Playing for Success, a partnership between the Department for Education and Skills, the Premier League (PL), Nationwide Football League, their respective clubs and local authorities. Football was also beginning to be used to combat antisocial behaviour, such as smoking, alcohol/drug misuse, glue-sniffing and making 'hoax' phone calls to the emergency services (Mellor, 2002). This was an extension to the alleged benefits of sport that have underpinned policy in successive governments. Where previously the political pursuit of 'Sport for All' was rooted in the perceived developmental qualities of sport that were being lost through a gradual erosion of physical education in schools and increased post–16 drop out, a new agenda was emerging in recognition of social structures and communities that had become more fragmented and were facing complex forms of multiple deprivation at a local level.

Specific reviews of the FitC scheme (Williams & Taylor, 1994; McGuire & Fenoglio, 2004) and studies of football's relationship with their local communities more widely (Brown et al., 2006) point to the breadth of work that was being encompassed within football club community departments. Despite being able to point to positive results from individual programmes, however, there have been regular calls for more evidence to support the claims that football-based engagement work has positive impacts on local communities and the people within them (Coalter, 2007; Tacon, 2007). Similarly to the wider critique of community development work failing to offer a bottom-up approach, football was also criticised for adopting top-down approaches. Very few 'community' initiatives were coming directly from football clubs themselves or the constituents to whom they were directly targeting their work (Taylor, 2004). Rather, the programmes were encouraged, or enforced, by central government, local authorities or organisations such as the Football Foundation or the PFA.

Independence and professionalisation

Victory by New Labour in the 1997 general election signalled a shift in politics. Adopting something they termed 'third way thinking' (see Giddens & Sutton, 2017; Blackshaw, 2010), it was believed that civil society could be rediscovered through holding those in power to account. By this time, the PL had been born and was developing at a rapid pace, increasing in power as it did. Consequently, the 'business of football' was under pressure to be accountable for the way it operated, how it was governed and the role played by media organisations, which was resulting in an exponential growth in turnover. In order to do this, the government and those in power within football claimed football should be viewed as a community asset (Mellor, 2008; Sanders et al., 2014).

Previously, the sport had been left to its own devices, as had many other industries. Following the Taylor Report into the Hillsborough disaster, however, football was developing from being politically classed as 'a law and order issue' into something of a 'cash cow', benefiting, as it was, from politically enforced change following the tragedy and commercial deals struck between the more powerful clubs and television broadcasting companies. Whilst stadium improvements were welcome, many football supporters increasingly felt they were being priced out of attending matches, and, thus, the relationship between clubs and their supporters was arguably altering. Supporters were becoming customers, consumers of a sporting experience. Those that could not afford it were not wanted. They became the responsibility of 'community' departments.

A drive by the New Labour government in using sport to help realise their social agenda alongside an increasingly experienced 'community sport' workforce led some football club community departments to set themselves up as independent charities, separate to the football clubs themselves. Hamil and Morrow (2011) identify that, in doing this, clubs were able to bring together all community-based activities under one umbrella organisation, benefit from claiming charitable status, have easier access to external funding (including government funding), work with other football clubs in pursuit of joint community goals, reduce the dependence on the team's on-field performance and create financial independence for community work. Notwithstanding these benefits, a key rationale for such a move was the realisation that clubs in financial difficulty could not sustain (or chose not to maintain support for) community work that was generally not perceived to be part of a professional football club's core business – yet, in many cases, had become an essential part of local service provision. This was happening at a time when the core business of seeking success on the field coupled with widening gaps between the bigger clubs and the rest, as increasing amounts of money poured into the football industry, produced a rush for more riches. Ever-increasing exposure on television and the financial rewards associated with it was causing some clubs to overinvest in things like player wages, without sufficient contingencies if on-field performances fell short leading to widespread fear of insolvency. In many cases, the first casualty was the community department and the main victims were those already socially excluded for whom statutory services had already failed.

Held up as leading the way for independent football community organisations is the Leyton Orient Community Sports Programme (LOCSP). The original three-way partnership between Leyton Orient Football Club, Sport England and the Arts and Leisure Department of the local authority was quite unique at the time. Each partner had their own rationale for engaging more local people in sporting activity, and the success of the programme saw it expand enormously between its beginnings in 1989 and its acknowledgment as Football Trust Community Club of the Year in 1995. Along with a number of other similarly successful football club community operations, LOCSP's achievements were built upon a bottom-up strategy that has been detailed elsewhere in this book.

This was based on the development of relationships between the organisation and 'target populations' through establishing shared interests and mutual benefits, whether that be with local residents, youth workers, coaches, criminal justice workers or any other individual working to maximise social cohesion and bring the community together (Taylor, 2004).

The reconfiguring of football club community departments, as independent and self-reliant entities, was seen as a key strength by Brown et al. (2006), whose work was prompted by evermore football clubs uprooting their position within local communities by building new stadia in new geographical locations, often on the outskirts of towns and cities. The research explored the impact of such moves as part of a wider investigation of football and its communities and, interestingly for us, raised questions about how football clubs defined their communities and how they effectively worked with different stakeholders. If the club moves from its traditional 'home', can it still engage effectively with the communities and partner organisations it leaves behind?

Furthermore, what about the different types of communities with whom the club engages: supporter communities, local neighbourhood communities, business communities and 'communities of need'?[3] To what extent are these different stakeholders seen as mutually exclusive? We must also ask who exactly has the power in these relationships to define and control the direction of resources, as well as what different stakeholders might want from the club. Is it the communities themselves, particular individuals within communities, the football club, their commercial partners, the independent community foundations and their staff, or is it directed by funders and the political agenda that is currently driving social policy?

The research by Brown et al. (2006) led to a number of recommendations, including the development of independent community organisations and more holistic approaches to community development and engagement. This has had two unintended consequences. First, a separation between 'the football club' and its 'community department' (Supporters Direct, 2010) and, second, an approach, by the community department, that focuses more on income generation in order to survive than the needs of the community. In this scenario, the football club operates as a business and the community department as a Corporate Social Responsibility (CSR) arm. The club's key stakeholders are its (paying) fans and sponsors, and the community department provides a platform for maximising exposure amongst other stakeholders that have become defined by professionally, politically and socially conceived demographic factors.

A few questions are raised from these consequences. For example, how does this compare to football clubs' positions within local communities in the past? Has increasing professionalisation of the community football industry led to distinct definition of and separation between communities of supporters, who are increasingly dispersed beyond the immediate vicinity of their club, and the communities the club supports, a more geographically bound client group whose reciprocal relationship with the club is based on (perceived) social needs and corporate responsibilities? In addition to this, Brown (2008) highlights that when thinking about the social value of football clubs, we need to differentiate between and understand the different roles of the 'direct' community interventions by a club's community scheme and the overall operation of the club as a local institution. For example, does having a community department defer or protect the club from wider responsibilities? There are, after all, plenty of issues with which we might associate professional football that can be argued to indicate social irresponsibility on the part of those running, supporting and playing the game. These include crowd violence, institutional and individualised racism, gender inequality, homophobia, sex and alcohol offences, corruption, gamesmanship and general role modelling. Of course, the extent to which these are problematic depends upon the value system deemed to be important within a particular culture (Blackshaw & Crabbe, 2004).

In some respects, these issues have meant community departments have had to take a more professional approach to their operations and, as part of this ongoing professionalisation, have developed more sophisticated means of monitoring and evaluation (M&E), a process that is explored in more detail in Chapter 15. Suffice to say, however, that the need for more evidence-based practice has helped facilitate more critical studies being carried out. Good examples include work by Parnell et al. (2013), Rutherford et al. (2014), Sanders et al. (2012) and Stone (2013). The other point to make here is that there has been a shift to focus on outcomes as well as outputs (Hindley & Williamson, 2013; Parnell et al., 2013).

Let me explain what I mean by that. Focusing on outputs is concerned with getting as many people involved as possible and is often evaluated through the production of quantitative data. While this has its place, I would argue that concentrating on outcomes – that is to say, the progress made by those involved in a programme – is just as, if not more, important. If people are turning up but not gaining anything, how successful is that scheme? There has also been a concentration on successes with a lack of critical analysis of the negative outcomes or outputs. For complete transparency, and in the interests of improving, the management of any community programme should also report on where the difficulties lie alongside celebrating the success.

THE ROLE OF FOOTBALL AUTHORITIES AND OTHER PARTNERSHIPS

The English Football League and Premier League

Since 2007, football club community programmes have been overseen and supported by the English Football League Trust (EFLT) and the PL, so it is worth reflecting a little on the work they do. The EFLT was established as a vehicle to distribute funding from the PL and some other sources in support of community work carried out within the English Football League (EFL). Beyond this, they also distribute monies obtained through commercial partnerships and government contracts. Since 2011, for example, the EFLT has been responsible for delivering the government-funded National Citizen Service (NCS) through the community departments of its league clubs. As with other realms of the football industry, the PL has an increasing part to play in community sport. For example, the PL currently has a communities strategy with the following aims:

- Use its ability in connecting with young people to help them realise their potential
- Inspire ambition in communities and schools
- Support young people to improve their skills on and off the sports field
- Invest in facilities and create opportunities in high-need areas

In trying to achieve these aims, the PL (2016) runs community schemes including Premier League Kicks, Premier League 4 Sport, Premier League Girls Football, Premier Skills, Premier League Enterprise, Premier League/BT Disability Fund and Premier League Works. This is an impressive list of schemes, and you are encouraged to go and explore what each of these schemes tries to achieve. However, for me, a couple of questions remain. First, why should the PL, whose primary role is to organise the football competition between the 20 Clubs, fund community-based programmes? And, second, if it is their role, is the 1.6 per cent[4] or so of their £3 billion revenue income an adequate financial commitment?

Should we be asking ourselves whether such involvement increases the dominance of the PL over 'flawed consumers' (Bauman, 2004) who have been priced out of engaging with their product through the more conventional means of match attendance? Or is it a case of an altruistic benefactor realising what differences can be made to lives that have been disadvantaged by continuing social change? Does it matter if the overall outcomes are of benefit?

The Professional Footballers Association

The PFA continues to support football clubs' community engagement work (PFA, 2016) through an agreement with clubs to engage players in community activities whilst highlighting their involvement in a positive and productive way. They recognise that support is needed for professional football players if they themselves, their clubs and the sport more widely are to benefit from their alleged status as role models. High-profile cases of players' illegal, immoral or deviant behaviour can tarnish the image of the sport and the positive work associated with community engagement programmes. More routinely, player community engagements must be managed to best match individuals with charitable events or campaigns from which both parties will gain benefit. Players must be well briefed because many invitations may put them outside their comfort zone in terms of familiarity with issues facing certain sections of society. In such cases, players, clubs and participants will gain little if the interactions seem awkward and/or players seem to lack the empathy for a particular community. To what extent have the changes in the social backgrounds of many professional football players had an effect on their relationships with local communities and supporter communities? Are professional football players and clubs' main stakeholders from similar cultural or economic backgrounds?

Case study: Sheffield United Community Foundation

Sheffield United Football Club's current community engagement is undertaken through the guise of the Sheffield United Community Foundation (SUCF). SUCF is the latest incarnation of a part of the club that began life as a FitC scheme. It operates as a charity that is funded through various sources independent to the finances generated by the football club's main business of competing in the national football league. This reflects a change in how such football club-based engagement work is funded more widely and responds to recommendations made by Brown et al. (2006) discussed earlier in the chapter.

The Sheffield United FitC scheme began in 1988, and according to the Sheffield United website, the purpose of FitC was as follows (SUFC, 2007) (Figure 7.1):

Although the website suggested that the FitC programme included forming wide links with local communities, the core of the work took place around the school timetable and had a focus on raising brand awareness amongst children through opportunities to develop their football abilities. There were also the financial rewards attached to charging for attendance at football coaching courses run by qualified football coaches and former players. This was how it remained for almost 18 years with more socially

---

What does United's FitC do?
- Encourage more people to play football – especially children
- Encourage more people to watch Sheffield United – again, especially children
- Forge links between local communities and Sheffield United
- Provide youth training qualifications up to NVQ level II

What are the current activities undertaken?
- In-school coaching programme
- After-school coaching
- Sponsored penalty shoot-outs
- Coaching on inset days
- Soccer Schools every school holiday
- Saturday Club
- Holiday Club
- Birthday parties
- Competitions - girls and boys six-a-side football
- Table football

How does Sheffield United benefit?
- More people are introduced to the Blades from a young age
- Develops a 'fan base' from a young age
- Public and community relations
- Enforces our equal opportunities policy by working with all members of the local community
- Gives the club first-hand contact to local talented youngsters for introduction to the Academy system
- Encourage more people to watch Sheffield United
- Make Sheffield United recognised nationally for its links and support it provides for the local community

---

FIGURE 7.1 Understanding FitC

directed initiatives during this period being undertaken by small independent community initiatives such as Football Unites Racism Divides working in partnership with the football club.

Sheffield United's brief promotion to the PL in the 2006/2007 season coincided with the introduction of the Kickz Programme (now rebranded as Kicks due to a copyright infringement), which was developed following discussions between the sport's governing bodies, the Football Foundation and the Metropolitan Police Service. Funding was provided through a combination of these bodies, with the original aim of working with young people deemed most at risk of criminal behaviour.

Changes in personnel at the board level within the club led to restructuring, and the Kicks agenda led to a widening of the club's reach in engaging with young people that required new and innovative engagement approaches. Consequently, there was a need to employ staff with a slightly different skill set – people who had youth work and community engagement experience as much as football coaching badges, something debated in more detail in Chapter 9. With this widening scope, the community side of the club became an incorporated charity and was rebranded as The United Initiative in 2008. Further subsequent changes in personnel, including the employment of a Business Development Officer, have led to greater operational independence. However, it was also recognised that a stronger symbolic link with the parent club was necessary, and The United Initiative was renamed the SUCF in 2013. This connection is reinforced and supported by a Service Level Agreement between the SUCF and Sheffield United Football Club.

The SUCF's vision is for a more active, healthy, educated, respectful and integrated society in Sheffield through the provision of a variety of interventions in the areas of sport participation, education, health and social inclusion. The head of the department has the belief that such interventions can encourage local people either to become a supporter for life and/or develop themselves to realise their full potential. The dual themes of brand awareness amongst young people and skill attainment still dominates the rationale for such work, but the latter has moved beyond just football skill development to incorporate a focus on developing individuals with whom they engage. This is, in part, the result of employing staff with a wider skill base and a realisation that the social inclusion agenda, explored in Chapters 3 and 5, has funding attached that football-based engagement programmes led by a strong local brand provide the dual goal of self-sufficiency and positive public relations.

The SUCF's stated aims are to

- Offer innovative programmes in the key areas of sport participation, health, education and social inclusion;
- Build links between the football club and the community using the appeal of football and sport in general;
- Use sport as a motivational tool to encourage, motivate and inspire individuals, regardless of background, to reach their potential;
- Promote healthy and active lifestyles through sport;
- Offer programmes aimed at developing personal skills, improving academic achievement and enhancing employability;

- Engage with people regardless of age, ability, race, religion, gender, sexual orientation or disability;
- Support pathways for player development from grassroots and community football; and
- Act as positive role models at all times, and be a valued contributor to community and personal well-being.

You may notice that these aims are not so dissimilar to the aims of the original FitC pilot programme. Any reference to hooliganism has clearly disappeared, but the core purpose is linked with education, training and employment, as well as building connections between the club and its communities. In recognition of increasingly diverse identity politics since the inception of this kind of work, in terms of intersecting understandings of structural difference amongst minority groups and their political will to raise awareness of particular issues related to their specific culture, engagement has also become about recognising such diversity and trying to overcome barriers faced by various minorities (as opposed to the more explicit focus on ethnicity in the initial FitC pilot programme).

Brand value in the community

The key advantage that the SUCF has over other agencies delivering similar programmes is the association with a professional football club. The brand value of Sheffield United may not be as high as other clubs (except within the established fan base), but associations with other parts of the football family, such as the PL, gives the organisation more authority – which may be lesser or greater with certain groups compared to others. Think about the kind of people that are attracted to football and to clubs at different levels of the league. Such limitations notwithstanding, the work is usually delivered by enthusiastic and committed staff. In fact, it is the relationship between the quality of the work on the ground and the reputation of the football club that builds credibility at the local level. It is, therefore, crucial to manage potentially negative actions on the part of the club, whether players, coaching staff or in the boardroom. The negativity surrounding former Sheffield United striker Ched Evans's original conviction for rape whilst playing for the club and the subsequent legal battles being a case in point as community programmes promoting equality (and attached community partnerships) would not be able to sit under the same brand that did not openly condemn such actions.[5]

SUCF's work spans across five strands: Participation, Education, NCS, Social Inclusion and Health & Wellbeing. Each strand has a number of projects and will be funded from varying sources. An overview of the amount of money we are talking about is detailed in Figure 7.2.

Much of the funding is sourced through having to bid to relevant bodies either to renew existing contracts or to develop new avenues of work. The majority comes from the PL, Football League Trust and the Big Lottery, but other sources include the city council, education providers, health authorities and private business. In addition, the

Strand Summary	2015/16 Income (£)	2015/16 Costs (£)
General Contribution	30,000	141,600
NCS Contribution	351,000	110,540
Participation Contribution	145,000	157,000
Health Contribution	0	22,080
Social Inclusion Contribution	89,000	74,000
Education Contribution	194,000	167,000
Total Contribution	**809,826**	**673,975**

FIGURE 7.2 Contribution analysis

club chairman has set up a business support network, 'Friends of the Foundation', with the aim of broadening the scope of delivery through various strands of work. Money is received as direct donations from local businesses ranging from car sales showrooms to carpet fitters and printing companies to public relations.

The Community Foundation employs a range of individuals including former players, qualified teachers, youth workers and football coaches. The majority are local people, some of whom have progressed from being participants or volunteers on various projects, as well as newly qualified graduates. The mix of individuals provides different qualities as cultural intermediaries in engaging different communities. The complexity of the staff structure is shown in Figure 7.3.

Where previously the FitC scheme operated under a small team of senior and junior coaches, the current structure includes more than 50 members of staff. Senior members of staff are employed on permanent contracts subject to the sustainability of funding levels, but the majority are employed on one-year rolling contracts, such is the precarious nature of community work.

As can be seen from the list of projects described on their website (www.sufc-community.com), the legacy of FitC remains. The participation and education strands are most developed, but, following the investment from the Kicks programme, engagement is becoming increasingly diverse. Much of the work focuses on young people from varying backgrounds and is linked to how the community engagement work has been funded over the years and the club's partnerships with other community-based organisations.

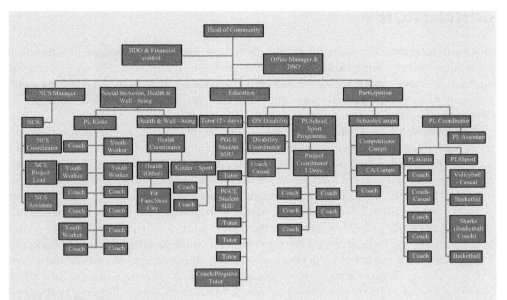

FIGURE 7.3 Community programme structure

This increase and growing reputation has had an effect on other organisations working in the community football development sector.

The future

The individuals and communities with which SUCF want to work and those with which they are able to work are still heavily mitigated by the kind of funding being sourced. It is the requirements of funders that tend to direct the work, but as the foundation has grown and matured, it has been better able to start pilot programmes for which further funding can be sought if they are shown to be successful.

As the club's community arm has attained an increasingly business-centred approach to charitable work, particular opportunities for future development have been identified by the SUCF. It is pertinent to pay attention to particular themes that have a national and political focus, such as the current health agenda. It has also been recognised that continuing pressure on local authority budgets has led private/charity organisations to become increasingly engaged to fill gaps in service provision that are not being served by statutory services. Such organisations are also in competition for funding from private/public organisations seeking to execute their CSR agendas. The SUCF's strength is the way in which it has developed its work as part of a recognised (local) brand. This could, however, also impede further development because there is a perception that the SUCF only offers football solutions. Furthermore, the connection with the football club may also prove disadvantageous due to an assumption that the SUCF have unlimited access to the perceived wealth that exists in football. A final threat that has been identified is related to ever-increasing competition within the field of community sport development, as existing providers become more professional, and new organisations form with their own expertise and specific agendas.

CONCLUSION

Since the inception of modern football, clubs have had an ever-changing relationship with their various communities. In the 1980s, problems surrounding the sport alongside changes in society more widely encouraged the development of a more instrumental engagement between football clubs and particular 'communities of need' through the development of FitC schemes.

The perceived success of these schemes led to the broadening of community engagement work through the use of football, around which there have been consistent calls for more evidence to support such work. In some locations, football club community departments became vital parts of local service delivery, leading to separation from the club itself. They now operate as mostly autonomous entities, having been set up as independent not-for-profit organisations linked to the parent club mainly through brand attachment.

Fitting perfectly with New Labour's 'third way' politics when they came into power at the turn of the 21st century, professional football clubs have incorporated community engagement work as part of corporate social responsibility activities, and the independent community departments have grown in income and output. Consequently, there has been a need to be more professional about M&E of the work. Funding is obtained through numerous sources, and whilst some will be specific to the local context, most come from a central governing body or political department and are used to meet localised demands as best they can. Community engagement work, thus, attempts to combine bottom-up and top-down approaches.

The enormous range of partnerships between football clubs, football authorities, commercial organisations and charitable entities demonstrates the complexity of the sector. As football club community organisations have grown in both experience and financial stature, however, there are potential consequences in terms of monopolising the work; potentially taking over areas of work previously undertaken by already-established and politically motivated, but less powerful (in terms of branding), community organisations. Ultimately though, success or failure of community engagement is heavily reliant on the individual relationships, background and interests of personnel involved, whether community coaches or club playing staff.

REVIEW QUESTIONS

1. Do you think problems in society are the responsibility of the football industry? Why? What solutions might football clubs offer that are different to other delivery providers?
2. What are the significant differences between a top-down approach initiated by the authorities and a bottom-up approach developed in consultation with specific communities?
3. How have football community schemes changed in terms of staffing, funding, target populations and overall aims?
4. What do you think are the advantages and disadvantages of creating an independent, not-for-profit community department?

5. What are the ways in which a football club interacts with different communities? How would you distinguish and define the communities with which a football club interacts?

FURTHER READING

Brown, A., Crabbe, T., Mellor, G., Blackshaw, T. & Stone, C. (2006). *Football and Its Communities: Final Report*. Manchester: Football Foundation and Manchester Metropolitan University.

McGuire, B. & Fenoglio, R. (2004). *Resources and Opportunities: A National Research Project for FitC*. Manchester: Manchester Metropolitan University.

Supporters Direct. (2010). *The Social and Community Value of Football: Summary Report*. Manchester: Substance.

NOTES

1 There is not enough space here to explore the global aspects of football and elite sport as a contemporary vehicle for community development. An excellent text in this field is Darnell, S. (2012) *Sport for Development and Peace: A Critical Sociology*. London: Bloomsbury.

2 Created in 1973, the Manpower Services Commission was a public body operating within the Department of Employment with a remit to co-ordinate employment and training services across the UK. They were most closely associated with the management of the Youth Training Scheme intended to help alleviate high levels of unemployment in the 1980s.

3 A term coined by Twelvetrees (2008) that categorises particular individuals and communities as 'in need' based on the belief that they are outside the social and political norms of other communities.

4 As of 2016, this is the percentage devoted to the programmes listed above. It is different to oft-cited official figures, which usually include solidarity payments to clubs further down the league structure. In May 2017, an agreement was struck in which the PL would commit £100 million a year to grassroots football. This equates to approximately 3.6 per cent of the increased £4.5 billion annual income as a consequence of new broadcasting deals for the period 2016–2019. The question remains: is this adequate?

5 This particular case was complicated by the player's continued denial of the charges and subsequent acquittal. But, whilst he was not guilty of rape within the legal framework, the whole incident left the club in a moral quandary.

REFERENCES

Bale, J. (1993). *Sport, Space and the City*. London: Routledge.

Bauman, Z. (2004). *Work, Consumerism and the New Poor*. Maidenhead: Open University Press.

Blackshaw, T. (2010). *Key Concepts in Community Studies*. London: SAGE.

Blackshaw, T. & Crabbe, T. (2004). *New Perspectives on Sport and 'Deviance': Consumption, Performativity and Social Control*. Abingdon: Routledge.

Brown, A. (2008). 'How can we value the social impact of football clubs?: qualitative approaches', *The Social Value of Football Research Project for Supporters Direct: Working Papers*. Manchester: Substance.

Brown, A., Crabbe, T., Mellor, G., Blackshaw, T. & Stone, C. (2006). *Football and Its Communities: Final Report*. Manchester: Football Foundation and Manchester Metropolitan University.

Coalter, F. (2007). *A Wider Social Role for Sport: Who's Keeping the Score?* London: Routledge.

Giddens, A. & Sutton, P.W. (2017). 'Reforming the welfare state', in A. Giddens & P.W. Sutton (eds.) *Sociology* (8th ed.), pp. 554–557. Cambridge: Polity Press.

Hamil, S. & Morrow, S. (2011). 'Corporate social responsibility in the Scottish Premier League: context and motivation', *European Sport Management Quarterly*, 11(2):143–170.

Hindley, D. & Williamson, D. (2013). 'Measuring and evaluating community sports projects: Notts County Football in the community', in K. Babiak, J. Paramio & G. Walters (eds.) *The Handbook of Sport and Corporate Social Responsibility*. London: Routledge, pp. 317–327.

Holt, R. (1989). *Sport and the British: A Modern History*. Oxford: Oxford University Press.

Ling, T. (1998). *The British State Since 1945: An Introduction*. Cambridge: Polity Press.

Mankiw, N.G. & Taylor, M.P. (2017). 'Supply side policies', in *Economics* (4th ed.). Andover: Cengage Learning EMEA.

McGuire, B. & Fenoglio, R. (2004). *Resources and Opportunities: A National Research Project for FitC*. Manchester: Manchester Metropolitan University.

Mellor, G. (2002). 'Can we have our fans back now? Football, community and the historical struggle of small-town clubs', in Singer & Friedlander, *Football Review 2000–01 Season*. Leicester: The Centre for Research into Sport and Society at the University of Leicester, pp. 34–37.

Mellor, G. (2008). ''The Janus–faced sport': English football, community and the legacy of the 'third way'', *Soccer & Society*, 9(3):313–324.

Parnell, D., Stratton, G., Drust, B. & Richardson, D. (2013). 'Implementing 'monitoring and evaluation' techniques within a Premier League FitC scheme: a case study involving Everton in the community', in K. Babiak, J. Paramio & G. Walters (eds.) *The Handbook of Sport and Corporate Social Responsibility*. London: Routledge.

PFA. (2016). *PFA Community Evaluation: Providing Inspiration & Opportunities through Positive Support*. London: Players Football Association.

Premier League. (2016). 'Programmes', *Premier League Website*. www.premierleague.com/communities/programmes.

Russell, D. (1997). *Football and the English: Of Association Football in England, 1863–1995*. Preston: Carnegie Publishing.

Rutherford, Z., Gough, B., Seymour-Smith, S., Matthews, C.R., Wilcox, J., Parnell, D. & Pringle, A. (2014). ''Motivate': the effect of a FitC delivered weight loss programme on over 35-year old men and women's cardiovascular risk factors', *Soccer & Society*, 5(6):951–969.

Sanders, A., Heys, B., Ravenscroft, N. & Burdsey, D. (2014). 'Making a difference: the power of FitC', *Soccer & Society*, 15(3):411–429.

Stone, C. (2013). *Football – A Shared Sense of Belonging?* Sheffield: FURD. Available at www.furd.org/default.asp?intPageID=535.

SUFC. (2007). 'FitC', *Sheffield United: The Official Website* (archived). http://origin-www.sufc.co.uk/page/Community/0, 10418~1082463, 00.html.

SUCF. (2016). *Leadership Manual*. Internal Document: Sheffield United.

Supporters Direct. (2010). *The Social and Community Value of Football: Summary Report*. Manchester: Substance.

Tacon, R. (2007). 'Football and social inclusion: evaluating social policy', *Managing Leisure* 12(1):1–23.

Taylor, N. (2004). ''Giving something back': can football clubs and their communities co-exist?' in S. Wagg (ed.) *British Football and Social Exclusion*. Abingdon: Routledge, pp. 47–66.

Twelvetrees, A. (2008). *Community Work*. Basingstoke: Palgrave Macmillan.

Williams, J. & Taylor, R. (1994). *The National Football and the Community Programme: A Research Report*. Leicester: University of Leicester.

CHAPTER 8

Community sport event management

Jo Marsden-Heathcote and Jude Langdon

SUMMARY

This chapter covers a range of aspects that mix the theoretical underpinning of event management with applied learning from the field of community sport. The value that events can hold for local sporting organisations can be crucial to their survival and be a part of a club's annual activity. The elements covered here will give insight into the processes involved in event management, offering suggestions for additional structures and tools to be utilised within the planning and delivery of community sport events.

AIMS

By engaging with this chapter, you will be able to

- Communicate an awareness of the processes required to plan and deliver a community sport event,
- Understand the benefits that can be gained from delivering community sport events and
- Apply planning tools and processes to community sport events.

INTRODUCTION

Event management has become a well-established professional field within the UK, seeing a rapid growth of sporting events over the last decade. The impact that sporting events can have at a major level is well discussed and researched. At a local, community level, the research is less evident, however, there are numerous, localised evaluations identifying the impact that sport events can have.

The purpose of this chapter is to present an overview of the sport event industry from a community sport setting. It will provide practical guidance to understand the planning and processes that are involved in event management. Even though each event may be unique, the tools that are used in successful event management will be the same. A sporting event can be so much more than 'just a game', and whatever its size, it can have considerable importance to the community. Local events have always been important; Brown, Brown, Jackson, Sellers and Manuel (2003) believe that local sporting events are deemed to have a certain 'intrinsic power' to activate people, remove barriers between groups and change people's attitudes and behaviour. They have an appeal due to their capacity to be fun and entertaining whilst offering a change in everyday life. They can involve and integrate diverse communities, increase awareness and promote all kinds of organisations and key messages (Taylor, 2011).

According to Tomlinson and Sugden (1994), the social identity of belonging to the same group is rarely more strongly felt than in competitive special events. Coalter (2007) and Sugden (2006) believe that to warrant the achievement of positive outcomes, sport event projects need to be strategically planned to ensure group development. To achieve positive beliefs, attitudes, intentions and behaviour, the social context and people's experiences with 'others' need to be pleasant and/or beneficial. Having a focus on social rather than just overly competitive sport encounters seems the most promising in using sporting events to develop communities. However, community development is not the only reason for running a sporting event. Sport itself has many benefits and has been, and will continue to be, discussed throughout this book, and events are a way of harnessing, kick-starting and promoting these benefits. But before we examine some of this, let's begin with the basics.

What is an event?

Events have played an important role in society for many years. The monotony of every-day life is broken up with all kinds of events, from traditional celebrations with strict rituals and celebrations to festivals and carnivals (Shone & Parry, 2013). Back in the 1990s, Getz (1997, p. 4) defined events as 'temporary occurrences … They have a finite length,

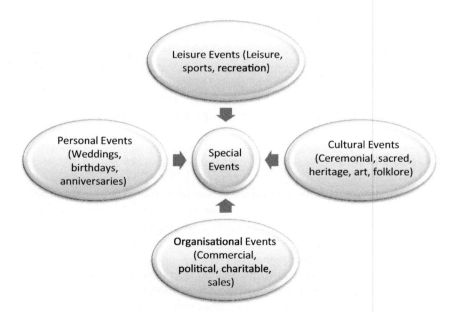

FIGURE 8.1 Categorisation of special events

Source: Adapted from Shone and Parry (2013)

and for planned events this is usually fixed and publicised'. More recently, Goldblatt (2011) focussed on the celebratory nature of events, which fits closely with events such as weddings, recognising them as 'a unique moment in time with ceremony and ritual to satisfy specific needs'. However, when considering sporting competitions and leisure events, this definition does not always fit.

Shone and Parry (2011), for convenience, categorised special events in Figure 8.1, and it is important to bear in mind, when considering this categorisation, that there are frequent overlaps.

PURPOSE OF YOUR EVENT

Event planning models are a useful starting point, allowing event organisers the opportunity of adding a more structured and ordered approach to the planning of events. There are a number of different models that authors have developed for event planning, however, there is no one model that fits all. It is dependent upon a number of different factors, first and foremost upon the event organiser to perhaps select and engage with a model they find useful, and one which they can understand, share with their colleagues/ stakeholders and amend/adapt where necessary. Therefore, it is useful to view the models as a reference point, offering a visual representation of the key areas of the event planning process. In an ever fast-paced industry, with pressures on effective use of time, shorter lead in times and an ever-increasingly competitive environment, it is vital that organisations utilise and maximise all their resources efficiently and effectively and manage and control their time management. Planning and the utilisation of event planning models may well be of assistance in this area.

> Because of the unique nature of each special event, planning is a process that must continuously occur from the start of the bid (initial idea) until the end of the event (evaluation and feedback).
>
> (Catherwood & Van Kirk, 1992, p. 5)

It is entirely possible for events to be produced and delivered without any formal processes or planning structure in place. However, as the events become larger, more complex and see an increase in resources – such as financial, staffing and time – a variety of different business management principles can be applied. Masterman (2009) believes that the key to minimising negative impacts and achieving positive impacts is in the effective planning of the event.

It is not possible to gauge if an event has been a success or not without having a clear purpose of what you want the event to achieve. Whether the purpose is to recruit new players, raise funds for a sports club or increase awareness of a new initiative, it is imperative to set aims and objectives. This will offer direction for the organisers of the event and provide a solid understanding so that through the planning process, decisions can be made based upon the aims and objectives.

Direct social impacts may be developed into long-term social outcomes. In other words, the different social experiences made at an event can be maximised to achieve lasting social consequences (Moscardo, 2007). For example, first contacts made at an event could be developed into trustful friendships or community networks, which have the power to make a considerable change. Importantly, within this process, sport and event activities are merely a starting point, a vehicle or booster for further activities that need to be strategically implemented to achieve wider social development outcomes (Misener & Mason, 2006; Sugden, 2006).

Case study: the School Games (2017)

What is the School Games?

The School Games is a unique opportunity to motivate and inspire millions of young people across the country by building on existing practices to provide more opportunities for those currently not engaged in competitive school sport.

Over £128 million of Lottery and Government funding is being invested to support the School Games. Nationally and locally, the School Games is being delivered through partnerships.

At a local level, the School Games will be delivered by schools, clubs, county sports partnerships and other local partners. There are almost 50 Local Organising Committees, which are chaired by Head Teachers, and these oversee the county festivals.

The School Games is made up of four levels of activity, as shown in Figure 8.2: competition in schools, between schools and at a county or national level.

LEVEL 4
National multisport
residential event

Progression into/through NGB performance system

LEVEL 3
Annual county/subregional
culmination of inter-school competition

↑ **LINKED** ↑

LEVEL 2
Regular inter-school competition
between schools at local level

↑ **FEEDS** ↑

LEVEL 1
Intra-school
competition

FIGURE 8.2 School Games' four levels of activity

Considering the case study of the School Games and the pathway structure shown in Figure 8.2, School Games is perceived by schools and School Games Organisers to be very successful in offering young people the opportunity to take part in a variety of sports and to progress through to higher levels of competitions and suitable community exit routes. There is increasing evidence of good practice in terms of forming school-club links, and of engagement with clubs and national governing bodies helping to link competition pathways (Sport England, 2013). Although this has a clear sporting focus, there is also evidence of developing skills of young people through volunteer roles.

Young Leaders have been the driving force for most, if not all, competitions at Levels 1, 2 and 3. They have enjoyed and revelled in having responsibilities and acting as mentors to younger children. They have been the biggest advocates of the School Games movement and values.

Aims and objectives

The aim of an event can vary in its complexity but ultimately acts as focus for the event organisers. It should be an overarching broad statement that covers the purpose of the event. The objectives, then, sit underneath the aim and show the actions that need to be met in order to meet the aim of the event. For example:

Aim: To increase the membership to the local cricket team through delivery of a Family Fun Day on June 20th

Objectives:

1 Distribute promotional materials at 10 local community points before the end of May
2 Recruit a minimum of five volunteer club members to assist in the delivery
3 Source 12 raffle prizes from local businesses
4 Add five junior members and five adult members for the start of the new season

The objectives should follow the SMART acronym designed by Doran (1981) and used throughout management industry and literature. This stands for Smart, Measurable, Achievable, Realistic and Time-related and allow for a level of measurement and control to be implemented. Relating back to the previous example, the promotional distribution objective can be monitored in the run up to the event. If, at the beginning of May, only two community points have received the promotional materials, then action can be taken to rectify this; potentially by adapting the marketing plan or adding resources, such as the number of people distributing the material, and ensuring that objectives are met.

PLANNING

Event management is the organisation and coordination of activities required to achieve the objectives of events (Bladen, Kennell, Abson, & Wilde, 2012). There are multiple facets and tasks that make up any event, with even the smallest events, such as a children's birthday party, comprising many different tasks that need to be undertaken. These will be before the party, during the party and following the party. As events grow in size, so does the list of tasks that need to be undertaken and additional complexities in an order in which they can be executed.

A basic event plan, below, has been adapted from Shone and Parry (2011) and covers the main areas required for planning a local sporting event. Areas of this will be discussed in greater detail throughout the chapter, however, ensure that all areas of the plan are monitored and adapted where necessary throughout the process.

1. Purpose – aims & objectives
2. Ideas of event concept
3. Consideration of stakeholders/partners, event dates, costs/revenue, venues, staffing
4. Detailed plan
   a. Operations: Staff and volunteers, venue, equipment, H&S, logistics
   b. Finances: budget, sponsorship, charges, income
   c. Marketing: promotion, schedules
5. Implementing the preparation plan ready for the event
6. Delivery of the actual event
7. Evaluation & legacy

Once the overall concept has been considered and a detailed plan has been agreed upon, there is a need to keep control over any actions, as well as understand the time connections between the actions. For example, it is important to realise that medals for a sporting event cannot be ordered until it is confirmed how many participants will be attending the event. There are a number of different tools that can be used such as a Critical Path Network, Work Breakdown Structure, however, a simple way in which this can be achieved is through use of a Gantt chart. An example in Figure 8.3 gives an idea of a basic Gantt chart for staffing that can be adapted to reflect the entire event plan and used to monitor event progress. The shaded areas represent when actions are planned to be undertaken.

Task/Action	Week 1	Week 2	Week 3	Week 4	Week 5	Week 6	Week 7	Progress
Confirm number of participants	■							Completed
Decide upon number of volunteers required	■							Completed
Advertise for volunteers		■						Completed
Select volunteers				■				In progress
Identify training needs					■			In progress
Training and briefing session							■	Booked in

FIGURE 8.3 Gantt chart

EVENT DESIGN

The size and level of sport events can vary enormously. Sport events can be 'held annually or more frequently, conducted on a single day or over a number of days, staged in a single venue or multiple venues, focused on one sport or recreation activity or involve a variety of activities' and can be conducted for participants of differing age groups or abilities (ASC, 2000, p. 3). Events can also be competitive or for participation and fun. In all events, it is the spirit of sport and taking part that are the most important factors, and as Masterman (2009, p. 3) points out, there is 'wider significance to society than just the staging of a sporting event'.

If your event has a competitive aspect, then you will need to consider the various competition formats that are universal and could be applied to your event. For example, knockout tournaments, leagues, round robins and mass participation festivals can all be used, with some more common than others at certain sized events.

LOCATIONS/VENUES

Event venues/facilities and sites can vary enormously. Depending on who the event is aimed at and the event type, the event team must think carefully about their specific venue and the logistical requirements of their choice. For example, older adults taking part in short mat bowls in a local church hall have very different on-site logistical requirements to a secondary school cross-country event taking place in a local authority green space.

It is important to stress that every event will differ in its individual nature, and aspects will result in very different logistical requirements. When selecting an appropriate event venue, one of the main factors you need to consider is if your audience can enjoy themselves in a safe and comfortable atmosphere – it is often easy to get enthusiastic about a fantastic venue and forget that the audience's enjoyment is key.

Important venue considerations:

- Will the participants/spectators like the venue?
- Can they find the location easily?
- Are the transport links adequate?
- What about the catering and general service?
- How large is the site, and how easy is it to navigate?
- What additional facilities are available?

Masterman (2004) states that educational institutions are possibly the first to offer most sports at the earliest ages, and schools, colleges and universities are all involved with events at intra- and inter-competition levels. Examples of some community spaces where sporting events can take place:

- Green spaces – including parks, playing fields, woods, trails, outdoor gyms, skateparks
- Education facilities – school halls, playgrounds, multi-use game areas, playing fields/ AstroTurf pitches, tennis/netball courts, swimming pools, etc.
- Local authority leisure centres
- Sports and social clubs
- Multifaith buildings – church halls or mosques
- Community centres

PARTNERSHIPS

To develop your event further, you may wish to consider working in partnership and creating links with key players in the community, for example, with local authority, the educational sector and/or the media (Chalip, 2004, 2006). All partners need to have a sound understanding of the purpose and aim of your sporting event so that they can plan, manage and support accordingly. They could, for example, engage in, contribute to or report about event-related activities such as street games, community fun days, tournaments or marketing campaigns. Such event-related sociocultural activities are likely to lead to additional positive outcomes such as an increase in community capacities and the communities' quality of life (Schulenkorf, 2011).

OPERATIONS

The planning of the operations section of an event can be daunting, but if taken step-by-step and linked to an appropriate plan, it can be more than achievable. One way in which to view the operations section is to visualise yourself as a customer at your event. From accessing transport, to getting to the event, to arriving and finding your way to the entrance, take yourself through the event step-by-step and note down all of the points in which an action needs to be taken to ensure that your customer has the experience that you want them to have. Ensure that you then transfer all of these actions to your Gantt chart and discuss with your event team.

Event logistics

The logistics of an event, put simply, is the transport/movement of resources and products. For a local event it is appropriate to think about this in two sections – the logistics of the customer and the logistics of the venue. Bladen et al. (2012) provide a model in Figure 8.4 that illustrates the detail involved within these areas and are useful when writing your event plan and Gantt chart.

HUMAN RESOURCES

There are a wide variety of roles that require human resource to be involved with community sport events, for example, management or operations. Gladden, Milne and Sutton (1998) suggest event teams should consider the following:

• Team management and liaison	• Finance and budgeting
• Media roles	• Risk management
• Catering and hospitality	• First aid provision
• Marketing	• Event operations
• Venue management	• Registration
• Crowd control	• Volunteer supervision and management

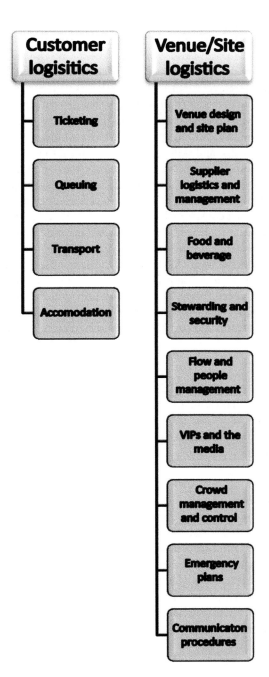

FIGURE 8.4 Logistics model

Source: Adapted from Bladen et al. (2012)

These diverse roles require a range of skills, experience, knowledge and, in some cases, accreditation or specialised training. The degree of complexity of these roles will vary according to the type, duration and size of the event, and the anticipated number of participants and spectators. Some roles require very little preparation or training and could be done on the day of the event, while others, such as venue management or team liaison, may require staff to be involved for long lead times prior to the event period.

Volunteers have always played a vital part in the sport and physical activity sector. Without them, most community sport and physical activity would not happen. Sport event organisers rely on the knowledge and skills of event volunteers to undertake some roles within a sporting event. This could be in the role of administering competitions; liaising with visiting teams; working with media and security organisations; managing hospitality and catering services; and/or providing services for athletes, sponsors, spectators and other event stakeholders. Every event must consider what training is required and who is going to deliver the necessary training to all staff. Volunteers who undertake training will develop new skills and increase their confidence in being able to put what they have learnt into practice.

If your event is working with children and young people or vulnerable adults, then all volunteers must have an up to date Disclosure Barring Service (DBS). The DBS helps employers make safer recruitment decisions and prevent unsuitable people from working with vulnerable groups, including children. For further information on this, go to www.gov.uk/government/organisations/disclosure-and-barring-service.

MARKETING

Selecting appropriate marketing methods will enable you to be more effective in targeting your offers to your audience(s). If you are managing a limited budget, you will find low-cost methods of marketing to be useful. Here are a few examples of different low cost methods (adapted from Sport England, 2017) that could be used:

1. Website presence
2. Strategically placed banners
3. Adverts/notices in free press/community publications
4. Good news stories/editorial submitted to local press
5. Articles in local organisation newsletters, e.g. schools
6. Use of social media such as Twitter and Facebook
7. Offering taster sessions/assembly activities in your local school
8. Working in partnership with other community groups that service your target groups
9. Getting in touch with your local college or university and requesting a marketing student for a work placement
10. Getting out into the community to develop relationships with clubs and groups; getting out and meeting people is a much more effective method of reaching new audiences and developing a community offer

Timescales for marketing need to be considered fully and will play a crucial part in the planning process – allow plenty of time. There are many different elements of marketing principles to consider that will link into your event, from promotional sales of entry tickets to recruiting a workforce. What is important with community sport events is being clear about what it is that you are marketing and to whom – this will be different for every event.

The event management team will need to have an understanding of their potential consumers and customers and ensure that the marketing mix meets the needs and objectives of the event. In this context, we can describe the marketing mix by the application (from an event perspective) of the 7Ps: Price, Product, Place, Promotion, People, Physical Evidence and Partners. The 7Ps help organisations to review and define key issues that affect the marketing of its products and services. For example, if you want to use social media to promote your event, then you need to ensure that your target group (e.g., the people that you are wanting to communicate this information to) actually use social media. You can use the 7Ps model to set objectives, conduct a SWOT (Strengths, Weaknesses, Opportunities and Threats) analysis and undertake a competitor analysis. It's a practical framework to evaluate an existing event (or new one) and work through appropriate approaches whilst evaluating the mix element as shown through the following questions:

Products/Services: How can you develop your products or services?

Prices: How can you change your pricing model or design a new one?

Place: What new distribution options are there for customers to experience your product? e.g., Where is the best location for your event, etc.?

Promotion: How can you add to or substitute the combination of media channels? Which is the best way to promote your event?

Physical Evidence: How can you reassure your customers? e.g., impressive event space, well-trained staff, great website, etc.

People: Who are your people, and are there skills gaps? How will you train staff and/or volunteers?

Partners: Are you seeking partners and managing existing partners well? You may need partners for funding and they need to understand the benefit to them.

Health and safety

Bladen et al. (2012) highlight that it is essential that the event manager and team are aware of any licences, permits and regulations that are related to health and safety before the event planning starts. It is the event teams' responsibility to ensure they have researched the relevant requirements and that they are in compliance with them. For example, licences for premises/music and performance rights/selling refreshments on the street.

In today's society, it is imperative that the appropriate insurance (fire, weather and special insurance specific to your event, for example, marquees often require special insurance) is obtained prior to the running of an event. Event insurance will typically cover such items as cancellation of the event, damage to property or premises, legal liabilities, damage to equipment and public liabilities. Careful research is required for all legal requirements, and you must ensure that all policies and clauses are read, understood and apply to your event.

According to the Health & Safety at Work Act (1974), employers (i.e., event organisers), site/venue owners and self-employed contractors have a statutory duty of care to protect the health and safety of those that may be affected by their work activity (Bowdin, 2001). The event team are responsible for ensuring that overall safety at the event is maintained so that, as far as reasonably practicable, people setting up, breaking down and attending the event are not exposed to risks to their health and safety. The Health & Safety Executive (2017) states that Risk Assessments should be completed to identify sensible measures to control the risks associated to your workplace or event. Risk Assessments should not be overcomplicated – most solutions will be common sense.

The Risk Assessment is used as a guide for your events team to develop 'Control Measures' with the view to hopefully eliminate the risk altogether. If this cannot be done, then the risks must be reduced to an 'acceptable' level. The benefits of having a written Risk Assessment are that hazards are identified and control measures are documented, which will reduce the likelihood of accidents occurring. There are many ways to portray the information, but it is important that the procedure is kept simple and that the 'whole picture' is taken into account. The Risk Assessment can be used as evidence in possible cases of litigation. For further information on how to assess the risks for your event, go to www.hse.gov.uk/event-safety/getting-started.htm.

Finance/resourcing

There are resources attached to the delivery of any event, whether that is staff, time and/or consumables, and it is vital to ensure that you match the resource available to the type of event that you hope to deliver. Consider the aims and objectives of your event in the planning stage, and try to list all of the resources that are required for that event to run successfully. For example, consider the resources that go into a five-a-side football tournament:

- Pitch hire (goals included)
- Event staff (paid & volunteers)
- Referees
- Equipment to mark out pitches/respect barriers
- Medals/trophies
- Administration to organise
- Marketing resources (time, social media, etc.)
- Refreshments
- Entry fee for each team
- Refuse collection
- Site set-up/break down

This is not an exhaustive list by any means, however, it covers some of the main points that are discussed here within this chapter, e.g., marketing, staffing, etc. Depending on the organisation, leading the event will depend on financial support; for example, a local authority may have access to a budget for delivering local sporting events, whereas a local sports club registered as a charity may be looking for funding through alternative means. This could come through a number of different avenues, from income generation through ticket sales, for example, or from sponsorship, or even from funding/grants.

Sponsorship

The business of sport provides some of the best examples of how sponsorship works, with some of the biggest sponsorship deals being linked to sporting events. However, the attraction for a local community sport event is slightly different than for a major event and comes in many different shapes and sizes. Sponsorship could be in the form of financial support to deliver the event, but could also include the donation of equipment, or staff to assist in the event. The latter could also be termed as 'in-kind' contributions, whereby an organisation offers non-financial support. Within local sporting events, this could range from facility hire for the pitches to the donation of drinks for the participants.

Funding

Funding can be available from a range of sources to support local and sporting delivery. These are largely to support 'not-for-profit' and charitable organisations, for example, local sporting clubs, but can also include education and local authority. It is often a good place to start when considering how to fund your event. You can research the funding opportunities that are available in your local area either through local authority, your local County Sport Partnership or even a web search. Funders such as National Lottery, Sport Relief and local authority small grants are good places to start your search. There are a number of elements that require consideration when looking at funding your event. These range from the appropriateness of the fund to time frames. For example, if your event is focussed on getting older people more active, but the fund criteria is for young people, an application for this particular funding stream would be unsuccessful. A flow chart highlighting the process for funding application can be viewed in Figure 8.5.

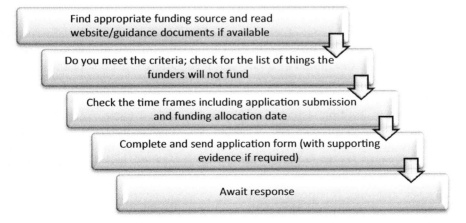

FIGURE 8.5 Funding application flow chart

MANAGING BUDGETS

The management of a budget is crucial to ensuring financial success within a local community event, and some key information on how to set up and manage budgets can be found in Chapter 11. If the event is to be paid for through external funding, sponsorship, etc., it is highly likely that there will be less potential flexibility in the finances. Therefore, there needs to be consideration of the event budget early on in the planning stage. This will then allow for a more comprehensive and well thought out justification of budget spend, rather than a more retrospective process. The budgeting process will include elements such as costing, estimating income generated (if any) as well as the allocation of resources across the event (Wilson, 2011). Budgeting ultimately forces managers to think ahead and plan where they consider the allocation of resources to be and then implement action to ensure that it happens. The budget can be written as a basic income and expenditure account to assist with planning and also as a control mechanism once the event has occurred.

Contingency planning

Contingency planning is a vital aspect of any event management – it is essential when planning and designing events that you have a contingency plan in place. Even the best-made plans are unlikely to ensure that nothing goes wrong. When a major problem does occur, event organisers are expected to be able to react quickly and appropriately. Event teams must be able to react, and this comes from anticipating emergencies, accidents and problems and formulating plans and training all staff (paid and voluntary) in what must be done to prevent any incidents.

A contingency plan should cover all possibilities that something could go wrong either in the build-up to the event, on the day, during the event or during the event break down. Bladen et al. (2012) identify that the key areas to consider are health and safety, people, venue and equipment.

Monitoring and evaluation (legacy)

The final element to the event process is to both review and also to assess/measure the success/impact. You'll find some approaches to monitoring and evaluation in the final chapter in this book but should be aware that it requires a reflection of the entire process, from planning to event break down and the efficiencies, operational considerations and organisational factors. In addition to this, there needs to be a way in which you can assess if the event itself has achieved what you set out to achieve. Here, it is useful to revisit your original event aims and objectives and consider how you can measure, or find evidence to support, that you have met them. Bladen et al. (2012) suggest that the method in which you evaluate the success of your event is the first stage to the planning process for the next event.

However, although this process comes at the end of this chapter, it is something that requires consideration within the planning stages. That is because you may have to include some processes or systems within your event to enable you to measure your aims/objectives. Whether you are aware of this or not, you will have been controlling elements of your event (e.g., your objectives) throughout the entire process, as discussed earlier in the budgeting section. Doing this more formally allows for greater structure to your monitoring and evaluation and could also be required for your funding purposes or to feed information back to partners. An example of this can be seen in the School Games case study. A Level 1 event requires schools to deliver an intra-school competition (where pupils compete against other pupils within the same school). In this instance, it may be useful for you to have registers ready to document which children have participated, total numbers, age, previous engagement with competition, male/female and number of Young Leaders involved. This information could then be used for a number of different purposes: as a celebration tool for both school and partners, to justify funding for the event, to share best practice within the industry, etc.

When considering the measurement of social impact of sporting events, this becomes more challenging and requires thought. For example, again with the School Games case study, how can a school measure if the pupils have developed 'Teamwork' (an element of the Spirit of the Games value)? Observational evidence could be gathered regarding the pupils' engagement with teams during the event, as well as asking the pupils if they feel as though they have developed their teamwork capabilities. These are two different ways in which the same element could be measured.

As mentioned in the partnerships section, through working with other organisations with a similar purpose to the event, it could be that a longer-term, strategic goal has the potential of being developed. This is an area that requires further development within sport in general, and how it can impact on social factors and assist with sustainability (Allen, O'Toole, Harris, & McDonnell, 2008), which touches on the concept of legacy.

CONCLUSION

This chapter has given a short insight into the processes involved in delivering local sporting events. Event management is an area where experience is invaluable, however, through utilising the event management models and theories discussed, you have now got the mechanisms to allow you to appropriately plan and deliver your own event. Remembering to be clear as to the reason for holding the event in the first place is the initial challenge, and then ensuring that you recognise the different ways in which you can achieve this. By optimising this through your choice of event, you can develop relationships with your customers. From an operational perspective, use of the Risk Assessments and logistics models will allow for a more practical understanding of the event, where health and safety is a priority. A method of preparation for the planning of a community sport event is to visit another event and view it from an organiser's perspective. You will then have a different viewpoint of the requirements of the many different facets of an event. It is an ever-changing environment where a need to be flexible is key; however, by following these principles with appropriate planning, you are giving yourself a great chance at success.

REVIEW QUESTIONS

1. Can you come up with your own definition to describe a community sport event?
2. Using the School Games case study, consider what the aims and objectives could be for a Level 1 event.
3. Linked to the case study, who do you think the partners are at a Level 2 event, and what are the benefits to their involvement?
4. What qualifications/training requirements will your workforce need in order to run a successful School Games Level 2 gymnastics event?
5. What risks do you think you need to assess in order for your event to run safely?
6. Using the case study, what income and expenditure costs would be linked to a Level 3 event?

REFERENCES

Allen, J., O'Toole, W., Harris, R., & McDonnell, I. (2008). *Festival & special event management*. Milton: Wiley.

Australian Sports Commission (ASC). (2000). *Volunteer management program: Managing event volunteers*. Canberra: Australian Sports Commission.

Bladen, C., Kennell, J., Abson, E., & Wilde, N. (2012). *Events management: An introduction*. Oxon: Routledge.

Bowdin, G. A. J. (2001). *Events management*. Hospitality, leisure and tourism series. Oxford: Butterworth-Heinemann.

Brown, K. T., Brown, T. N., Jackson, J. S., Sellers, R. M., & Manuel, W. J. (2003). Teammates on and off the field? Contact with Black teammates and the racial attitudes of White student athletes. *Journal of Applied Social Psychology, 33*(7), 1379–1403.

Catherwood, D. W., & Van Kirk, R. L. (1992). *The complete guide to special event management: Business insights, financial advice, and successful strategies from Ernst & Young, advisors to the Olympics, the Emmy Awards and the PGA Tour*. New York: John Wiley & Sons.

Chalip, L. (2004). Beyond impact: A general model for host community event leverage. In B. Ritchie & D. Adair (Eds.), *Sport tourism: Interrelationships, impacts and issues (Aspects of tourism)*. Clevedon: Channel View.

Chalip, L. (2006). Towards social leverage of sport events. *Journal of Sport & Tourism, 11*(2), 109–127.

Coalter, F. (2008). *A wider social role for sport: Who's keeping the score?* London: Routledge.

Doran, G. T. (1981). There's a SMART way to write management's goals and objectives. *Management Review, 70*, 35–36.

Getz, D. (1997). *Event management and event tourism*. New York: Cognizant Communication.

Gladden, J. M., Milne, G. R., & Sutton, W. A. (1998). A conceptual framework for assessing brand equity in Division I college athletics. *Journal of Sport Management, 12*(1), 1–19.

Goldblatt, J. (2011). *Special events: A new generation and the next frontier* (6th ed., Wiley event management series; 13). Hoboken, NJ: Wiley.

Health and Safety Executive. (2017). *Getting started*. Retrieved from www.hse.gov.uk/event-safety/getting-started.htm.

Masterman, G. (2004). *Strategic sports event management: An international approach.* Hospitality, leisure and tourism series. Oxford: Elsevier Butterworth-Heinemann.

Masterman, G. (2009). *Strategic sports event management* (2nd ed., Olympic ed.). Amsterdam and London: Butterworth-Heinemann.

Misener, L., & Mason, D. S. (2006). Creating community networks: Can sporting events offer meaningful sources of social capital? *Managing Leisure, 11*(1), 39–56.

Moscardo, G. (2007). Analyzing the role of festivals and events in regional development. *Event Management, 11*(1–2), 23–32.

Schulenkorf, N. (2011). Intercommunity sport events: Vehicles and catalysts for social capital in divided societies. *Event Management, 15*(2), 105–119.

Shone, P., & Parry, B. (2010). *Successful event management: A practical handbook* (3rd ed.). Andover: Cengage Learning.

Shone, P., & Parry, B. (2013). *Successful event management: A practical handbook* (4th ed.). Andover: Cengage Learning.

Sport England. (2013). *Sainsbury's School Games evaluation: Executive summary.* Retrieved from www.sportengland.org/media/4252/school-games-executive-summary-2013.pdf.

Sugden, J. (2006). Teaching and playing sport for conflict resolution and co-existence in Israel. *International Review for the Sociology of Sport, 41*(2), 221–240.

Tomlinson, A., & Sugden, J. (1994). *Hosts and champions: Soccer cultures, national identities and the USA World Cup.* Aldershot: Arena.

Taylor, P (eds). (2011). *Torkildsen's sport and leisure management* (6th ed.). London: Routledge.

Wilson, R. (2011). Financial management in sport and leisure. In Taylor, P (eds). (2011), *Torkildsen's sport and leisure management* (6th ed.). London: Routledge.

CHAPTER 9

Community coaching

Pippa Jones and Val Stevenson

SUMMARY

This chapter discusses the role of community coaches and the range of contexts in which they are expected to operate. The chapter extends current participant development models to include individuals who are currently not active at all. Finally, the chapter argues that in order to be effective in a range of settings and with a range of participants, and non-participants, it is essential that the community coach becomes a 'social performer' who understands the identity of those being coached and who needs to adopt different, and appropriate, roles in differing community coaching situations.

AIMS

By engaging with this chapter, you will

- Be able to discuss the concept of a 'community coach' and identify the broad range of contexts within which they may operate,
- Be familiar with the coaching domains of children, adolescents and adults,
- Have explored the impact of political ideology and policy on community sports coaching,
- Start to identify the broad range of coaching skills, knowledge and attributes required to develop participation within a range of community sports settings and
- Appreciate the complexity of the volunteer, part-time and full-time community coaching workforce.

INTRODUCTION

Coaches within a community setting are likely to be expected to work with a variety of populations in a number of contexts. There is a high probability that coaches will have to cater for young people, adults and ageing populations, those with a tradition of participating and those who are not comfortable with sport and physical activity (PA). Indeed, you may have to do all of this at the same time! So what does this mean for those who may wish to coach within a community setting? Coaching in the community requires us to think differently about our coaching, and that is the overall aim of this chapter.

WHAT DOES COACHING IN A COMMUNITY SETTING MEAN?

A brief review of coaching research highlights that, at a basic level, there are two ways in which people in communities engage with sport and PA, either for performance or for participation, and, it follows that, in order to support these 'performers' or 'participants', two models of coaching have emerged: performance coaching and participation coaching. Because of the focus on community within this book, together with the fact that the majority of the population who engage in sport and PA at a community level are participants and not performers, this chapter will focus on participation coaching. This is not to completely ignore performance coaching, however. While Cronin and Armour (2015, p. 959) claim that participation coaching is 'the act of coaching participants that are less intensely engaged in sport than performance orientated athletes', it is wise to remember that some community coaches work with participants who may be progressing towards performance, and, likewise, some community coaches work with participants who have previously been at performance level. To try and highlight how this may look, the International Council for Coaching Excellence (ICCE) (2013) has developed a sport participant spectrum (Figure 9.1), which demonstrates how some participants may move to and from different categories or 'domains'.

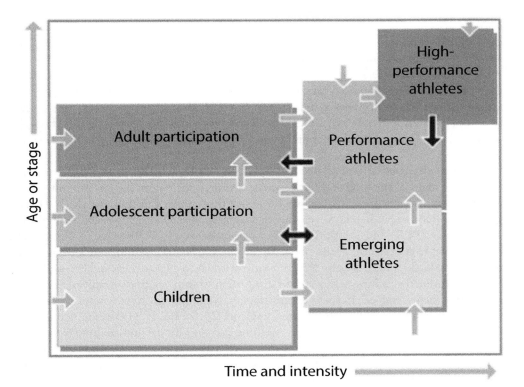

FIGURE 9.1 Sport participant spectrum

One problem with using this spectrum to define where a community coach may work, however, is that it is predicated on a role for coaches where the participant, at whatever level, is fully engaged with sport or PA from the outset. Of course, the majority of people *do not* participate in sport and PA. For this reason, when trying to define what a community coach is, or who they need to be, it is perhaps more fruitful to work with the alternative model of participant development offered by Collins et al. (2012): the 'three worlds' model of participant development.

In their Coaching Plan for England (2017–2021), Sport England affirms the need for 'coaching to change' in order to address the health and societal issues found amongst non- and low-level participants. A new vision for coaching emerges, 'Improving a person's experience of sport and physical activity providing specialist support and guidance aligned to their individual needs and aspirations'. This new definition is reflected within the three definitions of excellence contained in the 'three worlds' model:

1. *Elite Referenced Excellence (ERE)*. Excellence in the form of high-level sporting performance, where achievement is measured against others, with the ultimate goal of winning at the highest level possible.

2. *Personal Referenced Excellence (PRE)*. Excellence in the form of participation and personal performance, where achievement is more personally referenced by, say, completing a marathon or improving one's personal best. This second category of excellence also includes not only 'the achievement of developmentally appropriate challenges within sport and physical activity across the length of the participant's lifespan', but also the achievement of goals that contribute to lifelong health and well-being. In this context, the achievement of a 'low level' sport and activity goal by a previous non- or low-level participant can be regarded as 'excellence'.

3. *Participation for Personal Well-Being (PPW)*. Taking part in PA to satisfy needs other than personal progression. Typical motivations for PPW might include the improvement of one's social life (e.g., making and keeping friends), the enhancement of one's social identity (by being a member of a high-status group or club), personal renewal (through activity that is fulfilling) and the maintenance of aspects of self-concept (staying in good shape).

One key characteristic of the model put forwards by Collins et al. (2012) is that the management of sporting excellence and sporting participation has, to date, involved the traditional sports organisations, such as UK Sport, Sport England and the National Governing Bodies (NGBs), however, the management of the extended second definition of excellence (PRE) and the third category of excellence (PPW) involves a number of organisations that have not, traditionally, been central to sport coaching. Success in these two areas will, therefore, require the community coach to engage with and be employed by less traditional coaching organisations in addition to working in nontraditional coaching environments. Indeed, in these circumstances, we might question whether 'coach' is the right terminology (Lyle, 2002; Sport England, 2016). Based on the points made by Collins et al., we have taken the ICCE coaching domains model and adapted it to more accurately reflect the dual role of the community coach (Figure 9.2). That is to say, a community coach has to engage those groups who are already involved within the more traditional sports structures at the same time as being approachable and appealing to those who do not currently participate at all.

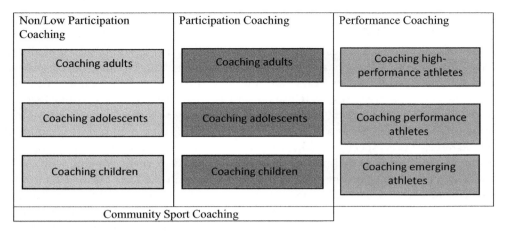

FIGURE 9.2 The dual role of the community coach

DEFINITIONS OF COACHING

We might surmise, therefore, that the role of a community sports coach lies somewhere between the more easily defined Physical Education (PE) or sports teacher, who introduces all young children to sport and PA within the formal and compulsory setting of education, and the performance coach who progresses athletes into recognised regional, national and international competition. Working in between these are, for example, the coaches who work in local sport clubs, run after-school and holiday sports programmes, work in institutions for both young and adult offenders and the coaches who work with ageing adults or General Practitioner (GP) referrals. The range of possible community settings is both vast and continually changing. Indeed, you may be able to think of a number of other settings a community coach may be asked to work with. However, whatever the setting, it is vital that any community coach appreciates the context and requirements of their chosen settings if they are to be effective in delivering a community programme. It is to a greater understanding of that context that we now turn.

UNDERSTANDING 'COACHING PHILOSOPHY' AND 'COACHING CONTEXT'

It would be fair to say that a key focus for any coach, including those working at a community level, is to try and develop a shared philosophy with the participants they are working with. Indeed, understanding, among other things, the reason someone is attending, what they want to achieve, their history with sport and PA or what they enjoy about sport and PA helps the coach to develop a shared set of values, beliefs, assumptions, attitudes, principles and priorities with that participant. This 'shared philosophy' should then underpin everything a coach does (Kidman & Hanrahan, 2011). Indeed, given that a coaching philosophy is central to a coach's behaviour and style (Cassidy, Jones, & Potrac 2009; Jenkins, 2010; Jones, Armour, & Potrac, 2004; Lyle, 2002), without such a shared philosophy, a coach runs the risk of delivering sessions that are out of step with the participants' wishes. This may sound straightforward, however, the practical challenges that face a coach in achieving a shared philosophy are substantial. First of all, to have fully considered these factors as part of the planning of any coaching is demanding, even for experienced coaches. Above all, time should be used for planning and delivering a safe and appropriate session (Cushion & Partington, 2016). Second, adding further complexity to this issue, there are situations where it may be difficult to understand the 'values, beliefs, assumptions and attitudes' of the participants. As noted in Chapter 3, for example, this is especially tricky if the coach comes from a different population or is not affected by the same issues as those being coached. A coach working with older adults in a community setting, for example, may not be in the same age bracket as the participants and may have different experiences or values in sport and PA. Similarly, a coach working with GP referrals may not fully understand the impact of illnesses and diseases of which they have no experience. In these sorts of circumstances, developing empathy, understanding and emotional intelligence to create a shared philosophy can be very challenging, and, yet, this is the cornerstone of the successful community coach. Third, it is not as easy within the community context, as opposed to some other contexts, to generate a shared philosophy with participants. For example, while we may argue that a teacher within a school will work to the vision and philosophy of the school or a performance coach will have clear external goals to work towards, i.e., competition success and so on, bringing together community goals can be much more difficult to achieve given the socio-demographic and other factors that influence involvement. The broader community context can give rise to a range of motivational aspirations within a group of participants. How a coach identifies and addresses different philosophies within a group is a key issue for those interested in managing and developing community sport.

So, can we develop a shared coaching philosophy?

If we are to accept that a coaching philosophy, which is inclusive and supportive, is a key requirement of a coach working in the community, we are, therefore, faced with the question: How can coaches develop such a philosophy? Before we can answer this, we need to be sensitive to the ways in which the beliefs and values that we currently hold may impact on the development of such a philosophy. As Cushion and Partington (2016) have argued, coaches emerge within the beliefs and values that they have experienced throughout their lives. So, what if these are at odds with the participants within a community? What if the coach's values and beliefs are different to those of the people we are trying to get to participate? It is, we argue, only by accepting that our philosophy may be different than those we are reaching out to, and that we may all to need to change our philosophy, that we might then begin to develop a shared philosophy. Those wishing to coach in a community may have to sacrifice their own philosophy (however strong that may be) just as much as those we are wanting to coach. This is similar to considering where coaching takes place. The person coaching on the pitch, court, park, AstroTurf or in the gym may feel very comfortable; they may even have fond memories of that place and an attachment to it. However, that view could be quite a contrast to the way others feel about it. So, should sport and PA always have to be delivered in these places?

Should we also change our philosophy about the settings within which sport and PA are delivered? Are there other settings that may be more appropriate, particularly for non-participants?

The second, and more complex, element to developing a coaching philosophy, we feel, is the notion of 'identity' and its relation to something called habitus. There are two parts of identity we want you to consider. First, the coach and the participants will each have an individual identity in terms of how each of them sees themselves. In addition to this, they will also have what is termed a social identity, which is how they think they are viewed by other people (Jenkins, 2010). Whereas personal identity is the personal self and the individual characteristics that mark each individual out, social identity is the way people define themselves through the interactions that they have with different groups (Brewer, 1991; Tajfel & Turner, 1986). Within a coaching context, the idea of identity has profound impacts for developing a shared philosophy. Consider, for example, that for some people, the point at which they feel most vulnerable – that is to say, when they feel other people are viewing them in a negative way, and they view themselves in a negative way – is during participation in sport and PA. These individuals will define themselves as 'not sporty'. This is not just for the session, but it will be a way of thinking that is also present in other areas of their lives. Then consider the coach. They are likely to define themselves as 'sporty'. Their identity is linked to sport and PA. It is what they do for a job, it probably transcends their professional life and it is part of their leisure life as well. It is likely, just like you, to have been central to their education. For this person, who they are and how they view themselves is linked to a positive view of sport. Critical to this, however, is that the coach has to understand the identity of those who do not recognise the positive experiences of sport and PA if any shared philosophy is to be established.

So, where does identity come from?

The identity of both a community coach and those we want to participate is not something either is born with. It is, in fact, something that we develop over time and comes from what Bordieu (1977, 1990) calls 'habitus', which is the way we call, unconsciously and routinely, ourselves to the world. Interestingly, because the habitus underpinning our identity develops over a long period of time, both can manifest in a conscious and unconscious way. In other words, as a coach, the way we present ourselves, in a conscious effort to maintain the identity we want, results in actions that may seem 'normal' to us but are not to others around us. In drawing all this together, when thinking about developing a shared philosophy with those we are trying to engage, it is essential that the coach reflects on their own social identity and 'habitus'. How has their development pathway from the moment they began to play and to coach influenced who they are and their notion of what sport and PA should be? Is this the same as those who they want to engage?

You may be reading this as a coach who has engaged largely with a performance environment, and you may have been influenced by the coaching practices used in that context. Those practices are unlikely to be relevant to the philosophy, identity and habitus of those in a community setting. Or, are you a coach who started their journey coaching children? How do you need to adapt your philosophy when you are asked to coach adults? To achieve philosophical congruence, or a shared philosophical vision, is to create a situation where participants and coaches share and understand each other's values, which is particularly challenging in an environment where community is a fluid concept with moveable membership (Blackshaw, 2010) and where the coach may not share the same social identity as those being coached. A modern community is ever changing, and this flexibility can be apparent in constantly changing personnel and constantly changing policies.

Could stigma help?

Jones et al. (2011) examine Erving Goffman's theory of stigma and, notably, use it to argue that a coach needs to take on the role of a 'social performer', adopting appropriate roles for different situations. Within a community context, this means adopting different roles to address the needs of different people and, therefore, maintaining a very flexible and adaptable coaching philosophy. For example, a coach working within a triathlon club may be dealing with young athletes who show promise, older master athletes who may succeed in global competitions and complete beginners who have come along to 'try a tri'. The needs of all these participants require the coach to adopt a 'social performance' specific to each person even though the social identity of each participant may be defined as being a 'triathlete'. A coach working in several different contexts will succeed by developing a social identity that is fluid, flexible and extremely adaptable. For example, a football coach working on a project in Tanzania was surprised to find the coaching environment unfamiliar. The football pitch was hard scrubland, and there were only two balls between 30 participants. The participants were not used to a structured session and often used unfamiliar methods, such as dance and singing, to warm up. Some of them wore football boots or trainers, but many were barefoot. The coach's first session was planned as she would have planned for a community session in the UK where there were plenty of balls, cones, goals and a grassy field and where the participants at least wore recognisable sports gear and most of them had football boots. She said: 'I had never seen anything like this and was expecting there to be, you know, cones, balls and all the usual equipment … but there just wasn't anything'. In Tanzania, she had to adapt very quickly in order to respond to the unfamiliar social space that she was entering. Spaaij, Magee, and Jeanes (2014) describe a football-coaching programme for the homeless where, on meeting the group, the experienced and very well-qualified coach 'felt completely out of my depth and desperately isolated as I had totally misunderstood the setting'. In this instance, the football content was very low on the list of reasons why the participants had voluntarily signed up for the programme.

THE COMMUNITY SPORT COACHING WORKFORCE AND THE POLITICAL IDEOLOGY THAT INFLUENCES PRACTICE

So, who are these coaches who are working across such varied and often unpredictable environments? Whilst the workforce includes a complex mix of unpaid volunteers, part-time employees, full-time employees and those who are self-employed, it is difficult to determine what knowledge, skills and attributes might be required to do the job (SCUK, 2009). The qualification framework for coaches in the UK barely addresses coaching context or philosophy and focuses on more fundamental issues of planning, session organisation and management, evaluation, safety and some technical content. Our concern here is that there is very little to prepare coaches for the complexities that they may face if they coach outside of a world that reflects their habitus. Many coaches enter the profession as volunteers and often from within their own sporting environment where they have been performers or are parents, so the workforce tends to reflect their field of 'sport' rather than the broader aspects of 'society'. Within an institution for offenders, or a school, for example, a sports coach may already be part of the full-time staff there and will, therefore, understand the 'context' within which they are working, or they may be a specialist brought in for specific activities with little to no understanding of the context but plenty of sport-specific technical knowledge. A coach working with GP referrals may be part of an institution or company that has a contract to deliver an appropriate programme who may have limited experience of working with people with identified health issues. A coach in a local football club may be an unqualified parent or former player with varied levels of technical knowledge and a coaching philosophy that may be linked to results and performance rather than the development of lifelong habits. In addition, there are several coaches and coaching organisations within the private sector that will deliver coached programmes according to market forces and external grant availability. Hartmann and Kwauk (2011) suggest that sports coaching is sometimes delivered with an assumption that the coach owns knowledge that is 'universal' and 'static' and can be transferred easily to any group. Hopefully through the first half of this chapter, we have highlighted that, in community settings in particular, this is far from the case. As the coach, understanding is vital for increasing participants and then delivering benefits to those people.

Case studies

Coaching children

In this first case study, we explore the work of two different coaches who are both working with children but in contrasting contexts. One is working within a sport-specific club setting where the children are being coached to improve performance, and the other is leading a project within a school working with children who have not enjoyed PE and sport. Many coaches start their careers by working with children and young people, and there are an increasing number of agencies employing sports coaches to work within school, after-school and community settings, often taking on the responsibility for delivery of PE curriculum as well as extracurricular opportunities. Earlier in the chapter, we looked at theories of social identity and habitus. It is likely that most coaches will feel familiar within a school or community sports club setting, as they will have previously experienced both environments. When you read about these coaches, consider the knowledge, skills, attributes and experience required to successfully engage the range of children involved.

Paul Greaves: Sheffield Trampoline Academy, based at multiple venues across Sheffield

The Trampoline Academy is affiliated with the NGB for gymnastics, the coaches are qualified to the requirements of the NGB and the club has achieved the NGB hallmark (Gym-Mark), which marks it as being appropriate and safe for young people. This academy identifies itself as one that provides a stepping stone onto the performance pathway, and, therefore, all the participating children will have the opportunity to progress to the very top of the sport if they show sufficient talent. This is achieved by offering two strands: one being the 'recreational programme', which is open to all young people between 5 and 17, and the other being the 'competition' programme, for which young people are selected from the recreational programme. This selection process is conducted by the network of coaches working within the academy and will be based on 'desire to compete and achieve' and the necessary parental support for this level of sport. This process is mostly completed before the age of 12, by which time it is almost certainly too late to progress onto the competition strand. Recruitment onto the whole programme is through the usual channels of 'word of mouth', social media, advertising and schools, and it is almost always full.

Within the competition strand, there is clearly a requirement for the coaches to have a deep technical understanding of the sport in addition to an empathy with a range of performers. They will also need to be able to deal with parents and caretakers, as they will usually be present because the children have been enrolled and need to be taken by an adult. The philosophy adopted by the coaches reflects the aspirations of the club and its position within an NGB hierarchy, measured by success at local, regional and even national competitions. Paul Greaves, high performance coach, suggested that, for many coaches, working within the competitive strand is more straightforward, as 'the performers are all at a similar level' and are progressing towards clearly defined competitive targets, whereas in the recreation groups, you have a 'very wide range and it is more about social engagement'. He suggested that for many of the competition technical coaches, working at a recreational level with participants, whose desire to improve performance is limited, can be challenging, as they find it difficult to 'understand people who don't want to improve'.

Linzi Gaywood: Longstone Tigers, Great Longstone Primary School, Derbyshire

In direct contrast to the Trampoline Academy, a rural School Sport Partnership in Derbyshire has implemented the 'Change For Life' programme within Great Longstone Primary School, targeting those children who are not usually involved in structured sport, who become 'Tigers'. The programme utilises young leaders to work with the children to develop an enjoyment of PA. The programme's coaching philosophy is not based on developing technical expertise but on support and encouragement and on creating a climate where any child can take part. Linzi Gaywood, who leads the sessions, explained that 'the programme works with children who are poorly co-ordinated, anxious about sport or simply new to the environment' and seeks to 'get them sold on sport' so that they might want to come along to other clubs within the school. The leaders need to 'understand anxiety in children and why some children do not want to compete'. They aim to encourage children to be active and healthy rather than to excel at a particular sport. Working in this programme, therefore, requires empathy and understanding of young people who are not engaged in activity, and this can be challenging for any coach who has always enjoyed sport and finds it difficult to understand non-participants. Success can be measured by the 99–100 per cent success rate in participants progressing to other clubs within the primary school. The young leaders are encouraged to talk to the 'Tigers' about what they don't like about sport and to encourage and support friendships within the programme. Participants learn skills that will help them to develop sufficient confidence to progress, but they can stay in 'Tigers' for as long as they like. The sessions take place during the school lunchtime so organisation is simple, and there is no need to send letters home to persuade children to stay after school or gain additional parental consent. It is a flexible setting where attendance is voluntary, and children participate in their school uniform without the need to get changed.

Children participating in the programme said 'it's better than PE because we can join in more' and 'it's nice being in small teams because we get to touch the ball'. The leadership programme for the older children is based around developing creative games, which they devise and deliver themselves under the supervision of the teacher, and the 'exercise message' is hidden behind an overriding theme of 'fun'. Some of the leaders were previously in the 'Tigers' programme themselves and, so, can readily identify with those children who do not feel comfortable in a sport and PA setting. This has helped to create a situation where 'participants and coaches share and understand each other's values'.

Coaching adolescents

In this second case study, we explore the work of three different coaches who are working with adolescents, but in very different contexts. One is working within a sport-specific club setting where performers are being coached to improve performance, and the other two are seeking to engage young people who have been marginalised and for whom participation in sport and PE has not always been a positive experience. Once young people reach secondary school, they begin to develop a deepening sense of who they want to be. For those for whom sport is already a key part of their social identity, in other words, those who have progressed into a setting where they are comfortable and reasonably successful, there is a possibility that they will continue to participate. However, by this stage, there are young people who have already been marginalised and for whom participation in sport and PA is not a part of their identity. When you read about these coaches, consider the challenges of engaging both young people who have been marginalised and young people who have set out on a performance pathway.

Chris Motley: junior coach, City of Sheffield Water Polo Club

City of Sheffield Water Polo club has a progressive player pathway for children who can start in the 'Mini Monsters' programme (aged 4+) through to its club junior programme and eventually, for those with sufficient talent, into teams that compete at the highest level in national competitions. Like the trampoline club in the first case study, it is affiliated to its NGB and has achieved the NGB hallmark, (SwimMark), marking it as safe and appropriate for young people. Coaches work with players as they progress from the junior into the senior programme, which requires a high degree of technical expertise. However, and just as important, they require an understanding of the complex issues and choices facing a young person during this phase of their life. It is a time when drop out from sport is at its highest as young people start to make their own choices about how to fill their time and, sometimes, because they are no longer making progress in sport. The formation of friendship groups and progress within sport is likely to determine the likelihood of them being able to access a traditional community sports club.

Chris Motley coaches players from junior into senior level at City of Sheffield Water Polo Club and explained his philosophy when working with adolescents as being to

> make sure they enjoy what they do as there are lots of other things for them to do at this age. I work on improving their skills, giving them mini targets because they need to improve if they are to stay with the sport.

He pointed out that as young people progress through sport, there will be natural wastage once they stop making progress, and for this reason, his philosophy also includes the need to 'buy into the idea of working hard' because otherwise they will not progress and keep up with the others. The social connections are essential, as Chris says they will always 'turn up to be with people they want to be with' but will not often be motivated to work by themselves. 'This is a team game, it's about building teams', and they want to belong to a group. As coach, he has to manage group dynamics, which means sometimes allowing them to work with friends and sometimes splitting friendship groups so the he can stretch them further. 'They are on a player pathway, they need to take things seriously as well as just chat'.

Chris and the other coaches within the club have all been performers at some stage in their lives and have a deep understanding of the sport's technical requirements. They have friendship groups associated with the sport and strive to recreate this within the younger players. As with the coaches from the trampoline club in the first case study, there is a preference for coaching players in a competitive environment, and the club has limited capacity to offer a recreational strand.

Lee Hible: Stocksbridge Community Leisure Centre and Saeed Brasab: Unity Gym Project, Sheffield

In contrast, the Street Games project, referred to in Chapter 5, set out to offer sporting opportunities to young people who were either unable to access traditional sport through lack of social and physical capital or who rejected the disciplined traditional coaching environment of those involved in competitive sport. The sport development officer at Stocksbridge Community Leisure Centre is managing a project as a part of the recently formed community trust, which has seen the centre reopen in response to demand from the community. Whilst bookings by local clubs at the centre are a potential barrier to participation for some, his project has developed, through support from Street Games, a programme of taster sessions in local schools, which link to 'doorstep clubs' at the centre. The clientele for these sessions are young people who 'aren't as good and don't do well at PE, they don't willingly join clubs'. The philosophy is to offer a variety of activities to get young people 'involved', and there is no emphasis on 'improving performance'. For example, when the boys in the club 'just wanted to play football', the coaches continued with this and 'didn't tell them to try something else'. This potentially challenges the traditional concept of a sports coach who seeks to improve performance and move participants along a notional 'performance pathway'. The coach's role within this setting is to understand the participants who do not progress along the traditional route and for whom sport has not always been positive.

This was further exemplified at the Unity Gym in multicultural Broomhall, Sheffield, an area marked by racial conflict and gang warfare in the early part of the 21st century. Saeed Brasab created the project in response to a need he identified as a 'lack of provision for young people, no youth clubs', and he set out to use sport as a 'tool to engage young people, to deal with conflict with groups who wouldn't usually see eye to eye'. He saw the area as 'where I lived, where I grew up', and therefore was able to 'identify' with the community.

Doorstep clubs have been established with support from Street Games, and the coaches who work on the project are often recruited from within the participants who volunteer initially. The key qualities in Saeed's coaches are 'shared cultural background', 'trust' and 'the ability to recognise the natural talents that young people have'. The key to their success is 'having a vested interest in the well being of the community', but 'having a sporting background is not enough, you need to understand youth work … it doesn't matter if you are fantastic at football'.

One of the shared visions of both the Stocksbridge Community Leisure Centre and the Unity Gym Project was that coaches needed to be passionate about developing the community and that this has not been achieved when coaches were simply brought in to deliver activities. They both felt that coaches succeeded where they gained the 'trust' of young people and were, therefore, able to deal with a range of issues affecting them.

Coaching adults

In this third case study, we explore the work of two different coaches who are working with adults in contrasting contexts. One is working within a swimming environment, coaching adults who want to improve performance, and the other is leading a walking football session, which is based purely on participation. As the population demographic has changed, the number of older adults has increased. The influential 'Baby Boomer generation', that is, those born in the years following the Second World War, has reached retirement and, with it, has brought changing perceptions of what it is to be old. This, in turn, has developed an entrepreneurial approach to creating and adapting age-appropriate activities. In 2011, walking football emerged to be followed by walking netball, which, in turn, developed from the 'Back to Netball' campaign. Alongside 'sport' for older adults, other activities such as 'chairobics' have emerged, all requiring coaches with very different knowledge, skills and aptitude. In addition, the number of GPs referring patients to exercise rather than medication has created a need for coaches who are able to deliver safe, structured activities for participants who may not have previously chosen PA.

Greg Unwin and James Blencowe: walking football coaches, University of Sheffield Community Sport Programme

The walking football club has been recently established as a part of the University of Sheffield Community Sport Programme and is part of the growing phenomena of walking sports, recognised by the Football Association (FA) in 2011 and offering the opportunity for older people to continue to play the game they love in a recreational environment with an emphasis on fun and participation. Greg Unwin and James Blencowe's role is to respond to the participants in terms of how much they would like to do, whether they would like to develop skills and to manage the game safely and fairly.

Several participants have been recommended to attend by GPs who are prescribing PA. There is a wide range of motivation, therefore, which the coach needs to manage, alongside a need to focus on health improvement. Both coaches are qualified to FA Level 1, but they manage the session by encouraging participation in a game with no technical skill development. They create a 'comfortable atmosphere' where there is encouragement to take part but no 'taught drills'. The participants identify 'getting fit, getting out of the house and playing sport' as their key motivation to be involved. The session is 'pay as you go' and is targeted at everyone from beginner to those who have previous playing experience. It is easy to make the link between this session and Bailey's PPW model identified earlier in the chapter. The key motivator for the participants is to take part in exercise, which will benefit their physical and mental health but that is also simply designed to be fun.

The coaches emerge as examples of Goffman's 'social performer' as they play a role in this session that is different from other, more technical personal and elite-referenced sessions that they also coach across a variety of sports. They both succeed in this particular context because of their ability to respond to a group of individuals whose shared social identity is through football, even though they may have very different individual identities. Unwin, although he was a good footballer as a junior, commented that he runs the session in a very informal way:

> It puts people off if I turn up with my whistle ... too many whistles and shouting make people drop out of sport. You know there are a lot of people playing sport and only a few of them are good ... people say 'I'm no good at sport' and I say that doesn't matter, just come and enjoy it.

Blencowe, on the other hand, has never been a footballer and has a background in trampolining: 'So many coaching skills are transferable, you need to be able to get on with people', and this is the essence of the walking football session where camaraderie and friendship prevails.

Wendy Figures: swimming coach, adult Swimfit, Yorkshire Outdoor Swimmers

Wendy Figures is an experienced swimming coach and teacher working within Sheffield. Whilst she still teaches children to swim, her main area of interest is now working with adults from beginners up to masters' competition swimmers and open-water swimmers. She delivers one-to-one sessions with 'adults who can swim and want to develop their front crawl for a triathlon' through to 'Swimfit' sessions in a pool where most of the swimmers can do front crawl but need to improve their technique. She recruits mainly through word of mouth and social media and works with swimmers from their mid-twenties to the over sixties, particularly in the rapidly growing area of outdoor swimming. At the 'top end', the masters' swimmers have good technique and are often former competitive swimmers, whereas the one-to-one sessions focus on individuals who are mastering the technical aspects of swimming. Technique is everything, and Figures explains that coaching adults is different because adults really want to know everything and enjoy seeing video footage of their strokes, which Wendy uses to help them develop. The coaching requests are specific to improving swimming and do not come from those who simply want to improve their health and fitness, although this is always an outcome of Figures's sessions.

In her one-to-one sessions, 'the client sets the agenda', but it will almost always be based on 'rotation and breathing', and Figures says 'they all need to do the same thing but completely differently'. Coaching a masters' squad is different because you are working with a bigger group who all do the same basic session but with differentiated lane swim and rest times. The one-to-one sessions are more enjoyable because 'I feel like I'm getting more quality', because 'one size does not fit all'.

The key thing in this context is that a high level of technical knowledge is required, and, whilst the coach needs to really understand and appreciate the needs of the clientele, their demands are sport specific. Swimming can only be 'coached' once the fundamentals have been mastered through a teaching programme, and there is, therefore, a distinction between teaching and coaching in swimming. A high level of knowledge is required so that the session is appropriate to the needs of the swimmer. However, Figures's swimmers are already engaged in some way and have requested coaching, and she does not need, therefore, to understand the requirements of those who are not engaged in swimming. However, she will constantly be changing people's perceptions of what it takes and supporting swimmers from their first steps into open water: 'I will swim round with them and chat about the wildlife' to the more advanced challenges of 'masters' competition and channel swimming. These sessions, however, all focus on technical improvement and, specifically, improving swimming.

CONCLUSION

It is clear to see that, from the range of contexts identified here, coaches need to be flexible, adaptable and able to understand the values and experiences of the participants with whom they are working. Goffman's 'social actor' may be able to respond to the varied needs of different people, but the key in many of these examples was that the coach emerged from within a community with which they were familiar.

REVIEW QUESTIONS

1. The ICCE and the Jones and Stevenson model acknowledges that the number and makeup of the domains within coaching are many and varied. How and why might this be?
2. How would you approach coaching a group whose life experience is different from yours and who do not share the same values and beliefs as you?
3. What impact would your own habitus and identity have on the way you might coach in a community setting?
4. How and when do you think technical sport-specific knowledge is important when delivering a community sports programme?

REFERENCES

Blackshaw, T. (2010). *Key Concepts in Community Studies*, Sage Publications Ltd, London.
Bordieu, P. (1977). *Outline of a Theory of Practice*, Cambridge University Press, Cambridge.
Bordieu, P. (1990). *The Logic of Practice*, Polity Press Cambridge in Association with Blackwell Publishers, Oxford.
Brewer, M.D. (1991). The Social Self: On Being the Same and Different at the Same Time. *Personality and Social Psychology Bulletin*, 17 (5), 47–482.
Cassidy, T., Jones, R. and Potrac, P. (2009). *Understanding Sports Coaching: The Social, Cultural and Pedagogical Foundations of Coaching Practice*. 2nd Edition, Routledge, London.
Collins, D., Bailey, R., Ford, P.A., MacNamara, A., Toms, M. and Pearce, G. (2012). Three worlds: new directions in participant development in sport and physical activity. *Sport, Education and Society*, 17 (2), 225–243.
Cronin, C. and Armour, K.M. (2015). Lived experience and community sport coaching: A phenomenological investigation. *Sport, Education and Society*, 20 (8), 959–975.
Cushion, C. and Partington, M. (2016). A critical analysis of the conceptualisation of 'coaching philosophy'. *Sport, Education and Society*, 21 (6), 851–867.
Hartmann, D. and Kwauk, C. (2011). Sport and development: An overview, critique and recontruction. *Journal of Sport and Social Issues*, 35 (3), 284–305.
International Council for Coaching Excellence, Association of Summer Olympic International Federations, Leeds Becket University. (2013). International Sports Coaching Framework, Version 1.2, Human Kinetics, Champaign, IL.
Jenkins, S. (2010). Coaching philosophy. pp. 233–242. In: Lyle, J. and Cushion, C. (eds.). *Sports Coaching: Professionalisation and Practice*. Churchill Livingstone (Elsevier), Edinburgh.

Jones, R.L., Armour, K.M. and Potrac, P. (2004). *Sports Coaching Culture: From Practice to Theory*, Routledge, London.

Jones, R.L., Potrac, P., Cushion, C. and Ronglan, L.T. (Eds) (2011). *The Sociology of Sports Coaching*, Routledge, London.

Kidman, L. and Hanrahan, S. (2011). *A Practical Guide to Becoming an Effective Sports Coach*, Routledge, London.

Lyle, J. (2002). *Sports Coaching Concepts, Part One*, Routledge, London.

Spaaij, R., Magee, J. and Jeanes, R. (2014). *Sport and Social Exclusion in Global Society*, Routledge, Oxford.

Sport England. (2016). A Coaching Plan For England. www.sportengland.org/media/11317/coaching-in-an-active-nation_the-coaching-plan-for-england.pdf.

Sports Coach UK. (2009). The Coaching Workforce 2009–2016. www.ukcoaching.org/resource/coaching-workforce-2009-16-0.

Tulle, E. and Pheonix, C. (Eds) (2015). *Physical Activity and Sport in Later Life, Chapter One*, Palgrave Macmillan, London.

Turner, J.C. and Tajfel, H. (1986). The social identity theory of intergroup behavior. *Psychology of Intergroup Relations*, 5, 7–24.

PART III

Functions and operations in community sport and physical activity

CHAPTER 10

Managing community sport and physical activity centres

Melissa Jacobi and Rebecca Peake

SUMMARY

This chapter will provide you with an overview of some of the areas deemed to be critical to success when managing community sport facilities in the dynamic and challenging environment evident in the UK in recent years. These include organisations' finance and staffing and are exemplified by three case study facilities situated within the city of Sheffield. Although Sheffield focussed, the concepts and challenges identified are transferrable across the country as well as mirroring similar situations in the wider global sector. Within the chapter, you find an introduction to the historical provision of sport facilities in the UK, overviews of the case study facilities and a consideration of the challenges and opportunities community sport facilities face.

AIMS

By engaging with this chapter, you will be able to

- Provide an overview of the historical development of public sector sports provision and community sport facilities,
- Consider the key resource requirements for the operation of community sport facilities,
- Identify key challenges and opportunities faced by community sport facilities and
- Identify elements of good practice and development opportunities available to community sport facilities.

INTRODUCTION

Key components in the delivery of community sport are the facilities and spaces in which sport and physical activity can take place. Ensuring that these facilities and spaces are in alignment with the needs of community groups is essential if facilities are to meet their financial and social objectives. The environment in which facilities are managed has shifted dramatically in recent years in response to policy and ownership trends. The non-profit sector in which community sport facilities operate has grown in terms of its front-line provision with a range of developments and changes being made in recent decades. Such changes will be explored during this chapter, followed by a consideration of what demonstrates best practice by the case study facilities. Finally, we will explore how community facilities can, in the future, prove themselves and become financially viable whilst remaining responsive to the local communities they serve. By understanding the key themes in this chapter, you will be able to identify critical success factors vital in this dynamic sector, which, as you will see, are in many cases transferrable across a range of areas.

Historical development

Before we can understand the immediate and future challenges for facility managers, it is important that we take a look back at the historical development of community sport provision, identify the key changes that have taken place and determine the reasons why the industry has needed to modernise. The formal provision of public sector sport and leisure opportunities has been influenced by a range of policies and strategies in recent decades including the Central Council for Physical Recreation's commissioning of the Wolfenden Report, 'Sport in the Community' in 1957, which saw, among a range of findings, the initial recommendation for a Sports Advisory Council (Haywood et al., 1995). Moving into the 1970s, the Labour Government's 1975 White Paper, 'Sport and Recreation', identified that the provision of recreation facilities were '... part of the general fabric of the social services', demonstrating a clear requirement for the provision of recreation activities for the general population (Adapted from Henry, 1993 cited in Wilson and Piekarz, 2016). The Sport and Recreation White Paper was published at one of the pivotal times in relation to sport and recreation facility development in the UK – the mid-1970s.

1974 saw the reorganisation of local government creating newer, generally larger, local authorities, which often included the creation of a Leisure Service or Recreation Department, providing a platform for the formalisation and strategic development of public sector sport facilities (Haywood et al., 1995). We can see this through the expansion of provision of public sector facilities during the 1970s; as Henry (1993) identified in 1972, there were 30 municipal (public sector) sport centres and 500 indoor swimming pools; by 1978, investment in sport facility infrastructure saw this increase to 350 sports centres and more than 850 pools (Henry, 1993 cited in Wilson and Piekarz, 2016).

Following the 1976 'IMF Crisis', a devalued pound (£) lead the 1976 Labour Government to request a $3.9 billion loan from the International Monetary Fund, which subsequently saw a change in orientation away from full employment and social welfare and towards much stricter controls on expenditure and inflation. The Conservative Government of 1979 continued this shift away from investment in infrastructure and towards a focus on the economic and efficiency side of provision – a move often referred to as the 'Marketisation' of public leisure services (Henry, 2001 cited in Taylor, 2011, p. 123). This included the introduction of Compulsory Competitive Tendering (CCT) of local government services from the late 1980s through to the mid-1990s, which was a significant landmark in the operation of sports facilities for the general population. Two acts (1988 and 1989) saw formal processes developed, enabling private organisations to submit tenders to run local authority services and facilities. Fundamentally, the local authority retained ownership of the facilities and retained a controlling interest in areas such as pricing, programming and opening times, but the operational side was handed over to private organisations to run the facilities. There were two key goals of CCT: first, to decrease the costs of running local authority sport provision by ensuring the facilities are run as efficiently as possible (with efficiency being judged solely on the 'bottom line') and second, to improve the service to users (adapted from Robinson, 2004). One of the issues with CCT was that initially, 60 per cent of sport and leisure management contracts were 'uncontested', and a further 22 per cent only had one external bid (possibly due to the way the packages of services were 'parcelled up' with some of the less attractive services/facilities being paired with more modern/profitable facilities) (Centre for Leisure research, 1993 cited in Taylor, 2011). Before the 1997 Labour election victory, commercial, contract companies had won over one quarter of all contracts (Taylor, 2011), which meant a significant change to the landscape of sport and leisure facilities for local communities. These organisations included non-profit distributing cooperatives such as Greenwich Leisure Limited who originated in 1993 to run local services such as leisure centres.

A change of government in 1997 saw the 'new' Labour Party effectively replace CCT with a duty to provide 'Best Value', which on a combination of quality and cost. This programme was introduced via the local government act (1999) and implemented in 2000, placing a requirement on local authorities in England and Wales to commit to the 'continuous improvement' of their services and operations with a key focus on the benefits that could be derived from concentrating on 'Economy, Efficiency and Effectiveness'.

As Robinson (2004) identified, the implication of 'Best Value' for a sport and recreation service was that they had to become more accountable to the communities they served, particularly in relation to 'Consulting' with them with regard to provisions. Consulting formed part to of the 4 Cs of 'Best Value', as identified in Table 10.1.

The Audit Commission conducted inspections of services and oversaw local authority reviews for 'Best Value', however, concerns they raised regarding different approaches being taken by local authorities saw the development of the Comprehensive Performance Assessment (CPA), which was proposed in 2001 and implemented in 2002.

TABLE 10.1 Best Value adapted from Taylor	
"C"	*Aspect of Best Value*
Challenge	Challenging whether the local authority should be offering the 'function' now and in the future, as well as challenging the way in which the service should be carried out.
Compare	Relates to the authorities' performance being compared to the performance of other organisations and authorities utilising a range of indicators, specifically the national indicators specified by the Audit Commission.
Consult	Requires authorities to consult with stakeholders including providers, users and non-users of the services.
Compete	To determine the 'optimal way of delivering services against agreed targets and objectives'.

CPA provided an overall assessment of a council's performance and focussed on six key areas including Education, Housing, Libraries and Leisure. CPA utilised centrally devised 'Performance Indicators' and assessments to rate local authorities as 'Excellent, Good, Fair, Weak or Poor'. A simplistic overview of the outcomes of CPA would suggest that those local authorities deemed to be performing well were given more autonomy and fewer assessments, whereas those with weaker performance were given more support. Further information on 'Best Value' and CPA can be found in Houlihan and Lindsey (2012).

CPA was replaced in 2009 by the Comprehensive Area Assessment (CAA), which provided an evaluation of how well communities were being served by their public services, with a focus on the 'outcomes' of provision in terms of the services and facilities provided by local authorities and their partners rather than the 'processes' by which they were provided, as tended to be the focus of CPA. This inclusion of partnerships and the focus on the 'area' rather than specifically the local authority demonstrates the shifting change of those involved in the provision of services for local communities, with less reliance on the local authority alone. In 2010, the election of the Coalition Government saw the abolition of CAA in a bid to remove what were perceived to be layers of bureaucracy and the costs associated with administering the evaluations; instead, local authorities were encouraged to be more open and transparent in relation to their provision and processes.

The recognition of the benefits of sport and physical activity to wider areas of life – such as to health in helping reduce obesity levels, which, in turn, helps reduce the demand on the National Health Service, as well as activities such as cycling being a sustainable method of transport – is reflected in the way that opportunities for participation in sport and physical activity are now provided in the UK. Under the 2015 Conservative Government, provision of sporting activities now falls under the remit of a range of government departments, as identified in Figure 10.1; a far cry from the method of provision in the 1970s where Leisure and Recreation Departments were almost exclusively responsible for provision.

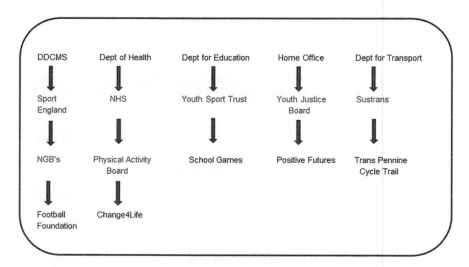

FIGURE 10.1 Government departments and sporting activities

Key: Government Department. Government Partner/Agency. Project Example.

DEVELOPMENT OF LEISURE TRUSTS

As has already been identified, over the last 25 years, local authority management of sporting facilities has moved from being exclusively the domain of 'in-house' or 'Direct Service Organisations' of local authorities to a sector with a variety of management models in place, of which 'Leisure Trusts' and private management companies play an increasingly significant role. There is no definitive definition of what constitutes a 'Trust', but it tends to be a generic term for organisations operating local authority facilities with a focus on community requirements rather than profit. In 2015/2016, the third sector provision (which includes trusts) increased to a level where the proportion of facilities being run by local authorities decreased to an all-time low of 20 per cent (Mintel, 2016). Mintel (2016) also identified that over the last decade (until 2016), the number of charitable trusts operating sport facilities increased from 17 per cent to 33 per cent, demonstrating the significant growth in this type of organisation. The range of organisations operating in this area is exemplified by Simmons (2003, p. 6): '… the scope of leisure trusts can vary from a single leisure facility at one end of the scale, through to an organisation encompassing the full range of leisure services formally administered by the local authority'. A detailed overview of Trusts, their structures and pros and cons of this type of organisation including the benefit of having exemption from business rates and value added tax can be found in Schwarz et al. (2015).

As is happening across the UK, the city of Sheffield has seen an increasing number of not-for-profit, Leisure Trusts, social enterprises and community organisations operating community sport facilities. Three such facilities are used as case study facilities in this chapter.

Case studies

The following case studies provide an overview of three community sport facilities in Sheffield; they will be used in the remainder of the chapter to provide examples of how the theories and concepts identified are implemented in real life. The use of these case studies will help you see how the differences in the historical past of a facility, as well as the varied communities they operate in, influences decisions and provision for the managers of these facilities.

Stocksbridge Community Leisure Centre

Stocksbridge Community Leisure Centre is a large centre originally opened by the old West Riding County Council in 1969, before transferring to Sheffield City Council following the local government boundary changes in 1974. Due to high running costs and budget cuts, it was proposed to be closed by Sheffield City Council in 2013. A campaign led by a community action group to save the facility from closure was ultimately unsuccessful, but after a period of three months, during which the facility was mothballed, a newly restructured community group reopened the dry side of the facility in October 2013. Now a registered charity, and a company limited by guarantee, '4SLC' operates the largest community run leisure centre in Sheffield (S36), and indeed, the South Yorkshire area. Facilities include a large indoor bowls hall, a multisports hall, two swimming pools, a fitness gym, meeting rooms and three squash courts, all run by a professional manager and a team of paid and unpaid staff. After four years of operation, it is now a sustainable enterprise operating without any subsidy from the City Council.

Zest

Situated in Upperthorpe in Sheffield (S6), Zest serves the whole of Sheffield but has a primary focus on the local neighbourhoods of Upperthorpe, Langsett and Netherthorpe. The Zest Centre serves as an integrated community service hub, offering a ramp-access swimming pool, gym, ladies-only gym, exercise classes, café, volunteer-led library, meeting rooms and office space available for hire, as well as providing services such as Zest for Work, which helps facilitate local people up skilling and gaining employment. Zest is a charity and community enterprise and is the trading name for Netherthorpe & Upperthorpe Community Alliance (NUCA). NUCA was established in 1997 as a community forum and by 1999 was successful in its bid to deliver an area regeneration programme (SRB 6/ERDF) worth £15 million, for which it was the accountable body. In 2007, Upperthorpe Healthy Living Centre Trust transferred full operational management of its centre to Zest. In 2008, NUCA adopted a new trading name of 'Zest' to reflect its increasing role in the delivery of public services. It now works with partners at a local and citywide level to deliver a wide range of services including the Department for Work and Pensions Work Programme, Smokefree Children & Young Peoples service in schools, Social Prescribing services and a wide range of volunteering programmes. The Zest Healthy Living Centre provides a local hub for a wide range of health, employment, sport, youth and community services (Zest Community, 2017).

U-Mix

U-Mix is situated in Lowfield, Sheffield (S2), an area with a mixed ethnic community and challenges both economically and socially. The U-Mix Centre opened in 2012 and includes two 3G football pitches with accessible changing facilities, a small dance studio, a running loop, a recording studio, a small gym, a digital media centre, a training room, a meeting room and a 'Positive Activity' multipurpose room, which includes a pool table, table tennis table, table football, PlayStation and Xbox, primarily used by youth groups.

The U-Mix facility was derived from the organisation Football Unites Racism Divides (FURD), who in the mid-1990s were delivering a range of football coaching activities and providing volunteering opportunities and youth work from a base called The Stables located in Sharrow (S2), but with a lack of facilities, these activities were predominantly undertaken on an outreach basis. Whilst the work FURD undertook was deemed to be successful and valuable to the community, it was felt that uniting the activities under one roof would be of benefit. Around 2010, a collaboration between FURD, Sheffield City

Council and Sheffield Futures (who became Sheffield Youth Work) applied for a My Place grant to build a purpose-built facility. They were successful and received £2.1 million to fund the build. The Football Foundation also provided £300,000 to fund the 3G pitches. In the summer of 2012, almost coinciding with the London Olympics, U-Mix opened.

CHALLENGES AND OPPORTUNITIES FOR COMMUNITY SPORT FACILITIES

All organisations, no matter what country or sector they operate in, face challenges from their external environment; challenges faced by community sport facilities vary depending on a number of factors, including location, history and funding partner objectives. There are, however, some common challenges, which were highlighted by Hall et al. (2003) in their work on Canadian non-profit and voluntary sport organisations. Whilst this might not be the most recent work available in the area of non-profit sport provision, Hall et al.'s (2003) work provides what is considered to be the most appropriate framework for this chapter. They identify that 'an organisations overall capacity to fulfil its mission depends on a variety of specific capacities' (Hall et al., 2003, p. 2). The most significant capacities in relation to an organisation achieving its goals and objectives are

- Financial Capacity,
- Human Resources (HR) Capacity and
- Structural Capacity, which includes
    - Relationship and Network Capacity and
    - Infrastructure and Process Capacity.

Although Hall et al.'s (2003) work is based in Canada and includes a range of different types of voluntary organisations within the primary research focus groups, these key areas are very much relevant to the operation of community sport facilities in the UK. Indeed, the areas of finance and HR are arguably the most significant for *any* organisation no matter which sector or country the organisation is operating in. Therefore, Hall et al.'s (2003) model is used as a framework for the discussion of the three case study facilities representing different types of community sport facilities operating in Sheffield, with particular focus on Finance and HR.

FINANCIAL CAPACITY

Financial capacity issues pose the greatest challenges for no-profit and voluntary organisations.

(Hall et al., 2003, p. viii)

As alluded to previously, financial capacity – or the ability to have enough available financial resources to be able to not only operate on a day-to-day basis, but also be able to plan for the future direction of an organisation – is vital to all organisations, not just community sport facilities. That said, community sport facilities have faced a range of challenges in recent years relating to finances. Some of these are outlined below.

As a result of cuts to local authority budgets, difficult decisions need to be made on how the remaining budget is spent; in Sheffield, these austerity cuts have totalled £390 million in seven years up to 2017 (Sheffield City Council, 2017). These cuts have led to significant reductions in funding available for a range of council services, including libraries and sport and leisure facilities. For the case study facilities, these cuts have meant significant changes.

The Healthy Living Centre/leisure arm of Zest was originally funded by Sheffield City Council. In 2008, between council funding and public health funding, Zest received around £230,000 per annum; this has reduced year on year down to £80,000 from 2017. This £150,000 reduction has largely been implemented in the last three years and has made the commercial focus of Zest evermore vital to help ensure a future for the whole organisation. They have consolidated their offering by focusing on services and contract work to effectively cross subsidise ongoing community business development and community development activities. They also utilise performance 'targets' across relevant service areas, including swimming lessons, and on payment-by-results employment contracts, balancing the need to be client centred whilst ensuring they are delivering effectively and efficiently to help sustain the core community service offer.

For U-Mix, operational funding for the first two years (2012–2014) was provided wholly by Sheffield City Council; this included staff wages as well as running costs such as heating and lighting. This allowed FURD to focus their attention on developing activities and partnerships as well as seeking additional funding to be able to cater for different groups or demographics. In their third year of operation (2015), Sheffield City Council had to halve the operational funding they provided due to cuts in local authority budgets; the fourth year (2016) saw no operational funding from Sheffield City Council, which means the facility has to become self-supporting. Due to the subsidy (particularly in the first two years) U-Mix was able to save an amount of money, which is currently being utilised, to help cover operational costs. U-Mix faces a further issue in balancing community and commercial operations; there is the opportunity to 'sell space' to generate income, particularly their 3G pitch, at commercial rates; peak-rate pitch hire is currently £35 for the general public and private organisations and £20 for community groups. Given the growing focus on needing to be financially self-sufficient, it would be easy to see how 'selling the space' to the 'highest bidder' might be attractive, yet FURD try to ensure that U-Mix is used for the purpose for which it was originally intended – carrying out FURD's community development and anti-racism work – which means that they try and ensure a flexible ratio of approximately 50 per cent private/community use. Hall et al. (2003) make a distinction between 'Outputs and Outcomes', where they identify that, '… outputs are secondary to the intended outcome of those outputs' (Hall et al., 2003, p. 6). For U-Mix, the fact that they could generate a higher level of turnover (increased output) would detract from their intended 'outcome' of ensuring access for disadvantaged groups and the focus of FURD of being able to use football to bring diverse groups together to enhance community cohesion and address the issue of racism in communities. The result is that the management of U-Mix must balance the need to increase income whilst still providing accessibility for the local community.

Initiatives such as asking the users of the traditionally free youth club to contribute a nominal amount (50p) towards the running costs were not been met favourably, again evidencing the issues and challenges faced by managers of community sport facilities such as U-Mix.

Funding applications present an additional challenge. In the words of the U-Mix Centre manager, there is a constant 'jigsaw puzzle of funding' from a wide range of sources (including Children in Need and Lloyds TSB), and, as such, the origin of the funding dictates the type of user U-Mix target with the funded activities. This relates to another issue raised by Hall et al. (2003), where they identify that '... funders tend to provide *project funding* which supports specific programs and activities, rather than *core funding*, which supports the organisation as a whole' (Hall et al., 2003, p. 21); they go on to suggest that one of the problems of project funding is 'danger of mission drift', suggesting that there is a need to tailor programmes and offerings of a facility to meet funders' mandates and requirements; 'consequently they (the organisation) must continually struggle to ensure that the character and mission of their organisation are not altered' (Hall et al., 2003, p. 23); this is clearly a significant challenge for U-Mix, who are underpinned by FURD core principles; by having to tailor activities to meet the needs of different project funders, they are arguably exposed to the risk of 'Mission Drift'. Increased 'Core Funding', such as that previously provided by the Council, would mean they could focus on their core objectives and desired 'Outcomes' rather than having to play the funding jigsaw puzzle, as they currently do.

Zest has some advantages in this respect; first, due to having a broad vision to improve the lives of the local community, they are more readily able to apply for different funding pots that are more likely to align with one of their operating areas, helping avoid 'Mission Drift'; second, the fact that they also provide contracted services to the outside means, to some extent, a more diverse and stable income base, and they become less reliant on dwindling local authority subsidies. Critically though, Zest has found a way to help generate some of the 'Core Funding' to support the core functions including business development. This is centred on (a) factoring in full-cost recovery, which includes recognising that management costs are not an add-on but a critical part of the whole. Where feasible, a 'management fee' is built in, and that recognises the true cost of running a community business, which can help funded posts or programmes to help sustain the organisation as a whole; and (b) delivering services with unrestricted income that may generate a small surplus or profit, which can be reinvested into business development, subsidising community services or building repairs.

For Stocksbridge Community Leisure Centre, the situation is slightly different. Their facility was taken over by a community group when the facility was due to be closed, so the group was aware there would not be any council subsidy to help contribute to operational running costs. This means Stocksbridge Community Leisure Centre needs to be self-sufficient financially in order to survive. For this type of community sport facility (particularly ones with swimming pools), the major challenge is to manage costs. Funding is used to run activities, gain qualifications for staff to support certain activities or (as has most often been the case for Stocksbridge Community Leisure Centre) as capital revenue for building renovations due to the ageing fabric of the buildings. These have included plant maintenance, replacement windows, changing room improvements and, critically for Stocksbridge Community Leisure Centre, sustainable sources of energy including biomass boilers and 300 solar panels to help ensure energy-efficient operation as well as income in the form of 'Renewable Heat Incentive' payments, which have helped offset the heating costs of the pools. It is the keeping control of costs that helps ensure the financial viability of the facility.

A further challenge for community sport facilities housed in older buildings (typically ex-Council buildings taken over by community groups) is the cost of maintaining the infrastructure of the facility. Zest requires £170,000–£180,000 in order to replace its leaking roof, and Stocksbridge Community Leisure Centre secured a £10,000 grant (match funded to £20,000) to refurbish their dry-side changing rooms. These examples demonstrate some of the significant issues for organisations operating in older buildings, meaning an additional burden of fundraising as well as managing the expectations of customers who often have the opportunity to spend their leisure time and disposable income in newer, often custom-built, competitor facilities such as budget gyms like Pure Gym or Snap Fitness (which has a brand new purpose-built gym just a mile from Stocksbridge Community Leisure Centre). The cost is often comparable for customers in terms of membership prices, but the community sport facilities offer a different type of experience in many cases, largely focusing on a personalised experience, whether it be in terms of customer service – being known by the members of staff or volunteers at the facility – or in terms of the offering being tailored to the requirements of specific area – such as the women-only gym at Zest where there is a high number of Muslim women looking for a suitable gym to exercise in.

HUMAN RESOURCE CAPACITY

> … human capital, staff and volunteers (are a community organisations) greatest resource.
>
> (Hall et al., 2003, p. viii)

As well as being one of the most costly aspects of running a business, the HR of an organisation, commonly referred to as 'the staff', can be one of the biggest strengths an organisation can have. The challenge for managers in any sector is to ensure that they recruit staff with a good work ethic as well as personal values that are aligned with the organisation.

In terms of community sport facilities, whilst staffing can be considered a challenging area, it is largely a challenge due to financial constraints rather than the staff themselves. Zest currently employs around 80 members of staff, however, due to the funding cuts, it has meant that the organisation has had to 'trim' staffing, with the vast majority of staff now on part-time contracts to help ensure that the organisation runs as leanly as possible. Stocksbridge Community Leisure Centre approaches staffing in a different way; from the original community action group and publicity surrounding the closure of the facility, around 300 people volunteered to help in the reopening of the facility – this has now settled at a core of around 60 volunteers, from a range of different backgrounds, who commit time on a weekly basis to ensure the facility can remain open and financially viable. Stocksbridge Community Leisure Centre operates with around 10 paid staff, paid lifeguards on casual contracts and the 60 volunteers who undertake roles ranging from cleaning, to reception, to snack bar operation and, critically, as 'pool responders' who work alongside the lifeguards to supervise the small pool where requirements of any required rescue would be significantly less than in the main pool. Indeed, the philosophy at Stocksbridge Community Leisure Centre is 'can a volunteer reasonably be expected to undertake this role?' If the answer is 'yes', then they will try in the first instance to utilise a volunteer rather than a paid member of staff to undertake the job/role, the rationale being purely to help ensure financial viability of the facility. This core of volunteers is a considerable resource; however, it provides a challenge in terms of maintaining the ongoing enthusiasm and commitment of the volunteers; this is managed carefully with full inductions and training as well as recognition events such as their Christmas party and awards night where volunteers are thanked, recognised and provided with a night out to help keep motivation high.

For both U-Mix and Stocksbridge Community Leisure Centre, there is an issue with those currently in management roles having previous limited experience in managing a community sport facility; their backgrounds and skills lie in different areas, however, some are very transferrable. The current manager of Stocksbridge Community Leisure Centre has a wealth of experience in the community sector; funding bid writing; as well as managing people, budgets and accounts. This enables him to see the facility as a 'business' first and foremost and bring a commercial mindset to the role; the specialisms of managing a 'sport facility' have been learnt along the way from consultation with other organisations or specialists. At U-Mix, the facility was originally meant to be jointly run between Sheffield Futures (youth service) and FURD, but the austerity cuts affecting the youth service meant that Sheffield City Council asked FURD to manage the whole facility. The small team of FURD staff means that they have a limited HR capacity, making running the facility, carrying out their community development and youth work activities as well as developing further business opportunities a challenge.

OPPORTUNITIES

The third element of Hall et al.'s (2003) framework deemed vital for the success of organisations is their **Structural Capacity** – effectively, an organisation's ability to capitalise on opportunities as they arise. Opportunities for community sport facilities differ from organisation to organisation and location to location; this is no different for our case study facilities; each has their own mechanism for operationalising provision and capitalising on opportunities. The key to long-term prosperity, however, relates to strategic planning, something Hall et al. (2003) refer to as 'Planning and Development Capacity'. The ability for an organisation to not rely on reactive management, and to be able to strategically plan for a sustainable future, is seen as being vital to long-term viability. For an organisation such as Zest, with a management team one step removed from day-to-day operational activities, there is the capacity in terms of *time* to be able to strategically plan and facilitate growth.

Zest sees itself as a niche organisation that understands the requirements and barriers facing the local community; this means it is able to enhance the opportunity for members of their community to access sporting facilities. The ladies-only gym and accessibility for disabled people, as well as hosting the citywide weight management programme, help to introduce traditional non-users to the organisation. They see the health agenda as an ongoing opportunity and an area they have a background and extensive experience in, which as envisaged will help ensure a viable future in this area.

The health agenda is also seen as a positive opportunity for U-Mix and Stocksbridge Community Leisure Centre, with U-MIX having identified possible avenues for funding streams and links to a local GP practice to help provide project funding for future activities. Stocksbridge see an opportunity to link to 'Healthy Living' funding to fund a Healthy Living Centre as well as expanding their offering further to possibly include outside facilities in the form of a 3G pitch if funding and access negotiations can be agreed. However, this sort of development relies on the previously mentioned 'Planning and Development Capacity' being available to the management of the community sport facility; for Stocksbridge Community Leisure Centre and Zest, in particular, this is available due to the skills, experience and time afforded to the management, due partly to the structure of the organisation, but also to the motivation and drive they have to see their organisations succeed and improve the lives people living in their local communities.

Essentially, the opportunities for community sport facilities lie in the ability to be able to identify and react to local customer needs and requirements because they are essentially *part* of the local community. Stocksbridge Community Leisure Centre exemplifies how a facility's operating budget requirements can be cut in half by simply *thinking differently*, being business minded and having the ability to not be constrained by a large council's way of managing a facility. The layers of management are significantly reduced, costs are controlled by utilising new and progressive forms of energy and a significant community commitment has been harnessed by a passionate group of local people with a wide range of skills and interests to ensure a community facility remains accessible to members of the local community.

GOOD PRACTICE

In terms of identifying good practice and areas for development from the case study facilities, it is clear that many of the key competencies held by the organisations are derived from the individuals who run the facility, usually those with a remit for planning and the strategic direction of the organisation. Operationally, a facility can continue to function on a day-to-day basis, opening the doors and running sessions, without too much trouble. However, long-term sustainability relies on the management of a facility engaging with strategic planning and ensuring there is sound financial underpinning for all decisions.

For example, at Stocksbridge Community Leisure Centre, the dry-side facilities (bowls hall, sports hall and gym) were opened first, giving access back to the community to part of 'their facility', however, the main focus for many local residents was the swimming pools (10 metre-learner pool and 25 metre-main pool). To them, the facility would not be considered fully open until they got access to swimming again; this brought with it major issues in terms of the costs associated with running a pool, potentially jeopardising the longer-term viability of the facility. The only way in which that could be considered was if the operational costs were brought down considerably; this meant two of the original campaign groups – now members of staff (General Manager and Buildings and Plant Manager) – considering an extensive range of alternative options for generating the energy needed to heat the pools. After in-depth research into a range of sustainable energy sources, Biomass Boilers and 300 solar panels were installed, with the Biomass Boilers heating the pools and solar panels providing 40 per cent of the electricity required by the facility as a whole. This progressive way of thinking, and a willingness to 'think outside the box', meant that the pools could be considered for reopening on a sound financial footing.

Staffing is another area with the potential for exhibiting areas of good practice. From the use of volunteers, which helps keep staffing budgets under control at Stocksbridge Community Leisure Centre, to the fact that Zest identifies one of its key competences to be its staff. The recruitment, training and retention of the 'right people', whether paid or voluntary, is crucial to any community sport facility. Given the challenges that some community facilities face in terms of competing with newer, purpose-built facilities having staff who understand the ethos of the organisation, the underpinning principles and philosophies that a facility such as U-Mix has and the need to welcome everyone into a 'community' facility is vital and something that is integral to and displayed at all three case study facilities.

Keeping a focus on the organisation's initial remit, objectives and core competencies is another element of good practice that can be derived from the case study facilities. At U-Mix, although the 'jigsaw puzzle' of funding is seen as a challenge, there is also the clear focus by the management of the facility on ensuring that 'Mission Drift' is avoided, which could be considered good practice but does not negate the challenges to sustainability this can provide.

Partnership work, utilising community support groups and projects such as Sheffield Cubed (a third-sector membership organisation who works to help their members win contracts for providing local services such as health and well-being activities, training and education) can bring significant benefits to organisations and facilities, where knowledge, expertise, resources and guidance can be shared. One of the benefits of being a member of an organisation such as Sheffield Cubed is that they are able to take a collaborative approach to securing larger contracts that would arguably be outside the capacity of individual member organisations – so helping to expand the opportunities for members. The more general ability to network and share knowledge can help community sport facilities navigate the challenging external environment.

Finally, the financial planning in terms of generating 'Core Funding', which could be seen as a challenge to find given dwindling financial support from the local authority for a number of community facilities being created by Zest by adding a 'management fee' to contracts and funding bids, is seen as an element of good practice, where it is practical and possible to do so (although it is acknowledged that with many funding sources, this may not be a possibility).

FUTURE VIABILITY FOR COMMUNITY SPORT FACILITIES

In terms of future viability for community sport facilities, the currently uncertain financial climate for organisations in many sectors – due in part to continued government spending cut backs as well as ongoing uncertainty with regard to wider economic climates (affected by more global issues such as Brexit) – means there is a clear need for community sport facilities (as for *all* organisations) and to ensure they operate in a commercial and 'business-like' way. In times of change, such as austerity and Brexit, it is perhaps understandable that organisations might not be keen to take risks or expose themselves to what could be considered 'precarious' ventures, however, there is a clear need for them to be brave and make decisions with a view to consolidating their financial position as well as their ability to continue to provide services for their communities.

There is no getting away from uncertainty being a problem for businesses; whenever there is a doubt over fundamental aspects of a business such as funding, it creates nervousness and concern over future viability. The summer of 2016 saw FURD negotiate their first lease for U-Mix; although there was the option to consider a longer length lease, after careful consideration, three years was identified as enough time to establish whether U-Mix is viable in the longer term, meaning that in the short-to-medium term, U-Mix will have a future, with the longer term to be decided based on the coming years. This clearly demonstrates a concern over the long-term viability of the facility due to the uncertain external environment, with financial viability being one of the key fundamental components.

A further challenge to future viability in relation to community sport facilities, which operate from what are often ex-local authority buildings, is the ageing nature of the buildings; for Stocksbridge Community Leisure Centre and Zest, this is a considerable and ongoing challenge. Should the fabric of the building (including the roof) or plant machinery (fundamental to the running of a swimming pool) suffer a malfunction or fail, then the ability of the facility to operate is immediately compromised. The cost of replacing roofs and plant equipment is considerable (£170,000–£180,000 estimated to replace Zest's roof and a swimming pool filter costing in the region of £20,000), which makes securing this sort of expenditure a major undertaking, and not something that can be overlooked if an issue arises. More generally, the condition of an ageing building can affect the daily operations of the facility as well as the customer experience. As previously identified, customers have a larger choice than ever when it comes to where to exercise, particularly in relation to dry-side gyms where budget operators provide new, purpose-built, 24-hour facilities at competitive prices; for community sport facilities in older buildings, where the changing rooms may be in need of refurbishment or the general décor would benefit from updating, there is a clear need for them to offer something different to the customer. Often, that comes in the form of understanding and 'caring' about the needs of the local community, identifying barriers and providing solutions to them as well as excellent customer service, which replicates the 'community' that these facilities are based in and exist to serve. Examples of this are the women-only gym at Zest and local volunteer staffing Stocksbridge Community Leisure Centre. As the Stocksbridge Community Leisure Centre manager identified, their front-of-house staff and volunteers know the majority of users by name (and at times, by member number), meaning customers are greeted by a friendly smile, a quick chat and a warm welcome rather than a swipe card or pin code entry door.

Managing costs are also key to the long-term viability of community sport facilities; sustainable energy methods have assisted in controlling costs, specifically in the case of swimming pools where heating is a major cost. As well as finding innovative ways of controlling staffing costs, the benefit for a facility such as Stocksbridge Community Leisure Centre being outside the control of a local authority means that there are fewer constraints on the use of volunteers, which is obviously a cost saved on paid staff. However, there is really only the ideal opportunity to develop a substantial volunteer base at certain times and in certain situations; such as in the case of Stocksbridge Community Leisure Centre when the threat of closure caused a wave of community support for the facility. The conversion of community action group members (interested in saving the facility from closure) into volunteers used to help operate the facility was a natural development. It would be much harder to develop such a volunteer workforce retrospectively; to ask individuals to undertake unpaid roles where they had previously been fulfilled by paid staff would be challenging and potentially seen as unethical. However, it has been shown with the recent conversion of several previously Council-run libraries to volunteer-led enterprises (again due to budget cuts in local authorities) that alternative methods of delivery have to be considered if community facilities are going to remain viable in future years.

An issue of sustainability arises from the ability to make long-term plans and to ensure future viability of community sport facilities. Managing a facility operationally is a full-time role, so the capacity for individuals to be involved in the longer-term planning is crucial, again, requiring time and skills best provided by those with experience in strategic management or commercial management.

In order for community sport facilities to remain viable in an external environment of uncertainty, a clear focussed strategic direction addressing the needs of the community that the facility serves must remain a priority. A control of costs and a focus on generating 'Core Funding' and income streams will ensure community sport facilities provide services for their local communities into the future. The competitive environment that exists in providing sport, physical activity and health improvement for local communities will remain. The position of these facilities within the community and the 'community feel' of facilities operated by the community for the community present a 'Unique Selling Point' that brings users into the facility rather than to commercial competitors.

CONCLUSION

To conclude this chapter, let's have a look at some of the key learning points from the areas we've covered. First, it's important to have an awareness of the historical background behind the development of a sector; an appreciation of what has happened in the past can give you a clearer understanding of what otherwise could seem confusing or unnecessary developments. So, the advent of CCT, meaning that organisations other than local authorities started to run sport facilities, was essentially the emergence of what today is a range of third-sector, non-profit organisations operating community sport facilities.

Second, in today's environment, there is a constant pressure on managers of community sport organisations to ensure that funding and income streams are maintained, that there is sound financial underpinning for all decisions and that there is a focus on 'Core Funding' wherever possible. Considering innovative ways of staffing and controlling staff expenditure is vital, as is trying to ensure there is the capacity and capability to strategically plan for the future.

Finally, it's important to understand that community sport facilities can often 'do things better' than they have been done in the past, but it is also important to remember that having independence, and not having to conform to the controls exerted by local authorities, means that legally, community sport facilities can operate in a different, more cost-effective way. That can bring with it the benefit of cost effectiveness, but also potentially not as attractive employment packages for individuals as might have been available in the past.

REVIEW QUESTIONS

1. What were the key historical developments in facility management?
2. Can you list the benefits and drawbacks of CCT and Best Value?
3. What are the opportunities for the new government's structure for sporting activity?
4. What are the key funding challenges for community sport facilities?

REFERENCES

Hall, M. H., Barr, C. W., Easwaramoorthy, M., Wojciech Sokolowski, S., & Salamon, L. (2003). *The Canadian Nonprofit and Voluntary Sector in Comparative Perspective*. Toronto, ON: Imagine Canada.

Haywood, L., Kew, F., Bramham, P., Spink, J., Capenerhurst, J., & Henry, I. (1995). *Understanding Leisure* (2nd ed.). Cheltenham: Stanley Thornes.

Henry, I. (1993). *The Politics of Leisure Policy*. London: CABI.

Houlihan, B., & Lindsey, I. (2012). *Sport Policy in Britain*. Oxon: Routledge.

Mintel. (2016). *UK Charitable Giving Market Report*. http://store.mintel.com/uk-charitable-giving-market-report.

Robinson, L. (2004). *Managing Public Sport and Leisure Services*. London: Routledge.

Schwarz, E., Hall, S., & Shibli, S. (2015). *Sport Facility Operations Management* (2nd ed.). Oxon: Routledge.

Sheffield City Council. (2017). *Council Faces Seventh Year of Budget Cuts*. Retrieved from www.sheffield-newsroom.co.uk/budget-cuts-1718/.

Simmons, R. (2003). *New Leisure Trusts*. Reading, PA: Institute of Leisure and Amenity Management.

Taylor, P. (Ed.) (2011). *Torkildsen's Sport and Leisure Management* (6th ed.). Oxon: Routledge.

Wilson, R., & Piekarz, M. (2016). *Sport Management the Basics*. Oxon: Routledge.

Wise, M. (1969). The Future of Local Government in England: The 'Redcliffe-Maud Report': Review. *The Geographical Journal, 135*(4), 583–587.

Zest Community. (2017). *About Us*. Retrieved from www.zestcommunity.co.uk.

CHAPTER 11

Finance and budgeting for community sport and physical activity

Rob Wilson and Daniel Plumley

SUMMARY

This chapter demonstrates the importance of financial management within a community sport management context. Provision is made to equip you, as managers, with the necessary skills to communicate, in basic terms, the financial sustainability at a place of work. The cyclical process of planning, decision-making and control, coupled with the analytical techniques that can be applied to management accounting information, enhances the tool-box of skills that any community manager possesses. The importance of this process should not be underestimated in both profit and not-for-profit organisations, regardless of size or stature. The main objective of all community organisations should be to operate within their own resources so that they can be sustainable and so that people can appreciate their value. The tools identified in this chapter, including budgeting, should help this process.

AIMS

By engaging with this chapter, you will be able to

- Appreciate why financial skills are an important part of a community manager's portfolio of skills,
- Articulate key financial terminology that is often applied to community sport,
- Understand the meaning of budgeting in operational, tactical and strategic community sport management contexts and
- Analyse budgeted against actual performance using recognised evaluation techniques.

INTRODUCTION

This chapter takes a look at the importance of managing finance in community sport settings. For all community sport projects, it is essential that the overall governance be underpinned by sound financial management so that everything runs successfully. Without needing to be a fully qualified accountant or having specific training in finance, all community sport managers should be able to answer two fundamental questions: First, is the selling price higher than the cost? In other words, will the project or initiative bring in more money than it pays out? Or, is the project or initiative operating within the resources allocated to it? If the answer is no to this question, then your projects and ideas could prove to be unsustainable.

The second question all managers must answer is: Can this project continue? In financial terms, this question relates to the organisation's ability to pay its creditors (people that it owes money to for goods and services). Many community projects will never take place due to an inability to meet these obligations because they have not considered cash flow and run out of money to pay its creditors before any revenue can be generated. Being unable to meet these obligations is not uncommon and is the reason why you see businesses, organisations and community projects going bankrupt or ceasing to run. Community sport managers must ensure that they can pay their bills as they fall due and understand how to negotiate payment dates that fit in with income streams. Moreover, the sustainability of community sport is an increasingly important component of a project plan or funding application, and you will need to demonstrate how you can generate the income to meet your expenses.

It is important, however, before we start, that we establish some ground rules; put simply, finance, and by definition, the purpose of this chapter, is not simply about numbers, and you won't need to be a skilled mathematician to understand finance or manage money. Instead, you need to understand the guiding rules and principles that help compile and structure a set of financial documents. As students, or managers who work within the community sport industry, it is important that you appreciate the importance of financial management and responsibility and that you can communicate key financial information to both the internal and external stakeholders.

A successful project cannot happen without sufficient financial support and, by definition, financial management. The most significant, and perhaps most routine error, in committing to undertake a new project or try to deliver a new community initiative is to do so without securing the necessary funding at an early stage. Financial viability should be the key issue of any event-planning process, and if the expenses far outweigh the income streams, then managers should not be afraid to cancel their project. In not doing so, they compromise the future of similar community projects, acquire a poor image for their organisations and reduce the ability for bidding groups to launch other projects and initiatives in the future.

Unfortunately, the sport industry has lagged behind other business sectors from a financial management point of view. For the most part, event marketing, planning and strategy have dominated sport management education and led to a growing maturity in such areas. Financial management has often been overlooked, anecdotally because individuals claim to have some sort of fear with numbers. There are still many managers and graduates with sport management or development degrees who struggle to even understand the basics of a budget or cash flow statement, let alone have the confidence to make informed judgements on the financial health of their event. Every organisation ranging from multimillion-pound operations through to small, local, voluntary/community organisations need to manage money and make routine financial decisions. Therefore, if organisations have to do it, the chances are that, should managers wish to be successful in employment, managers will have to understand, communicate and use financial information too.

FINANCIAL TERMINOLOGY

Understanding the nature and application of finance is usually a question of understanding the terminology that financial experts use. Demystifying this terminology is the first step in managing finance effectively, as it will help you to understand what things mean and why they are important. Understand this, and I'm sure you will be able to apply it later on in the chapter.

Let's start at the beginning. Essentially, there are two types of accounts: financial and management. From the section before, you should have noticed that financial information can look two ways. When looking backwards, i.e., into the past, it is normal to examine financial accounts, as they are prepared for external use and are based on historical information; they are also required by law. A set of financial accounts will, for example, illustrate the past financial position and financial performance of an organisation.

However, should a manager wish to be more proactive and examine future trends and issues, they will need to examine more forward-looking (future) accounting information. Such information will not be found in financial accounts, hence, there are management accounts, i.e., accounts that look forward and are based on providing information for managers to help with the planning, decision-making and control of organisations. Unlike financial accounts, management accounts are not a statutory requirement. It is important that managers understand the distinction between the two types of accounts, as they dictate where they should look for information. Financial accounting and reporting is beyond the scope of this chapter, as we are examining the tools that you can use to *manage* finance. Consequently, we will focus on management accounting and how to plan, make decisions and control finance.

In reality, managers should appreciate that they will plan their operations, consider the implications of their decisions and control their organisation in such a way that they reach (in most cases) their organisation's objectives. In order to plan and make effective decisions, a manager will have to adopt the principles of good management accounting and, in particular, budgeting.

FINANCIAL PLANNING AND CONTROL

The concept behind financial management is not the simplistic idea that you need to manage profit but, more importantly, how to monitor, evaluate and control the income and expenditure. It is vital for managers to understand the changing values of the community sport industry and recognise that a large number of projects are provided to achieve social objectives, which operate at a loss, and which will normally require a government/local authority subsidy to operate. This does not mean, however, that proper financial planning and controls are not important. It is vital that managers have an understanding of the costs of the products and services that they offer in order to operate as effective business entities to generate profits, or to ensure that tax payers' money is not being wasted on frivolous plans or ideas that have no plan to become sustainable.

Many community projects will rely on funding from national, regional or local government; funding from quangos such as Sport England or the Arts Council; sponsorship;

or flexible credit terms from suppliers. However, using money from a third party is normally based on the simple assumption that the organisation's future returns will be sufficient to cover the borrowing or meet other objectives. Problems often occur when organisations fail to meet their financial obligations. Consequently, as you read in the introduction, an organisation's ability to pay its debts as they fall due is usually the difference between financial success and financial failure. If managers are to make effective plans and decisions, they need to control their organisation's finances.

Before a project progresses too far into the planning process, it is essential to assess its financial viability. This will mean setting out a financial plan to balance the cost of running the project against any existing funds and prospective income. Several draft budgets may need to be compiled before producing the final version. Initially, the budget will be based on estimates, but it is important to confirm actual figures as soon as possible to keep the budget on track and to exercise something resembling financial responsibility.

Any decision that is made to go ahead with an event will be a managerial one and, therefore, rather subjective. These decisions, however, can be made more reliable with a thorough understanding of the finances involved and the ability of the project to meet its financial obligations. What is more, the decision that determines whether a project is financially viable will ensure that effort (and money) is not wasted. Already in this book, you will have read about the importance of facility, event and project management and event design and production; these stages are vital for the operational success of a project or the provision of a service but will only yield success if they have sufficient financial resource to be implemented.

USERS OF FINANCIAL INFORMATION

Financial information will be useful to a wide variety of stakeholders. These will often span several sectors, and each will have slightly different needs for the information. For example, the Board of Directors of Intercontinental Hotels Group PLC will want to see how much profit they have made from trading activities and see how each arm of the business is performing so that they can make future investment decisions and consider returns to shareholders. York City Council will want to know how much subsidy they have to provide in order to keep all of their leisure services running across the city so that their council taxpayers get value for money. The Chairperson of the Cheltenham Swimming and Water Polo Club will want to ensure that enough money is being received through subscriptions and funding to cover their running costs.

Generally, information relating to the finance of an organisation is of interest to its owners, managers, trade contacts (for example, suppliers), providers of finance (for example, banks and funding bodies), employees and customers. All of these groups of people need to be sure that the organisation is strong, can pay its bills, make a profit (if it is commercial) and remain in business.

BUDGETING AND COMMUNITY SPORT

Budgeting is a subject area that takes its roots from the fields of management accounting, as it helps manage plans, make decisions and exercise control. Budgeting can be shown to be part of the overall planning process for an organisation by defining it as 'the overall plan of an organisation expressed in financial terms'. These plans might involve trying to achieve a predetermined level of financial performance such as a surplus of £x over the year or having sufficient cash resources to be able to replace the equipment in a gym. Organisational business planning can be summarised as an analysis of four key questions:

1. Where are we now?
2. How did we get here?
3. Where are we going? and
4. How are we going to get there?

To illustrate the link between general organisational planning and budgeting, the question 'where are we now?' can be modified to 'where are we now in financial terms?' Similarly, the question 'where are we going' can be modified to 'where are we going in financial terms?' To diagnose where a business *is* in financial terms requires the ability to be able to 'read' an income statement, a balance sheet and a cash flow statement. To predict where a business is going is difficult (as is any attempt to predict the future), but techniques such as compiling an expected income statement, balance sheet and cash flow statement can help to focus attention on the business essentials.

BUDGETING AS A LOGICALLY SEQUENCED PLANNING PROCESS

A key point about budgeting is that it is an ongoing process rather than a time-limited, one-off event. The actual mechanics of drawing up the numbers involved in a budget are but a small part of the overall budgeting process. By bearing in mind that budgeting is designed to help an organisation with planning, decision-making and control, it is possible to appreciate that budgeting is a continuous part of life. This point can be reinforced by viewing budgeting as steps in a logically sequenced planning process, as shown in Figure 11.1.

Figure 11.1 can be reinforced by a commentary on each of the nine stages of budgeting:

1. Define your organisational objectives
    The first question to ask when involved with any financial planning is 'in monetary terms, what are we trying to achieve?' Organisational objectives will vary according to the nature of the entity. A community sport club that exists for the benefit of the members may desire nothing more than to break even or to make a small surplus to maintain its existing facilities. Whatever the objectives of an organisation, they need to have certain qualities that enable them to be measured. These qualities are contained within the 'MASTER' mnemonic:

    Measurable   e.g., a surplus of £3 million in the financial year, or simply to break even;
    Achievable   the organisation must have the capability to attain its objectives: capability means staff, other resources and a competitive advantage;
    Specific   objectives must be specific, e.g., £3 million profit, not 'to do well this year';

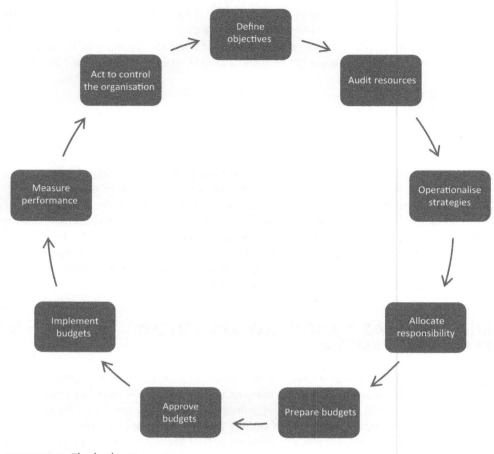

FIGURE 11.1 The budgeting process

Time-Limited	objectives must have a stated date for being achieved;
Ends-Related	objectives must relate to achieving outputs (ends) rather than describing means (how);
Ranked	ideally, objectives should be ranked in priority order.

2. Audit resources

    The audit of resources is a 'reality check' on the objectives. Its purpose is to ensure that the objectives and the resources required to achieve them are internally consistent. Where there is a discrepancy between the objectives and the resources available to achieve them, two courses of action are possible. First, the objectives can be changed so that they are compatible with the resources. Second, the gap between the resources available and the resources required can form the basis for prioritising capital investment such as increasing the capacity of a stadium or identifying training and development needs to ensure that your staff have the skills to deliver what is required of them.

3. Operationalise strategies

    Having defined what you want to achieve and having confirmed that you have the resources to deliver the objectives, the budgeting process evolves to consider the day-to-day tactics to be used to meet the objectives. In small community organisations, these might include the marketing plans, funding requirements, customer care protocols and opening hours. If organisational objectives can be regarded as 'what' we wish to achieve, then operational strategies can be regarded as 'how' we plan to achieve the objectives.

4. Allocate responsibility

    Successful achievement of objectives does not happen by chance, nor does it happen as a result of a mechanical exercise. Community sport is primarily a service industry, and the most important people in determining the extent to which objectives are met are an organisation's staff. In order for people to see where their contributions fit into an organisation's overall plan, they need to have agreed responsibility for particular areas of work. Agreed responsibility is particularly important in situations where staff can be rewarded, or indeed punished, on the basis of their performance – remember that this could be particularly difficult when managing volunteers. If it is known and clearly stated 'who is going to do what and by when', then there is the basis for a meaningful comparison of actual performance compared with planned or expected performance.

5. Preparation of budgets

    It is worth noting that the actual preparation of budgets does not occur until the midpoint of the budgeting process. This is important because it makes the point that budgeting is not an isolated process and is integral to overall business planning. When preparing a budget, there are two important considerations, namely 'how much' income or expenditure, and 'when' the income or expenditure will occur. To illustrate the point, consider a four-day event running from Thursday to Sunday. There will be peak times such as during weekend and off-peak times such on a Thursday when people are at work. Thus, in order to make sure that the appropriate level of resource (for example, staff) is in the right place and at the right time, it will be necessary to plan the predicted level of activity on a day-to-day basis. Doing such an exercise will enable managers to plan ahead for situations where expenditure is greater than income, and there is insufficient cash to meet the shortfall. Having identified situations requiring management attention, strategies can be put into place to deal with them such as negotiating an overdraft facility at the bank, rescheduling expenditure on capital items or simply not paying creditors on time. The important point of note is that the process of budgeting identifies potential problems in advance of them happening so that pre-emptive action can be taken.

    It is unlikely that at the first time of asking, the figures produced in the preparation of budgets will deliver the outcomes required. Therefore, managers may be asked to revise their budgets in such a way that the desired outcome is achieved. In practice, there are five ways in which a budget can be revised:

    *   **Increase revenue and keep costs constant**. This could be achieved by increasing prices, increasing throughput or a combination of the two methods. The key

assumption here is that any increase in price will not be offset by a reduction in demand.

- **Decrease expenditure, and keep income constant**. This could be achieved by making savings on non-essential expenditure or reducing the quality of the service on offer (for example, fewer staff on duty).
- **Increase income *and* decrease costs**, as the first two bullet points are not necessarily mutually exclusive.
- **Alter the financial outcome required**. It may be the case that it is not possible to bring the required outcomes and the budget into line by using the first three bullet points. Therefore, rather than alter income and expenditure, management may decide to alter the financial outcome required. This approach can work both positively and negatively. If staff provide managers with a budget that exceeds the required bottom line and the assumptions underpinning the budget are correct, then it would make sense to increase the overall budget target accordingly. A much more likely scenario is that the targeted outcome cannot be met by revisions to income and expenditure, and management agrees to settle for a reduced financial outcome.
- **Change the overall business objectives**. It may well be the case that it is impossible to arrive at an acceptable solution to a budget using the first four steps. Under these conditions, it may be that the required outcomes and the organisation's capabilities are not compatible. The only remaining alternative is to change the organisation's objectives.

The significance of preparing a budget, comparing it to business objectives and taking corrective action where appropriate indicates the importance of achieving internal consistency. Using the budgeting model described thus far ensures that what an organisation wishes to achieve in overall terms and the financial consequences of doing so are consistent. If potential problems can be identified at the planning (input) stage, pre-emptive action can be taken by drawing up plans to deal with adverse circumstances. Clearly, this approach has a greater chance of success and is more desirable than trying to deal with situations reactively, as they materialise without prior warning. The process of modelling the financial consequences of various scenarios until an acceptable outcome is achieved is known as an 'iterative' approach, or, in less scientific terms, 'trial and error'.

6.   Approval of budgets

Once an acceptable match has been achieved between an organisation's business objectives and the financial consequences of those objectives, a line needs to be drawn under the preparation of budgets stage. The point at which this line is drawn is at the approval of budgets stage, which effectively puts an end to the various iterations of the budget and leads to the formal adoption of the budget the organisation wishes to pursue. It is recognised good practice for the approval of a budget to be formalised in the minutes of a board or committee meeting. Furthermore, budgets should be approved in advance of the financial period to which they relate. The wider significance of a budget being approved formally is that those who have compiled it and those whose performance will in part be judged by it know exactly what their responsibilities are. This, in turn, has two benefits. First, if you know what is expected of you, then evaluation of performance can be objective rather than subjective. Second, expectation generates accountability, which, in turn, gives managers the focus to concentrate on those things that are important in terms of meeting the organisation's objectives.

7. Implementation of budgets

As a logical consequence of a budget being approved, it can be implemented with effect from the date to which it applies. For example, if an organisation's financial year operates from 1st April to 31st March, then it would be a reasonable expectation for the budget to be approved by the committee or board at least a month before the new financial year started. A less-than-ideal situation would be an organisation entering a financial period without an approved budget, which would be the managerial equivalent of a boat trying to operate without a rudder.

8. Measurement of performance

To reinforce the notion of budgeting being integral to overall business planning, it is vital to realise that the budgeting process does not end once the preparation and implementation phases are over. Once the budget is operational, it is essential that periodically (say, at least monthly, or weekly in some cases), a check be made between how the organisation is actually performing compared with how it is planned to perform. One of the greatest motivators in life is feedback, and the same is true in budgeting. Management accountants use the mnemonic CARROT as a way of categorising the features of good-quality information for feedback purposes. Each component of CARROT is explained below:

Concise	Information fed back to managers needs to be to the point;
Accurate	Feedback is used for planning, decision-making and control purposes, therefore, it follows that feedback should be error free;
Reliable	Similar to 'accurate', the same results of an actual versus budget comparison should be obtained if different people carried out the analysis, i.e., the source information is robust;
Relevant	Different levels of management require different levels of information, therefore, feedback should be presented in terms that are relevant to the intended recipient;
Objective	Feedback should be concerned with verifiable factual evidence and not with individual interpretation of findings;
Timely	There is a trade-off between timeliness and accuracy; nonetheless, feedback should be received in sufficient time for it to be of value in terms of planning, decision-making and control purposes.

9. Taking action to control the organisation

If we accept that rational decisions require information that meets the requirements of the CARROT mnemonic, the final stage of the budgeting process is to use the information to inform the direction of the organisation and control the event. It is highly unlikely that there will be a perfect match between budget and actual comparisons, so the first decision to make is whether overall variance is within a tolerable range. If variances are tolerable, then significant changes in policy will be unlikely. By contrast, if variances are considered to be so significant that the organisation is 'out of control' (in financial terms), then proactive management action may be needed. On a positive note, if performance is considerably ahead of target, it may be prudent to revise targets upwards. If, however, actual versus budget comparisons reveal a significant shortfall in performance, corrective action may be needed.

Budgeting is a process designed to help managers make sensible decisions about running their organisations and is particularly important when organisations have limited financial resources, as is usually the case in community sport. It helps to inform decisions, but clearly budgeting is not in itself a decision-making process. Compiling a budget is an iterative process. It is unlikely that the first draft of a budget will produce an acceptable result. Various scenarios will be modelled, and differing assumptions will be tested until an acceptable solution is found. Figure 11.1 is a simple model of an ideal process; in practice, the numerous iterations will result in a more complicated picture. However, the basic point is that each step of the model is a reality check on the previous step, which is designed to ensure that an organisation's overall plans and the financial consequences of those plans are internally consistent.

Although Figure 11.1 implies a step-by-step approach to compiling a budget, in reality, some steps are seamless. For example, defining your objectives (Step 1), conducting an audit of resources (Step 2) and devising operational strategies (Step 3) are likely to be interrelated and to occur simultaneously.

COMMON METHODS OF BUDGETING

In this section, 'methods of budgeting' refers to types of budgeting processes and behavioural aspects of budgeting. In terms of budgeting processes, there are two common ways in which budgets tend to be compiled. The most frequently used budgeting process is 'continuation' budgeting (or business as usual), and the other, somewhat more rare, process is 'zero-based budgeting' (ZBB). Continuation budgeting refers to situations whereby the business objectives of an organisation do not change significantly from one financial period to the next. An example of a continuation budget might be a voluntary club openswim meet whose main aim is to break even and to provide a service to the membership – you should note here that these types of budgets will be rarely used for one-off events but may be considered for events that occur as part of an annual calendar of activity.

If the club's basic operations lead to a situation whereby the selling price is higher than the cost, then apart from increasing spectator tickets and secondary spending prices to keep up with inflation, there is no point wasting time and resources on a more complicated approach to the organisation's finances. Continuation budgeting is also referred to as 'incremental' or 'decremental' budgeting. Incremental budgeting refers to a situation whereby an organisation increases its income and expenditure, usually by the rate of inflation, in order to pursue its existing policies. Decremental budgeting refers to a situation whereby an organisation agrees either to a standstill level of funding (a cut, in real terms) or an absolute decrease in funding. An example of a simple continuation budget for a swimming club's open meet is shown in Figure 11.2.

The basic assumptions in Figure 11.2 are that the club will pursue the same policies from one year to the next and will increase income and expenditure by the rate of inflation (in this case, 3 per cent). Thus, all that has happened to the numbers in the budget

INCOME	This Year	Inflation	Next Year
Spectator Tickets	1,450	3%	1,494
Other Ticket Sales	250	3%	258
Sponsorship	1,700	3%	1,751
Catering	220	3%	227
Merchandising	130	3%	134
Total Income	3,750	3%	3,863
EXPENDITURE			
Voulunteer Kit	700	3%	721
Pool Hire	2,500	3%	2,575
Marketing Activities	136	3%	140
Administration	342	3%	352
Total Expenditure	3,678	3%	3,788
SURPLUS / (DEFICIT)	72	3%	74

FIGURE 11.2 Open-swim meet continuation budget

is that they have increased by 3 per cent. There are some advantages and disadvantages of using continuation budgeting, and these are highlighted below.

Advantages of continuation budgeting:

- Continuation budgeting is intuitively simple and easy to understand.
- It is an effective use of resources if business objectives, infrastructure and strategies have remained unchanged.
- It is quick and easy to update figures and budget templates that are readily on hand.
- It requires less staff resources and, therefore, costs less than ZBB.

Disadvantages of continuation budgeting:

- The overall rate of inflation within a country does not necessarily equal the rate of inflation within a particular industry, and, therefore, the use of the headline inflation figure to increase budgets is somewhat crude.
- Continuation budgeting does not encourage growth in real terms; in Figure 11.2, the net position is that the business stands still. Businesses need to grow in real terms to remain competitive and to have the resources to maintain their operating infrastructure.
- Changes may be occurring within the marketplace, which requires change such as the application of Internet technology and e-marketing. By not taking advantage of business opportunities as they present themselves, standing still may actually be going backwards relative to your competitors.
- There is the danger that if income and expenditure budgets are not challenged occasionally, then targets are 'soft' rather than a fair test of an organisation's capabilities. Managers can build 'slack' (unnecessary expenditure) into budgets, which can be 'rewarded' when budgets for the next year are confirmed without detailed scrutiny.

Despite the fact that continuation budgeting is by far the most commonly used budgeting technique in all industries, if an organisation is facing a fundamental change to its operating circumstances, a more analytical approach may be needed. Rather than starting with last year's budget (or one that you have found elsewhere) and updating it, the ZBB starts with a blank sheet of paper and challenges every item of income and expenditure. An example of ZBB questions might be

1. What is the purpose of this expenditure?
2. On what exactly will this expenditure be made?
3. What are the quantifiable benefits of this expenditure?
4. What are the alternatives to this proposed expenditure?
5. What would be the outcome of cutting this expenditure completely?

In order for funds to be allocated to a given item of expenditure, a robust defence would have to be made for the expenditure through the five questions listed above. If some expenditure was not defendable, then it might be cut and be reallocated to more deserving areas of an organisation's activities. As an example, consider the case of the community sport event we considered earlier. As part of its agreement with volunteers, it runs its own laundry to wash and iron volunteers' kits. The laundry will make use of staff, space, equipment, energy and consumables – all of which cost money. Furthermore, in the long run, equipment will need to be replaced, and service contracts will have to be in place in case machinery breaks down. If commercial laundry facilities were available locally, which could match the quality of service provided in-house at a cheaper price, then not only would the club save money, it could also use the staff, space and other resources released on more important business objectives. Alternatively, it may be even more cost-effective to simply buy additional kits and benefit from discounted prices. Clearly, using the ZBB approach would be a more rigorous way of questioning existing business practices than simply accepting that the club has always provided an in-house laundry and will continue to do so.

The purpose of ZBB is the allocation of resources in a systematic manner that is consistent with an organisation's wider business objectives. It makes an implicit assumption that people within an organisation act rationally and prioritises business objectives rather than personal agendas – sometimes this can be a very ambitious assumption. Compared with continuation budgeting, ZBB is resource intensive and, therefore, can be wasteful if there has been no significant change in business objectives and operating procedures. It is, therefore, unsafe to make sweeping generalisations about one budgeting process being better than another. As in many instances of using applied management techniques, the best methods to use are the ones most appropriate to the circumstances faced by an organisation. Therefore, if a business is stable with no major changes on the horizon, continuation budgeting might be the best method to use. By contrast, if a business requires a major strategic overhaul or if you are planning a new or larger event, then ZBB approach might be the best method to use. Like many things in life, compromise can help to keep most of the people happy for most of the time. So too, a business could use continuation budgeting most of the time, but once every three or five years, a ZBB approach could be used to challenge the status quo and reallocate resources to where they are most needed.

In addition to being familiar with methods of budgeting such as continuation or ZBB approaches, it is also important to realise the human dimension of budgeting. Sport and physical activity is a people business, and ultimately, the extent to which business objectives are realised depends on the extent of staff motivation towards meeting targets. One of the great demotivators in life is having targets imposed on you from above (top-down) without consultation. Equally, for management, there is nothing more depressing than letting staff set their own budgets and finding out that the so-called 'bottom-up' budgets do not deliver the organisation's overall business objectives. The compromise approach is for a participatory budgeting style whereby all staff whose performance will in part be judged by meeting the budget have some influence in the compilation of the figures by which they will be judged. There are no hard and fast rules about when to use 'top down', 'bottom up' or 'participatory' methods. Good managers need to have a broad range of skills and techniques. Furthermore, these skills and techniques should be used in a context-sensitive manner, contingent upon the particular circumstances of the business and its operating environment.

APPLYING BUDGETING TO WORKED EXAMPLES

Community sport operators should report a summary of their financial transactions in two, or sometimes three, standard formats:

- The income statement (or income and expenditure statement in the case of non-profit organisations),
- The balance sheet (if the event is running through an established company) and
- The cash flow statement.

The income statement is a measure of an organisation's financial performance, the balance sheet is a measure of financial position and the cash flow statement illustrates how the cash available to an organisation has changed over a given period of time. In financial terms, the answers to the questions 'where are we now?' and 'where are we going?' can be seen by constructing an income statement, balance sheet and cash flow statement to show the change between the starting point and the ending point. In this section, examples of both the income statement and cash flow statement are modelled, and issues relating to them are discussed (should you wish to read about the balance sheet, you should follow up with some of the additional activities at the end of this chapter).

1. The income statement
    Figure 11.3 is the first two columns from Figure 11.2 and shows how a swimming club might produce a summary of its income statement for its event. The key message emerging from Figure 11.3 is that the club is planning to make a surplus of £72 during the year.
    The problem with Figure 11.3 is that a year is a long time, and it is unlikely that income and expenditure will occur at the same rate throughout the year. Indeed, as this statement reflects the event, it is likely that it only reflects the final position, and the budget does not tell you when profits or losses will occur. Many events are

INCOME	This Year
Spectator Tickets	1,450
Other Ticket Sales	250
Sponsorship	1,700
Catering	220
Merchandising	130
Total Income	3,750
EXPENDITURE	
Voulunteer Kit	700
Pool Hire	2,500
Marketing Activities	136
Administration	342
Total Expenditure	3,678
SURPLUS / (DEFICIT)	72

FIGURE 11.3 An income statement

seasonal and will have peaks and troughs in terms of their level of activity. This, in turn, has implications for other areas of management such as staff scheduling and cash flow management. If the data in Figure 11.3 were to be allocated over 11 months on the basis of when such income and expenditure were predicted to occur, the monthly budget would appear like the example shown in Figure 11.4. Remember that this is a relatively small swimming event, and you may well have to include much more data – the principals are the same though!

Two important points emerge from Figure 11.4. First, simply by looking at the surplus or deficit per month, it is clear that the events' position in the calendar is a factor in the events' financial fortunes. Income is received from sponsors in February and again during the event in April in the form of spectator ticket sales and other ticket sales, while expenditure exceeds income in October, November and December and again in March and May – this negative cash position must be managed. Second, a simple table of figures is not particularly helpful to somebody reading the budget. It would be much more helpful if the numbers were explained by a series of notes such as the examples that follow.

Income

Spectator ticket sales will occur in April, and we expect 580 spectators to purchase tickets at an average price of £2.50 (£1,450). (Last year, 500 sales were @ £2.50 = £1,250).

	1	2	3	4	5	6	7	8	9	10	Total
Other Ticket Sales	0	0	0	0	0	0	0	250	0	0	250
Sponsorship	0	0	0	0	0	1700	0	0	0	0	1700
Catering	0	0	0	0	0	0	0	220	0	0	220
Merchandising	0	0	0	0	0	0	0	130	0	0	130
Total Income	0	0	0	0	0	1700	0	2050	0	0	3750
EXPENDITURE											
Volunteer Kit	0	0	0	0	0	0	700	0	0	0	700
Pool Hire	0	0	0	0	0	0	0	0	2500	0	2500
Marketing Activities	0	0	136	0	0	0	0	0	0	0	136
Administration	0	100	100	42	0	0	100	0	0	0	342
Total Expenditure	0	100	236	42	0	0	800	0	2500	0	3678
SURPLUS / (DEFICIT)	0	-100	-236	-42	0	1700	-800	2050	-2500	0	72
Cumulative	0	-100	-336	-378	-378	1322	522	2572	72	72	72

FIGURE 11.4 Swim meet budget sub-analysed by month

Expenditure

Pool-hire costs are based on a discounted rate and are paid in May, after the event has taken place. Costs are £2,500. (Last year, pool hire was £3,700).

In practice, it would be expected that all items of income and expenditure would be qualified by a written explanation. By providing a brief written commentary to the key figures and assumptions that underpin the budget, it is possible for those people who look at it to have a much clearer idea of the organisation's plans. If the club planned to make a profit of £72 (financial performance), then it follows that the club's overall financial position would increase by £72.

For most sport managers, budgeting tends to start and end with a budgeted income statement, sub-analysed on a monthly basis (Figure 11.4). This is a perfectly acceptable level of skill for most managers. However, for those with ambitions to have full responsibility for all aspects of an organisation's financial performance, skills are also needed to be able to produce and act upon budgeted income statements (balance sheets) and cash flow statements.

COMPARING ACTUAL AND BUDGETED PERFORMANCE

The ultimate purpose of budgeting is to assist managers in the planning, decision-making and control of a business. To achieve this aim, periodic comparison of actual performance compared with planned or budgeted performance is required. Figure 11.5 is an example of how such a comparison might be presented to the managers of an organisation.

The layout of Figure 11.5 has a deliberate structure to it, and each component is explained in turn below:

'Actual' income and expenditure refers to entries made to an organisation's accounting system, which are supportable by documentary evidence such as invoices, receipts, staff time sheets, etc. 'Actual' figures are drawn from the financial accounting systems and can be supported by an audit trail of evidence.

'Incurred' (or 'committed') expenditure refers to expenditure that relates to the financial period in question that we know has been made but, as yet, has not been billed for. This sort of data can be picked up from documentation such as purchase order forms. The 'Incurred' column tends to be used for expenditure only – it would be unusual to have incurred income.

The 'Total' column is simply the sum of the 'Actual' and the 'Incurred' columns.

'Budget' refers to the approved budget for a given financial period.

'Variance' is the difference between the 'Total' column and the 'Budget' column.

'Direction' is a reference to whether the variance on any given line of the budget is favourable (F) or unfavourable (U). One characteristic of good information is that it is relevant to the intended recipient. For non-finance specialists, spelling out whether a variance is F or U is a helpful aid to understanding the underlying meaning of the figures.

'Note' is a cross reference to a written qualitative explanation of a variance. Numbers in isolation do not explain a variance, and, therefore, it is sometimes useful for a written explanation to accompany some of the more significant variances.

INCOME	Actual	Incurred	Total	Budget	Variance	Direction	Note
Spectator Tickets	1,450		1,450	1,350	100	F	1
Other Ticket Sales	250		250	0	250	F	
Sponsorship	1,700		1,700	1,800	-100	U	2
Catering	220		220	200	20	F	
Merchandising	130		130	100	30	F	
Total Income	3,750	0	3,750	3,450	300	F	3
EXPENDITURE							
Voluunteer Kit	700		700	600	100	U	4
Pool Hire	2,500	0	2,500	3,000	-500	F	5
Marketing Activities	136		136	140	-4	F	
Administration	342	50	392	400	-8	F	
Total Expenditure	3,678	50	3,728	4,140	-412	F	
SURPLUS / (DEFICIT)	72	-50	22	-690	712	F	6

FIGURE 11.5 Actual versus budget comparison

Event Budget Report

To: Swimming Committee

From: Event Manager

Date: 10th September 20XY

Re: Actual v Budget Notes

Note 1: Spectator Ticket Sales

Spectator ticket sales (580 at £2.50) were 40 ahead of target (540 at £2.50). More spectator ticket sales have been achieved by encouraging people who attended the event in the past to return this year.

Note 2: Sponsorship

Following the renegotiation of last year's agreements with our clubs partners we were able to secure £1,700 in sponsorship (£100 below our target). This unfavourable result was due to one company having to reduce its involvement due to market pressures.

Signed

Event Manager

FIGURE 11.6 Budget report

To illustrate how qualitative explanations can help to explain the meaning of variances, presented above is an example of two of the notes that might have accompanied the actual versus budget comparison (Figure 11.6). Note how it is written in the form of a report and can easily be cross-referenced to Figure 11.5.

Any chairperson/director reading the above report would be able to grasp the basic point that the event performed ahead of budget and had secured future discounts for the benefit of the club. At this stage, the actual versus budget comparison would be noted, and no action would need to be taken, other than to congratulate and encourage those responsible for delivering the better-than-planned performance.

CONCLUSION

The purpose of this chapter was to demonstrate the importance of financial management within a community sport management context. While any detailed analysis was beyond the scope of the chapter, provision is made to equip managers with the necessary skills to communicate, in basic terms, the financial sustainability of an event. The cyclical process of planning, decision-making and control, coupled with the analytical techniques that can be applied to management accounting information, should enhance the toolbox of skills that any event manager possesses. The importance of this process should not be underestimated in both profit and not-for-profit organisations, regardless of size or stature. The main objective of all community organisations should be to operate within their own resources so that they can be sustainable and so that people can appreciate their value. The tools identified in this chapter, including budgeting, should help this process.

The income statement (balance sheet) and cash flow statement equip managers with information that can determine the financial performance and position of an organisation and demonstrate the difference between profit and the typically scarce resource of cash. In addition, it can be determined whether the event should be held and whether you or your competitors can pay their debts as they fall due.

It is not possible within one single chapter to cover all event finance information and budgetary techniques. However, you should have grasped the idea that financial management is important enough to be considered an integral part of any event. Other skills are required to come up with a marketing campaign or a training and development plan, but only those who understand finance can establish whether they are financially viable, worthwhile or even necessary in the first place. The best way to ensure that you develop the full range of financial management skills is to achieve a thorough understanding of the theoretical concepts involved and some tangible experience of event finance in practice.

REVIEW QUESTIONS

1. Who do you think are the most important audiences for financial information (1) in a private commercial organisation, (2) in a local authority event team and (3) in a voluntary organisation?
2. What are the benefits and drawbacks of using a continuation budget for an annual community sport event?
3. What are the benefits and drawbacks of using a ZBB for a community sport event?
4. Why is it important to compare budgets with actual performance, and how frequently should a manager do this for (1) small events, (2) annual events and (3) major events?

FURTHER READING

For guidance on recording and reporting financial information and for more detail on performing a thorough financial health analyses, see Wilson, R. (2011). *Managing Sport Finance*. Routledge, Oxon.

For more information on general event funding and financial planning, see Ferdinand, N. & Kitchin, P. (2017). *Events Management: An International Approach (2nd Edition)*. Chapter 7; Financing Events. Sage, London.

CHAPTER 12

Leadership and management in community sport organisations

Rebecca Peake and Melissa Jacobi

SUMMARY

Numerous academics have attempted to define leadership and management generally and in the context of specific industries. Indeed, if you visit a library, you will find entire sections dedicated to understanding what is meant when we use these terms. This chapter is designed to do the same by exploring the concept of leadership and management in community sport organisations (CSOs). It is by no means a definitive guide, and we would encourage those with an interest in these areas to build on what we develop in this chapter by engaging with the guided reading at the end.

AIMS

By engaging with this chapter, you will

- Be introduced to leadership theory,
- Be given an overview of management theory,
- Be able to understand how management and leadership are observed in community sport and physical activity (PA) and
- Engage with specific examples of leadership and management in community sport.

WHAT DO WE MEAN BY MANAGEMENT?

While the term 'management' is frequently used in various settings, there is often an assumption that it is understood and, moreover, applied consistently. Indeed, a frequent approach to defining management is to explain how the word is used but not what the word means. For example, Torkildsen (2005, p. 7) maintains that 'management is a word that can be applied to most situations in life: it is the act or art of managing'. Rather than this approach, here we are aiming to find a definition that enables us to use a word correctly in all appropriate situations and, perhaps more importantly, clarify how it differs from other, possibly similar, terms. For us, management can be defined as *the function of efficiently and effectively co-ordinating resources to accomplish goals and objectives*. To give you some examples, the management tasks that would be associated with this definition include setting goals and objectives, planning, co-ordinating, organising, staffing (recruitment, training and development), leading or directing and, finally, controlling. To make this more specific to the setting of community sport and PA, some examples of management tasks you will be expected to engage with include developing goals and objectives in an area that is varied and often hard to define; engage with corporate policy and organisations; plan, control and direct an organisation's resources in order to achieve objectives; and monitor and evaluate your success in meeting those objectives. Indeed, you will notice many of these tasks are covered in greater detail in other areas of this book. This 'type' of management is frequently referred to as 'strategic management'. In other words, strategic management is an ongoing process of setting goals and objectives, planning, monitoring and analysis.

THE CONTEXT FOR MANAGING AND LEADING IN THE COMMUNITY

There are other chapters in this book that aim to delve much deeper into the context of community sport, however, there are a couple of points we would like you to keep in mind as you read the rest of this chapter. First, in his discussion of voluntary organisations, Handy (1990, p. 9) noted that 'we add confusion to the pain if we unconsciously think that there is one thing called a voluntary organisation and to try to think up rules for running it'. This is a vital point to grasp for anyone looking to manage and lead in community sport. As has been noted in other parts of this book, there is no one type of CSO; by definition, CSOs are reflective of, and, therefore, as diverse as, the communities in which they operate. As such, there is no set formula for the effective management and leadership of community sport. This chapter will consider management and leadership within the diverse area of community sport, CSOs and the individuals who manage and lead in this area.

 Formalised 'management' roles within voluntary organisations often centre on members of committees or boards including the President, Chairperson, Vice-President and Vice-Chairperson, Board or Committee Member, Secretary, Treasurer, Registrar and Volunteer Co-ordinator. Operationally, management activities may also be undertaken by Co-ordinators, Coaches, Team Managers, Assistant Coaches, Referees or Umpires, First-Aid Officers, Equipment Co-ordinators, Ground Marshals, Competition/Results Secretaries, Social Organisers, Fundraising Co-ordinators, Newsletter/Communications/Website Co-ordinators and General Helpers. These are different, of course, from the organisations within the community sport and PA sector that may pay members of staff. In either scenario, it is not recommended that management be considered as restoring or maintaining normality, which, according to Drucker (1965), is the situation of the past. Rather, the priority of 'management', in order to be effective, is an attempt to understand the circumstances of the future in order to direct their organisations into tomorrow. In doing this, however, a common mistake of managers is that they pay little attention to management issues and fail to recognise them. Simplified, things normally go wrong only because they have been omitted from consideration (Blair, 1996). You will now be beginning to understand how difficult the role of a manger is.

WHAT CAN WE LEARN FROM MANAGEMENT THEORY?

In 1909, Taylor published 'The Principles of Scientific Management' and started this paper by quoting then president of the United States, Theodore Roosevelt: 'The conservation of our national resources is only preliminary to the larger question of national efficiency'. Based on Taylor's background (in engineering), his focus was on production and efficiency gains. In order to achieve this, he proposed that by optimising and simplifying jobs, productivity would increase. He also advanced the idea that workers and managers needed to cooperate with one another. He found that by calculating the time needed for the various elements of a task, he could develop the 'best' way to complete that task. Taylor (1911) developed four principles of scientific management. These principles, known simply as 'Taylorism', can be summarised as

- A science for each element of work, which replaces the old rule of thumb method;
- Scientific selection, training and development of the employee, matching workers to their jobs based on capability and motivation and training them to work at maximum efficiency;
- Cooperation and monitoring of performance, providing instruction and guidance; and
- Allocation of work to ensure division of the work and the responsibility between the management and the workers. The managers spend their time planning and training, allowing the workers to perform their tasks efficiently.

Whilst some of these concepts may be appropriate for a community sport context, due to the focus on production and manufacturing rather than a service or the development of people, this style of management is best suited to an 'industrial' setting for which it was designed rather than in community sport and PA. In 1916, Fayol published the 'Fourteen Principles of Management' accompanied by a list of the six primary functions of management, to be considered alongside one another. These primary functions were forecasting, planning, organising, commanding, co-ordinating and controlling (Fayol, 1916). Fayol's work, arguably one of earliest examples we have on a 'theory of management', is still considered, over 100 years later, as one of the most comprehensive. Consequently, he is considered one of the founding fathers of the modern concept of management.

The theory of management saw little change until the 1950s and 1960s when 'People Management' – frequently referred to as Human Resource Management – emerged. This theory suggested that a manager should focus on the needs and motivations of individuals within organisations and place a greater emphasis on employee involvement in the functions outlined by Fayol. This is far more in line with the management of employees and volunteers in community sport and PA, and it is to this topic that we will now turn.

THE MANAGEMENT OF PEOPLE

Management of community sport and PA involves a considerable amount of working with others: facilitating and co-ordinating. The management of people is an essential facet of management. Within community sport and PA, a substantial number of the people you will manage will be volunteers, so it is worth noting that the concept of volunteering goes beyond simply unpaid work. Let us briefly explain what we mean by this.

Cnaan, Handy and Wadsworth (1996) outline several dimensions of volunteering, which highlights how complex this area of management is. One dimension, which is perhaps the most obvious, is choice. Your volunteer workforce will range in the choice they feel they have. Some will have free will, and some will feel relatively un-coerced, however, some will feel obliged to volunteer. A parent might feel obligated to volunteer – perhaps because their children play on a team – but would prefer to volunteer informally by not accepting a designated role such as that of team manager. Another dimension to volunteering is remuneration, which could range from none at all to none expected, all the way through to reimbursement of expenses or the inclusion of a stipend or low pay. Frequently, for example, a volunteer may take on the role of coach, and the need for formal coaching qualifications may result in an expectation that the club will reimburse expenses incurred in acquiring a qualification. Or, once the coach is qualified, they may be able to demand a fee. Finally, one dimension often ignored is the structure within which volunteering takes place. Volunteering can take place in both formal and informal organisational settings. Volunteers contribute their time through both formal and informal settings and may volunteer for more than one organisation and in more than one role at varying levels of frequency, from as little as once per year (e.g., an annual sport event) to a number of times per week (e.g., coaching a local team). With variation in the extent to which volunteers commit, there will be variation in the management of these volunteers reflecting their role. For example, volunteering for a specific sport event will require specific recruitment, training and management of the role during the event. A role coaching Walking Football, with over 50s, on a weekly basis would require support and management from the Football Association (FA), potentially from their regional development office (see Chapter 2 for more information on this).

When considering unpaid workers, it is often the case that sport volunteers are simultaneously owners and managers of Voluntary Sport Organisations (VSOs) as well as workers and clients of the organisation. Organisational behaviour – the study of the way people interact within groups – of members of VSOs is unique, as members are concomitantly the 'owners' and 'clients' (players and parents of junior players) of their organisation. Some members take on management roles by running for office and in so doing take on responsibility for managing the work of other members in operational roles. Importantly, each of these 'organizational roles comes with its own set of behavioural expectations' (Pearce, 1993, p. 151). In these situations specifically, individuals in management roles rarely view themselves as managers; they are members of the management committee or board with responsibility for the governance of the organisation and its assets. The division of roles into managerial and operational levels emphasises that some volunteers often have direct managerial responsibility for other volunteers. 'The implications are clear: to learn and to progress, first recognise the key management and leadership challenges, get into action, reflect upon and learn from your experiences – and be seen to have done so' (Pedler et al., 2012, p. 3).

LEADERSHIP

In the same way that the term management has been discussed and deliberated, despite decades of academic research on the topic, there has yet to be a unanimously accepted definition of 'leadership'. As such, as early as 1991, Roast (cited in Northouse, 2012, p. 1) noted that 'in leadership literature more than 100 definitions of leadership have been identified'. As a term, it is seen to have different meanings and connotations depending on the individual or context. Often included in a definition of leadership is, rather obviously, the ability of an individual to 'lead' a group or team, however, the words motivation, vision and inspiration are also regularly linked to the term. For example, Byers, Slack and Parent (2012, p. 85) state that 'leadership is a complex notion that generally refers to an individual's ability to direct, motivate and "lead" other individuals and groups in a desired direction or behavioural pattern'. Adding more insight to our discussion, Beech and Chadwick (2004, p. 80) outline a number of characteristics of leaders in their definition by claiming that 'effective leaders are likely to be those who identify the greatest need in their followers – whether it be for guidance, training, motivation or whatever – and provide it'. If people are to follow you, then we must acknowledge that underpinning much of the work of any leader is the ability to influence others. In doing so, however, Oakley and Rhys (2008, p. 106) claim that it is important that this influence is 'in the pursuit of organisational goals', and, importantly, it is recognised that 'although all managers should be able to lead, not all leaders will be managers, as leadership is not necessarily related to the position in the organisation' (Taylor et al. 2011, p. 342). It is worthy of acknowledgement that leadership is an important aspect of management – the ability to lead effectively is one of the factors that produces an effective manager.

We feel that it is important for you to observe the variety of definitions of leadership. However, the favoured definition of leadership for this chapter is that leadership is an individual's skills, character and ability to understand and influence others in the pursuit of organisational goals. For CSOs, it is vital that individuals in leadership roles, or those looked at to provide leadership for a group or organisation, are able to inspire employees, volunteers and participants to facilitate the long-term development and success of the organisation. A community sport leader may be the member of a team playing in a recreational touch rugby team or the fixture's security within a hockey club.

LEADERSHIP SKILLS AND CHARACTERISTICS

When observing individuals who excel in leadership, the onlooker frequently notices reoccurring skills and characteristics. The skills and characteristics shared are akin to the terminology originally cited in the definition of leadership and include such words and phrases as motivational, inspirational, visionary, honesty and integrity, excellent communication skills, self-awareness and self-confidence. What is clear from the plethora of literature related to leadership is that individuals who exhibit leadership qualities do not have to hold a senior role within an organisation; it might be hoped that senior positions are held by those who possess leadership qualities, however, the ability to lead most definitely does not 'come with the promotion' to a senior position. Informal leadership also exists, and this is when individuals with no seniority or position demonstrate leadership characteristics and undertake leadership responsibilities. Staff, at any level within a community sport and PA setting, are just as likely to possess – and indeed, require – leadership qualities as those in management positions. The ability to motivate and lead a group to achieve a common goal can be derived from individuals holding a range of job roles – it is about the qualities, skills and abilities of the individual rather than the job role they undertake or the position they hold.

This area of work was supported by research conducted by McCrae and Costa (1987) into the Big Five personality traits of a leader, and they found that in terms of an individual's personality, there were five key traits, which are frequently observed in leaders:

1. Neuroticism
2. Extraversion
3. Openness
4. Agreeableness
5. Conscientiousness

Interestingly, of all these traits, extroversion was the most closely linked personality trait to effective leadership. In short, a confident and dynamic personality is most likely to be a key requirement of leaders, rather than appointment in a leadership position. This reinforces trait theory, which will be discussed later in the chapter.

LEADERSHIP STYLES

Vecchio and Boatwright's research (2002) into different leadership styles provides further insight into leadership by outlining the relationship between different levels of education, gender and job experience to their acceptance of directive and supportive leadership. In particular, their findings showed that employees with a lot of experience or higher levels of education (or both) desired less structure and, therefore, did not respond well to directive leadership, which involves goal and deadline setting, monitoring and evaluation of roles undertaken with largely linear communication channels. There was also a gendered element to their findings, with Vecchio and Boatwright (2002) finding that although males preferred directive leadership, females preferred supportive leadership where there is more two-way communication and joint agreement of goals where workers are facilitated to become comfortable in their role and position in an organisation or group. Adding to the complexity of leadership, in this research, older employees were found to be more comfortable with directive leadership when compared to younger employees. In an organisational context with a range of employees or volunteers, this provides a challenge in terms of identifying the most appropriate style of leading members of a team towards achieving the desired goal. Should a leader set firm targets and deadlines? Should they monitor progress towards an objective regularly? Or, should they lead in a more inclusive communal way? This type of leadership dilemma moves us towards exploring the different styles of leadership that different forms of research have helped to develop.

Styles of leadership range from autocratic to laissez-faire; the style a leader adopts depends on their personality, but also on the culture of the organisation and the employees themselves. A number of leadership styles are outlined in Table 12.1.

TABLE 12.1 Leadership styles		
Style	*Overview*	*Community sport context*
Autocratic	Autocratic leaders have full control of their team or group. They identify and allocate the goals, priorities and actions for members of their team and monitor their achievement, or otherwise.	Autocratic styles are commonly observed in dangerous situations to avoid accident or injury. It, therefore, may be observed in an extreme sports setting. Additionally, coaches in young children's sport may adopt an autocratic style of leadership.
Paternalistic	Paternalistic leaders act as a type of 'father figure' for their subordinates. They will decide the goals, priorities and actions for the group, but unlike a typical authoritarian leader, a paternalistic leader will often explain their reasons for decisions, although there is no room for discussion. The paternalistic leader *will* make the decisions, and team members are expected to display their loyalty by adhering to decisions made.	Traditionally, this type of leadership may be observed in the initial inception of a community sport intervention aiming to combat youth crime. The group leader may wish to gradually hand over responsibilities to the group members, and, therefore, the comprehension of decisions would enhance the effectiveness.
Democratic	Democratic leaders share decision-making opportunities with the group or team they are responsible for. This process is often thought to compromise the speed of decision-making, but to the benefit of the motivation level of the team. Democratic leadership is most effective with experienced, educated and skilled individuals who are able to offer insightful suggestions or recommendations on required areas.	Democratic leadership is most effective with experienced groups. It is likely to, therefore, be most effective in settings like Masters or Veterans sport. A group of experienced athletes at a local Fell Running group may have a club chairperson acting as a democratic leader, but decisions are made by the committee and in consultation with members of the group.
Laissez-Faire	Laissez-Faire leadership underpins leaders who consciously decide to delegate responsibility for decisions to managers and teams. It is seen as being a very 'hands-off' approach to leadership where teams have the freedom to organise themselves as they see most appropriate. Criticism can relate to ill-defined roles, particularly for managers, but can be effective for highly motivated and experienced teams.	Laissez-Faire leadership may be observed in a community sport setting where adults participate in social, yet competitive, sport. A ladies 'Back to Netball' team or Men's five-a-side team participating in a local Powerleague football competition are examples.

ARE LEADERS BORN OR MADE?

The debates surrounding theories of leadership have developed in sophistication over the period of time it has been studied, progressing from the 'great man theory', which considered 'men' to be effectively 'born' into leadership, through to more recent consideration of 'transformational' leadership, where an individuals' needs and personal goals are as important to a leader as the success of the group or team. This section will explore the evolution of these approaches and apply them to the community sport and PA setting.

Great man theory

The great man theory is based on the premise that leaders are 'born' and dismisses any argument to say leadership is a skill that can be developed by an individual. The concept suggests that there are certain innate qualities a leader needs to possess in order to be an effective leader, which largely focuses on personality. One of the main criticisms of this theory focuses on the fact that if leaders are indeed born, then it could be expected that anyone born with the right qualities would be expected to find themselves in a leadership role. This is not always the case, as we have noted above. It is also apparent, specifically in more recent decades, that women are equally as capable of becoming great leaders as men, which was something – as the name suggests – that was not advocated by this theory.

Trait theory

Trait theories are based on a similar premise to the great man theory in that leadership is identified as a series of distinguishing qualities or attributes an individual possesses. Over the years, research has identified an extensive range of attributes or traits leaders hold including intelligence, self-confidence and determination. Earlier in the chapter, we touched on the work by McCrae and Costa (1987) where the 'Big Five' personality traits of leadership were identified. This is an example of a trait theory. Building on this work, Judge et al. (2002) identified that, in relation to leadership, 'extroversion' was the most strongly connected personality trait. There is little disputing that leaders typically possess a range of traits that often include key attributes, such as decision-making capabilities or extroversion. However, concern has been expressed about the fact that a comprehensive set of traits has yet to be established. The list of traits relating to leadership seems to continue to expand, and, for some, this is seen to dilute the concept and, perhaps, signals that there is no definitive set of traits.

Behaviourist theory

As the name suggests, behaviourist theory focuses on what a leader actually does (how they behave) rather than their personal qualities. This approach moves us away from the idea of leaders being born with characteristics or traits and focuses on how leaders act towards others in various situations. The theory suggests that a person can be taught how to react or behave in a given situation, meaning that a person can, in theory, 'learn' how to behave like a leader. For behavioural theorists, the behaviour of a leader is the best predictor of their likely success in leadership roles, rather than the identification of his or her personal traits or qualities, and, in that regard, research has identified that leaders typically engage with two types of behaviours, those being 'task' behaviour or 'process' behaviour.

Task behaviours involve the leader completing tasks to help their followers or team achieve a goal, such as writing an implementation plan. Process behaviours, on the other hand, are used by leaders to help individuals within the group feel at ease in situations by creating a no-blame or failure-tolerant culture. How a leader combines task and process behaviours to influence their followers is the main focus of behaviourist theories. Similar to criticisms of trait theories, however, criticisms of behaviourist theories include the fact that, despite significant research focussed on identifying a key set of leadership behaviours that would be consistently effective, consistency has not been possible, meaning that there is no clear formula for successful leadership behaviour.

Situational leadership

Unlike behaviourist theory, situational leadership focuses on the suggestion that leadership can and should be tailored to the situation. For example, in high-risk situations, an autocratic leadership style may be better, or a leader who is able to be decisive and command immediate responses from followers would arguably be more effective than a participative style. Importantly, situational leadership style requires leaders to be adaptable to a range of situations, followers and employees. There are, arguable, two key areas of focus for situational leaders. First, a diagnosis of the situation, including the task to be undertaken and the competency or experience of the individual(s) being asked to undertake the task, is crucial. Second, having done this, leaders must adapt their leadership style to meet the requirements of both the task and the individual being asked to undertake the task. Underpinning this is that, it is possible, within the same organisation or team, different leadership styles could be required depending on the situation. Criticisms of situational leadership have included there being a lack of primary research in the area to thoroughly interrogate the theory and provide a definitive overview of how situational leadership can be modelled. There has also been concern regarding how situational leadership differs and can be adapted between individuals and group situations. (For further reading on situational leadership, see Graeff [1997, 1983], Vecchio [1987] and Bosse et al. [2017].)

Contingency theory

Contingency theory is a development of the situational leadership theory but focuses on identifying the key variables to identify the best leadership style to suit a particular situation. Fiedler's (1964) research emphasised the importance of the leader's personality in relation to the situation in which they are required to lead. The two key 'styles' associated with this theory are 'task'- (focusing on the task on hand) and 'relationship'- (concerned with dynamics and interpersonal relationships) motivated styles. Three particular characteristics stand out with this theory. First, there has to be some understanding of the relationships between the leader and the members. How much trust and confidence do the group have in their leader? Second, there needs to be clarity with regard to the task and the method used to complete it. Finally, the power the leader has and, in particular, how much reward and punishment the leader can excerpt over members of the group will influence decision making and the success (or not) of the leader (Northouse, 2007).

As with the other theories, there are criticisms of contingency theory, and these centre on the lack of clarity surrounding why individuals with 'positive' leadership styles can be effective in some situations but not in others. There is also a concern that there is no development of modifications when a disparity arises between leaders and situations in a work environment.

Transactional theory

Transactional theory, developed by Berne in 1950, is often discussed in relation to the workplace and is based on the premise that leaders provide a 'contract' with their employees or followers that is generally formulated around employees providing a service or undertaking a role for which the leader will remunerate them with rewards, typically in terms of salary. Transactional leadership relates to supervising and organising teams or groups to achieve goals; both rewards and punishments are utilised depending on the situation. Transactional theory has been widely criticised, however, ranging from critiques that identify that transactional theory assumes all followers or employees are the same and have the same motivations as well as the fact that it pays no regard to social values or an individual's personal emotions. So, for example, how do we explain volunteering through transactional theory? There is also a question of how transactional theory could ever motivate people beyond basic remuneration. For example, there is no explanation regarding the development of individuals or recognition of wider ambitions.

Transformational leadership theory

Transformational leadership is, essentially, the opposite of transactional theory. Transformational leaders are visionary, inspiring and inclusive of those who follow them. They are focussed on achieving the goal with a team, but also on ensuring all individuals involved succeed in their assigned areas too. Transformational leaders can inspire positive changes in subordinates and are interested in helping them achieve their personal ambitions and goals. They inspire creativity and encourage wider development and enquiry by their followers. Transformational leaders can be 'infectious' in their leadership and inspire subordinates to achieve significantly higher results than anticipated or expected. Criticisms of transformational theory are limited in number; the approach could be considered to be currently 'in favour', meaning that there are limited negatives identified to date about this approach.

Case studies

Dronfield Netball Club

Dronfield Netball Club (DNC) is a community sport club based in Dronfield Sports Centre, North-East Derbyshire. The club originated in 2012 when a small group of '30-something' friends decided they wanted to do something a 'bit social and a bit active' as a means to increase their exercise levels. One of the women had previously had a background in netball, although she had not played for a number of years, and suggested hiring a court at the local sports centre to have a social 'game' of netball. Everyone enjoyed that initial session, and so, arrangements were made to book the hall again and 'bring a friend', increasing attendance to 12. Over the next four years, DNC grew and developed to include four competitive adult teams in local and county leagues, a recreational adult team, 100 children attending sessions weekly, several children selected to attend county netball training and a waiting list for both children and adults. Coached sessions for adults and juniors are run each Saturday between 2.15 pm and 6 pm, with participating ages being from 5 to 50, with mixed boys and girls sessions in the junior age groups.

Management of Dronfield Netball Club

The club is 'managed' by volunteers who offer their time weekly, operating under the remit of the DNC committee. Typically, as suggested earlier in the chapter, the vast majority of the committee and regular volunteers are players and/or parents of players at the club. Committee and club roles now include Chair, Treasurer, Secretary, Head Coach, Welfare Officer, Administration Manager, Junior Co-ordinator, Coaches, Team Captains and Parent Team Managers.

The hours required and, therefore, contributed to running the club by the core volunteers, particularly in relation to the junior section, can be very time-consuming. To give this some context, one weekend in April 2016 saw coaching sessions delivered 2.15–6 pm on the Saturday then a junior tournament away from Dronfield between 10 am and 4.30 pm on the Sunday with largely the same individuals present throughout both days. This meant relying on four Coaches, the Administration Manager and the Junior Co-ordinator to be working pretty much constantly on 'voluntary' netball activities over the weekend, as well as parents to transport children to training and to the tournament. As others have noted in various chapters of this book, this turn of events is not unusual; the scenario is replicated regularly throughout the year and clearly provides an insight into the level of commitment and time required organising this CSO.

The management of weekly operations at DNC is carried out by a range of volunteers, all of who have full-time jobs and the majority of who have families too. This means that time is scarce to undertake the administrative and financial requirements of running a club of this size. Essentially, DNC is 'managed' by a range of individuals, all of who have time pressures and none of who are identified as a 'manager' per se, or have any form of formal training (aside from the Coaches and Welfare Officer). However, the 'appointment' – relatively recently – of the Administration Manager and Junior Co-ordinator, both of who have excellent organisation and communication skills, means that they are looked to for direction and information on a regular basis; although still volunteers (and parents of junior members), these individuals possess many of the key skills and attributes required of effective managers and, at times, leaders.

In relation to Fayol's Six Primary Functions of Management, the Head Coach tends to take the lead in terms of Forecasting and Planning, with a range of other committee members and volunteers taking up the Organising, Co-ordinating and Controlling elements to the best of their ability within their own capability and knowledge levels as well as time constraints. Commanding does not tend to figure as a function within DNC, unless it ever relates to a Health and Safety situation. The management of communication within the club has been enhanced by using technology – specifically social media in the form of Facebook – to communicate with club members. Details of matches and tournaments as well as communicating results and changes to sessions are promoted widely through the club's Facebook page, and two of the adult teams have closed Facebook groups to allow easier communication and discussion between team members.

Leadership in Dronfield Netball Club

As a CSO, DNC has a range of stakeholders, which include club members, the facilities used for training, the leagues different teams are affiliated to, England Netball as the sport's National Governing Body and East Midlands Netball. This means that communication needs to ensure that all key stakeholders are fully informed of the direction of the club as well as operational management issues. Typically, the head coach leads the club and provides the vision and the netball knowledge to inform recommendations and future plans. Generally then, the committee and other regular volunteers will look at ways to ensure smooth implementation and management of these plans wherever possible. In more recent months, the Administration Manager has taken the lead with implementation and now shoulders much of the responsibility for organising and co-ordinating. In some ways, this means that although as a club, numbers have increased in terms of individuals volunteering at the club, the onus still falls on 'a few', just perhaps a different few than previously.

The committee works very much in line with a democratic leadership style, with discussion of recommendations or suggestions being made at regular committee meetings and, if necessary, a vote deciding the final direction of a decision. This means that processes can be slow to get moving if a meeting is not scheduled for a number of weeks. However, because those involved in the running of the club are there voluntarily, and it is something of a core principle for the club that decisions are made as a group, this is a principle that needs to be upheld for consistency and inclusion reasons. In this regard, it is in line with Vecchio and Boatwright's (2002) research and their finding that females preferred supportive leadership, where there is more two-way communication and joint agreement of goals. This is very evident within DNC; all of the committee members and key volunteers are female, and on occasions, when decisions have been made outside a democratic setting without consultation of the wider group, there has been discontent and ultimately the committee has tended to reverse these decisions to ensure the demo-cratic nature of the club, and the operational side of the club is able to meet the vision of those providing direction. It is a constant juggle to ensure that the resources, particularly in terms of time and availability of key volunteers, can meet the needs of a dynamic, growing and competitive club.

In terms of Leadership Approaches, as previously identified, the Head Coach tends to provide leadership, direction and suggestions related to goal setting for the club as a whole as well as individuals and teams. Her natural leadership approach tends to be transformational leadership, as there is a definite understanding of the needs and motiva-tions of individuals within the club as well as having a clear direction for the club in mind.

Nunny's funky boots

Katy Nunn (Nunny) set up Funky Boots, a friendly women's social football club, who meet every week for a kick about. Funky Boots gives women of all ages and abilities a chance to get into football in a fun, non-competitive, social environment. The club has blossomed into a session that is open and welcoming to women of all ages, experience, fitness levels and abilities to feel comfortable to come and learn to play or rekindle an old passion for the game. Funky Boots, run by Katy, is made up of a diverse mix of women with different abilities, some of who played years ago at school, some who have played throughout their lives and, for many, some of whom football is a new sport that they have never played before. Funky Boots participants include women from Brazil, Germany and across the UK, with ages ranging from 18 to 60. Since launching in 2011, the FA Mars Just Play initiative has been one of the UK's most successful grassroots foot-ball initiatives and this year celebrated one million attendances at sessions up and down the country. Katy was recently celebrated by the FA Mars Just Play as someone who inspires and motivates their local community to get involved with the Just Play initiative.

Social media is the main vehicle of communication, with a private Facebook page being used as the principal medium; this is managed and controlled by Katy, and the closed nature of the group means others can also post freely. The group meet weekly throughout the year, and participants have ranged in age from 18 to 60. Katy man-ages the team, ensuring pitch booking, equipment and finances are managed. In this respect, whilst Katy's position is the group leader, decisions are typically made dem-ocratically. An example of this was when the group decided to change the size of the repeat-booking pitch, which would result in an increase of weekly fees by £1; the group voted on the change. The annual tournament date is also determined using Doodle, a polling website, and the date that most players can attend is selected. Technology is also used for the day-to-day management of the team, as Katy uses the Teamer app to co-ordinate teams and assess availability. Informal leadership and a laissez-faire approach is adopted for weekly sessions; experienced players will allocate the teams, and another will take the weekly fee (Figure 12.1).

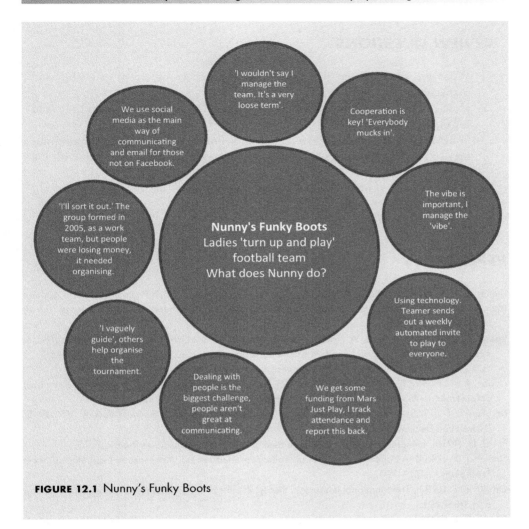

FIGURE 12.1 Nunny's Funky Boots

CONCLUSION

This chapter has highlighted both the difficulty and importance of defining what we mean by leadership and management. The concept of management and leadership is often 'taken for granted' by those with a responsibility for leading and managing. What we have tried to highlight through this chapter is the complexity of these concepts, but also the importance that must be placed on understanding them if we are to reach desired objectives. This is the case whatever the size of the organisation, as we have aimed to highlight through the case studies.

REVIEW QUESTIONS

1. What are some of the similarities and differences between leadership and management?
2. How can we apply different theories or principles of management to sport and PA in the community?
3. What impact does the high percentage of volunteers that make up the community sport and PA workforce have on any management and leadership within a community context?
4. What are the similarities and differences between the different leadership models?

REFERENCES

Beech, J., & Chadwick, S. (Eds.). (2004). *The business of sport management*. Pearson Education, London.

Blair, G. M. (1996). *Starting to manage: The essential skills* (IEEE Engineers Guide to Business, Vol. 8), New Jersey.

Bosse, T., Duell, R., Memon, Z. A., Treur, J., & van der Wal, C. N. (2017). Computational model-based design of leadership support based on situational leadership theory. *Simulation, 93*(7), 605–617.

Byers, T., Slack, T., & Parent, M. (2012). *Key concepts in sport management*. Sage, London.

Cnaan, R. A., Handy, F., & Wadsworth, M. (1996). Defining who is a volunteer: Conceptual and empirical considerations. *Nonprofit and Voluntary Sector Quarterly, 25*(3), 364–383.

Drucker, P. F. (1965). Is business letting young people down. *Harvard Business Review, 43,* 49–55 (November–December).

Fayol, H. (1916). General principles of management. *Classics of Organization Theory, 2,* 15.

Fiedler, F. E. (1964). A contingency model of leadership effectiveness. *Advances in Experimental Social Psychology, 1,* 149–190.

Graeff, C. L. (1983). The situational leadership theory: A critical view. *Academy of Management Review, 8*(2), 285–291.

Graeff, C. L. (1997). Evolution of situational leadership theory: A critical review. *The Leadership Quarterly, 8*(2), 153–170.

Handy, C. B. (1990). *Understanding voluntary organizations: How to make them function effectively*. Penguin, London.

Judge, T. A., Bono, J. E., Ilies, R., & Gerhardt, M. W. (2002). Personality and leadership: A qualitative and quantitative review. *Journal of Applied Psychology, 87*(4), 765.

McCrae, R. R., & Costa, P. T. (1987). Validation of the five-factor model of personality across instruments and observers. *Journal of Personality and Social Psychology, 52*(1), 81.

Northouse, P. G. (2007). Transformational leadership. *Leadership: Theory and Practice, 4,* 175–206.

Northouse, P. G. (2012). *Introduction to leadership: Concepts and practice*. Sage Publications, London.

Oakley, B., & Rhys, M. (2008). *The sport and fitness sector: An introduction*. Open University/Routledge, Abingdon.

Pearce, D. W. (1993). *Blueprint 3: Measuring sustainable development* (Vol. 3). Earthscan, London.

Pedler, M., Burgoyne, J., & Boydell, T. (2012). *A manager's guide to self-development*. McGraw-Hill Education, UK.

Taylor, F. W. (1911). *The principles of scientific management.* Harper & Brothers, New York.

Taylor, A., Cocklin, C., Brown, R., & Wilson-Evered, E. (2011). An investigation of champion-driven leadership processes. *The Leadership Quarterly, 22*(2), 412–433.

Torkildsen, G. (2005). *Leisure and recreation management.* Routledge, Oxon.

Vecchio, R. P. (1987). Situational leadership theory: An examination of a prescriptive theory. *Journal of Applied Psychology, 72*(3), 444.

Vecchio, R. P., & Boatwright, K. J. (2002). Preferences for idealized styles of supervision. *The Leadership Quarterly, 12*(4), 327–342.

CHAPTER 13

Enterprise and innovation in community sport

Jo Marsden-Heathcote and Andrew Finney

SUMMARY

The world is ever changing, and with the advancement of technology, this is even more apparent. This chapter takes a look at how this creates potential opportunities for those more enterprising individuals within the local sporting environment. Not only does it consider why entrepreneurial activity is useful in sport, but also offers processes that show how to develop yourself in an enterprising manner and how to start up and enterprise.

AIMS

By engaging with this chapter, you will be able to

- Develop an understanding of what entrepreneurship is and why it is important,
- Communicate the reasons why community sport utilises enterprising behaviours,
- Have a greater understanding of your own potential enterprising values and
- Apply a number of practical processes and tools to assist in the development of enterprise in community sport.

INTRODUCTION

The world of work is constantly evolving. No longer does a 'job for life' exist – if it ever did – in the UK. Working lives have been expected to involve more frequent changes of employer, industry, occupation and possibly even employment status (employee/free-lance/contractor). A number of changes in the nature of work have developed over the last 30 years, exacerbated by technological change, a more diverse workforce and the workplace structure. This is reflected within the world of community sport.

This chapter examines the importance of entrepreneurship and enterprise within a community sport setting, together with the growing importance and influence of social enterprises within this sector, contemplating how 'being enterprising' in sport can facilitate and develop the use of innovation to overcome emerging challenges and struggles at a local level within sport in combination with how enterprise and innovation can influence the landscape of what community sport looks like, activities that are available and how they can be delivered.

The entrepreneurship and sport management disciplines have grown significantly over the past decade. Sport is an entrepreneurial process, as innovation and change are key elements (Ratten, 2011). Alongside this, the sporting landscape has changed considerably too, and, following the recession in 2008, a remarkable pressure on leisure time and greater competition for people's attention and time has emerged. This shift in social patterns has given rise to new activities, with previously popular pursuits declining in interest. Health and fitness has always been a dynamic industry and one in which new trends are a regular feature, so it comes as no surprise that going to the gym is one of the most popular physical activities for UK consumers (Mintel, 2017). Sport is a little more stable, but activities such as mountaineering have seen an increase in once-a-week participation in 2005/2006 from 67,000 up to 110,200 in 2015/2016 (Sport England, 2016). Kitesurfing has also seen an increase from 2008/2009 of 11,600 up to 18,400 in 2011/2012 (of once-a-month participation) (Sport England, 2016).

Alongside this is a harsh realisation of publicly funded sport having to deliver a more sustainable and responsible sport sector. As has been noted many times throughout this book, the change in government from Labour to Conservative saw a change in how publicly funded sport was delivered at a local level. A shift from local authority delivery mechanisms then became County Sport Partnerships. Sport England's Towards an Active Nation Strategy (2016) has a focus on how it can bring benefits to people and to society through outcomes such as physical and mental well-being; individual development; and social, community and economic development. The hope is that this will get more people from every background regularly and meaningfully involved in sport, yet deliver a more productive, sustainable and responsible sport sector. Is this an outcome of a trying and challenging decade, or is this a new beginning for sport starting in the community? Will this allow ventures and enterprises to deliver what it is that the communities need and want? Consequently, this chapter will take a look at what we mean by enterprise and being enterprising alongside some practical ways in which you can develop entrepreneurial activity in sport within your local community.

ENTREPRENEURSHIP

The development of entrepreneurship is necessary for a healthy economy and for keeping economic wealth through the creation of jobs. Entrepreneurs can improve the competitiveness of an economy as well as create new wealth. As industries change and develop, it is through entrepreneurship that the economy continues to grow. According to Ratten (2011), changes in sport have required entrepreneurship. Such a rapid development in technology such as the Internet and digital television has meant that sport marketers have had to change the way they advertise through the media. In addition to this, as the global economy has weakened with the various recessions, sport marketers have had to recreate the way and the methods in which they advertise. When considering the sport sector, entrepreneurship is critical, as it allows for the consumers' changing demands along with increased emphasis on innovation (Ball, 2005).

The following case study highlights the journey of a small enterprise within the health and fitness industry, developing their entrepreneurial activity based upon both personal and consumer demands. This will be referred to throughout the chapter.

Case study: Mel Gibbons – personal trainer
www.melpersonaltraining.com

In her late 30s, Mel embarked on a journey to change her lifestyle. Being an overweight mum of two in the nursing profession, Mel decided that she needed a change. She joined a boot camp and learnt about High Intensity Interval Training, healthy nutrition and how she could incorporate all of this into her lifestyle. And it was successful. She realised that the results of the journey that she had been on were something that was desired by so many of her friends, family and women in general that were stuck in the same perpetuating lifestyle as she used to be. And importantly, she really believed in it and enjoyed it. So she became a personal trainer.

Mel began by working for the organisation that she had previously been a customer for and honed her talent. She specialised in pre and postnatal training groups and gradually developing her customer base. The demand for her services grew organically and allowed her to then move to becoming an independent, self-employed personal trainer. Mel had a real transformation story to tell about her journey, and her interpersonal skills including empathy from her nursing background gave her the ability to relate to the needs of her largely female customer base, and in turn, she saw her demand grow.

The promotion of Mel and her business originated through word of mouth, but as demand grew, she needed a more efficient way of communicating with her customers. Although she had a website, this wasn't as efficient in delivering information that her customers needed. It was then that she tried social media as a method of communication (mainly Facebook), as many of her female customer base (ages 25–39) were using it on a regular basis. This also gave Mel a way in which to celebrate her customers'/groups' success in a public way and encourage new customers.

As the business developed and grew, there was an increasing need for Mel to develop and grow as well. She had to ensure that she was meeting the needs of her customers by branching into group exercise such as 'Insanity', 'PiYo' and even linked with the 'This Girl Can' campaign to deliver 'Soccercise'.

Defining entrepreneurship

There is no one universally accepted definition used to describe an entrepreneur or entrepreneurship; however, there are a similar number of elements that make them up. An entrepreneur can be described as someone who creates and innovates and demonstrates initiative (Bolton and Thompson, 2013). They can also be considered as someone who finds and puts new ideas into effect. Factors that we tend to associate with an entrepreneur include identifying and meeting unmet demand or needs, an element of risk-taking as well as developing networks that enable change to happen.

Most contemporary definitions of entrepreneurship have a focus on the creation and development of new ventures and organisations. Having the ability to recognise opportunities is a common theme of entrepreneurship definitions, and Shane and Venkataraman (2000) define entrepreneurship as involving the discovery, evaluation and exploitation of opportunities.

Many theories have been used to explain entrepreneurship, particularly how and why it occurs. They include economic, psychological and social perspectives and the potential influence that can be had on the prevalence of entrepreneurism. The influence of personality traits, for example, that someone possesses can lend themselves to being more entrepreneurial (McClelland, 1961). Economic theory considers the impact that economic situations have on entrepreneurship. It comes from the perspective that the economic situation needs to be ideal to encourage the rise of new ventures. There is evidence to support that entrepreneurship is more evident in times of economic crisis. It is interesting to note that since the 2008 recession, the Office for National Statistics (ONS) has indeed recorded an increase in the number of sports businesses/enterprises that are running in the UK (ONS, 2017). More specifically, since the funding supporting primary school physical education and sport delivery altered in 2013/2013, the ONS (2017) identified an increase in the number of businesses relating to sport and education by over 70 per cent from 2013 to 2016.

ENTREPRENEURSHIP IN COMMUNITY SPORT AND PHYSICAL ACTIVITY

Sport-based entrepreneurship is defined as any form of enterprise or entrepreneurship in a sports context; examples of this could include when an entity in sport acts collectively to respond to an opportunity to create value. Entities involved in sport can include individuals, organisations or communities. Community-based entrepreneurship can occur when sports teams, organisations or players partner with community organisations. The key point here is that entrepreneurship in sport is dynamic and will have an impact on the economy and society through community development. Sport events and teams, for example, can encourage the development of a community by encouraging participation in sport and sport-related activity (Ratten, 2011).

Traditionally, most sport organisations sit within the public, private and not-for-profit sectors. However, restrictions in funding have contributed to the development of more local, community enterprises, which could be classed as social enterprises due to their impact on their communities. But, what do we mean by social enterprise? Social enterprises are hybrid organisations that trade goods and services with an aim to improve social, environmental, economic and cultural outcomes in a financially sustainable way. Social enterprises can vary greatly, but a good way to describe them is on a scale with traditional charities at one end and traditional businesses at the other, with a variety of social enterprises occupying the space in between.

What's it about?

Simply put, it is about having a purpose, trade to generate profit and impact. Every social enterprise should have a clear social and/or environmental purpose at the heart of what they do and have their mission statement articulates this. It is a clear and simple summary of what they do and why they do it, and it helps to remind their teams and customers alike. Where social enterprises differ from the average charity is that they generate the majority of their income through trade, selling products and services to customers, and not by raising funds through grants and donations.

Where social enterprises differ from the average 'for-profit' business is that they will reinvest at least 50 per cent of their profits directly back into achieving their 'social mission' as opposed to maximising profits for shareholders and other investors. We can see this illustrated nicely in Figure 13.1.

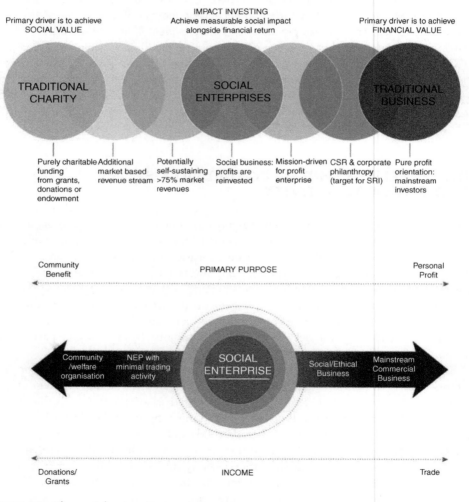

FIGURE 13.1 The social enterprise spectrum

By understanding how well they have been operating, organisations can measure the difference they are making and use this information to 'prove and improve' their impact. Through operating in this way, social enterprises offer a unique combination of social purpose and financial independence, providing a new option for both customers and suppliers alike. You may not be aware, but they are well established within our communities, from community buildings to the major high streets, offering banking services, food and drink outlets and department stores. Some of the most famous examples of social enterprises include the John Lewis Partnership, the Eden Project and Jamie Oliver's Fifteen restaurant.

There is scope for social enterprise structures to take different forms, ranging from the relatively informal and simple to the highly formal and sophisticated. This includes incorporated and unincorporated structures and potentially having charity status. Did you know that many university Students' Unions are also social enterprises? Profits from their commercial outlets such as food outlets and bars are reinvested into student services like the support services and societies.

Social entrepreneurship in sport encourages change in existing social issues such as those highlighted earlier within Sport England's Towards an Active Nation Strategy (2016). Sport can bring communities together, improve physical and mental well-being and make a significant contribution to the economy (Sport England, 2016). Hopefully by now, you will have a better understanding of the entrepreneurial nature of sport. The remainder of the chapter will focus on your entrepreneurial mindset, capabilities and finding your entrepreneurial potential.

BEING ENTERPRISING

Let's dispel a common belief first: an individual can be entrepreneurial without having their own business. There are a number of skills, behaviours and attributes that are linked to 'being enterprising' and are relevant to all parts of society. An important element is to raise your own awareness of your enterprising capabilities. Throughout this section, we'll look at your potential for being enterprising and consider your own capabilities in relation to this.

Gibbs (1993) listed a range of skills, traits and attributes that are displayed by entrepreneurs, similar to that in Table 13.1. It is hard to think that one person could display

TABLE 13.1 Entrepreneurial behaviours, skills and attributes

Skills	Attributes	Behaviours
Creativity	Self-motivation	Professionalism
Problem-solving	Independence	Using initiative
Decision-making	Confidence	Flexibility
Organisation	Driven	Risk-taking
Negotiation	Adaptability	Commitment to achieving goals
Communication	Resilience	Opportunity-seeking

Source: Adapted from Gibbs (1993).

all of these competencies, however, what is interesting is, for those of you with a sporting background, you may be surprised to find that you can relate to a good number of these, considering your experiences with sport.

VALUES

Knowing and understanding your values can help you to stay focussed, guide the future decisions that you make and inspire you to drive your idea in the long term. Although values can change over time as your idea matures, identifying these now ensure that you have the foundation for your future vision. By recognising these in yourself, it can help you decide on what idea to develop as your own enterprise or what employers you would love to work for throughout your career. Values are the things that matter to you and make you 'tick'! They can reflect your ambitions, passions and enthusiasm. It can be difficult to think of your own values. By looking around you or at the items you own, it can help you gain insight into the qualities and values that are important to you. Table 13.2 provides a list of steps that you can use to reflect on and identify your values.

This section has not only been about raising awareness of your own skills and values, and, therefore, having the potential to become someone who could be successful in a venture, but also how considering this wide range of skills, behaviours and attributes can be developed through starting your own venture. Interestingly, there is research that examines gender gap and tries to understand the reasons why there is such a disparity in the number of males in senior roles within organisations compared to females. One of the main thoughts is that men's perceptions of their own capability of performing at that level within

TABLE 13.2 Understanding your values

Step 1	Step 2
Think about something you use every day, and write what you like and admire about it.	Next, think of a business, product or service, and write what you like and admire about it.
Step 3	**Step 4**
Highlight six words that you feel represent your values. Remember, there are no right or wrong answers!	Come up with ten alternatives of those six words.
Step 5	**Optional Step 6**
You now have 60 words! Try to prioritise six–eight words that best describe your values.	Text ten family members or friends whose opinion you value. Ask them to text you three words describing what they like or admire about you. It's time to compare … do any of the words match your top words from Step 5? Is there commonality from the respondents? This is a great way to find out if your top values are similar to what others think they should be!

an organisation successfully are higher than those of women, and this is also reflected in business owners (Kelley et al., 2015). According to the Department for Business, Innovation and Skills, in 2013, 20 per cent of single-person businesses were owned and run by women. This has seen a sharp increase since 2008 and continues to rise year on year (FSB, 2016). Hopefully women are not only recognising their own skill set and potential, but also seeing that starting an enterprise allows for a varied and extensive set of competencies to develop throughout the experience. Within community settings, and in this growing dynamic environment of sport and physical activity, there is the capacity to look at your setting, your local area and the people within it and to highlight a demand that is currently not being met.

IDEA GENERATION

For some people, the thought of having to be creative and come up with new ideas is an incredibly challenging concept. Rae (2007) believes that 'creativity involves imagining a new reality, and innovation is required to make it work ... (by) developing ideas into applications and solutions'. However, it is not necessarily a skill that cannot be developed; it is less of a fact of possessing the skill and more about engaging the correct mindset to stimulate creative behaviours.

Idea-generating techniques

A number of idea-generating techniques exist that can assist in the concepts that could lead onto developing new products and services. You may have heard of some of the ones listed below:

* Brainstorming/Idea Shower
* SCAMPER
* Rule Reversal
* Mind Mapping

You can find further detailed instructions on how to undertake these at www.mindtools.com.

However, these are mainly only useful if you are clear of a problem that needs solving. When you are thinking about community enterprise, and the ability to meet the ever-increasing changes and demands of local areas, then you need to consider not only your own skills, but also more so your interests, knowledge and contacts. These are all important when scoping out a new business venture. The most successful of entrepreneurs recognised that they couldn't achieve it all without having support and connections to others. Therefore, it is useful to consider your personal potential. Ask yourself these questions:

* What are my interests?
* What is important to me?
* What contacts do I have?
* What knowledge do I possess?

When looking at the case study, Mel's motivation for her business came down to a number of different factors. She had found something that she was very passionate about that had a profound impact on her life and also lifestyle. And this gave her the drive and confidence to set up on her own. Not only this, but she recognised that she was not on her own with wanting to change her lifestyle and become healthier. Through some informal market research, she was able to 'scope' her idea and see if the demand (need) was there in the location in which she wanted to base herself. However, this is not always the case.

Can my idea work?

Having a great idea does not necessarily mean that it can make a good business. And even having a good business concept does not automatically translate into a viable business opportunity. So, it is important that you are aware of not only what is happening within the sport industry, but also within community sport; it is arguably more important to be aware of what is happening at a local level. You need to ask yourself a number of different questions:

- Is this actually a good idea?
  Speak to people. Ask as many people as possible and sound them out about your thoughts: people from different organisations, your customers, your neighbours, etc. It will allow you to look at the need/problem from a number of different perspectives.
- Who is your customer?
  This is sometimes not as easy a question to answer, as your customer could change or develop across the lifespan of a business. However, as a starting point, consider which grouping of people would be most likely to use your service/product.
- How many of your customers exists?
  Now that you are aware of who your customer is, you need to know if there is going to be enough demand from your potential customers to make this idea viable. This is a tough question to answer, but you can look at similar activities and usage levels to gauge potential interest. Again, talking to your potential customers at this point not only helps you to understand how many people could potentially be interested in your service/product, but also starts the process of promoting it – you are sowing the seed of your business idea.
- Why will they use this service/product?
  This is an important question, as it can be the basis for the promotion of your service/product and how you communicate with your customers. It would be beneficial to try to get an understanding of your customers' relationship with sport/physical activity. If you have this information, you will be able to communicate more effectively with your customers why they would want to use your service/product.
- Is there anyone else delivering the same business (competitors)?
  This has some links to the questions above: In your local area, search to see if there are other deliverers of the same service/product. If someone is delivering the same as you are intending, is it to the same type of customer? Is it in the same area? Will it have the same focus as yours? Basically, is there room for your business as well?

Not only will this information help you in assessing the viability of the business, it will also assist you in cementing the values and reasons for your business. You can then use this information to communicate and promote your business more effectively with your customers. Any marketing text will show you how to utilise a number of marketing tools, which provide a strategic and analytical approach to idea appraisal. These tools can be used in a number of ways. A SWOT (Strengths, Weaknesses, Opportunities, Threats) analysis, for example, can help you understand better your own strengths and weaknesses as a potential business, but also the possibility of opportunities available to you, as well as highlighting potential dangers and threats to look out for.

PROMOTION

How you promote your business is crucial, as it encompasses your communication methods with your customers and your potential customers. Here, it is critical to ensure that the focus is always the customer (Drucker, 1999). Using the lessons and guidance from this book and elsewhere, you can utilise the promotional methods that are most likely to be used by your target market (customer), but also that will engage them. Consider the Sport England 'This Girl Can' campaign that aimed to prompt a change in attitudes and help boost women's confidence. It used social media as a method of communication, telling the real story of women who play sport by using images that are the complete opposite of the idealised and stylised images of women we are used to seeing. They did this to overcome barriers and encourage triggers to get more women more active (Sport England, 2017).

STAFFING

For many start-up community enterprises, there will be one person at the forefront, setting up the business and delivering it as well. However there could come a point in the near future where you need to employ staff. When considering the possibility of employing staff, think about the types of roles that you need performing and if they can, first, be covered by volunteers. Volunteering in support of sports teams, clubs and other organisations is one of the most commonly undertaken types of volunteering in England. Within 'sports volunteering' exists an extremely wide range of roles – coach, captain, secretary, chairperson, treasurer, administrator, fundraiser, washing the kit, transporting children and a range of other more niche and sport-specific activities (Nichols et al., 2016). However, it could be that you have a specialist, or time-consuming, role that requires an employed staff member.

There are a number of factors to consider in respect to employees to ensure that you are operating within the law; for example, elements such as contracts, working hours and national minimum wage:

- An employee must be given written terms of employment, which can either be a simple printed form or a detailed legal agreement. Non-European Union nationals will require a work permit to be able to work in the UK. For a short-term employment contract, you can adapt the same one for your employees.
- Regarding the national minimum wage, any worker over the age of 25 is entitled to £7.50 per hour worked; those aged between 21 and 24, inclusive, are entitled to £7.05, between 18 and 20, inclusive, are entitled to £5.60 and those aged under 18 are entitled to £4.05 (these figures are reviewed each year). Employers are under a duty

to keep full records of payment to their employees, and it is important to ensure that you have these correct from the start.

- Anyone working for you is entitled to work a maximum of 48 hours per working week unless they sign something explicitly revoking this protection. This may be in exceptional circumstances; for example, at children's holiday period or if you are working events.
- The nature of sport and physical activity means that there is a high chance of working with children and/or vulnerable adults. Therefore, to ensure that the safety of your customers is a top priority, you will need your volunteers and employees to complete a Disclosure and Barring Service. It's against the law for employers to employ someone or allow them to volunteer for 'regulated activity with children' if they know they're on one of the barred lists.
- Get employment insurance – you need employers' liability insurance as soon as you become an employer. Your policy must cover you for at least £5 million and come from an authorised insurer. Employer's liability insurance will help you pay compensation if an employee is injured or becomes ill because of the work they do for you.

FINANCE

It is important when contemplating the set-up of an enterprise to consider the financial aspects. If your business isn't going to generate any money, it won't be successful, so you need to be very clear on how you will make a profit. Use it to your advantage – your plan will be incredibly useful when it comes to securing loans and investments, but that's not its only use. It's also a personal tool to help you understand your objectives. Before you decide how much to sell your services/products for, you need to work out how much each one, or each hour of service, costs you. The challenge here is that most examples centre on a product being produced. A considerable proportion of community sport enterprises are services, and, therefore, consideration of costs and pricing from this perspective is a little different. You need to consider elements such as the affordability of your target market, competitor costs for the level of expertise to be delivered or if it will be of no cost and income generated elsewhere. Whatever the situation, you need to consider those costs linked to the delivery of your service; this could be in time, getting to the venue, hall hire, etc. The price you charge customers for a service/product must be higher than its cost and include enough money to cover the extra costs of running your business (for example, petrol, bills, rent, etc.) and your essential personal costs. For more information on budgeting and financial systems, see Chapter 11.

Personal survival budget

A survival budget shows the amount of money you need each month to live on. To work it out, add up all the money you spend, and take away any money you get as income from sources other than your business. You may have to make guesstimates on some items to consider this from a monthly perspective, but try to be as realistic as possible. It is always useful to consider a potential backup option, for example, cutting the magazine subscriptions or moving in with parents for a year to lower your costs. Table 13.3 illustrates a personal survival budget.

A	Estimated costs	Monthly cost (£)
	TABLE 13.3 A personal survival budget	
	Mortgage/rent	
	Council tax	
	Gas, electricity and oil	
	Water rates	
	All personal and property insurances	
	Clothing	
	Food and housekeeping	
	Telephone	
	Hire charges (TV, DVD, etc.)	
	Subscriptions (clubs, magazines, etc.)	
	Entertainment (meals and drinks)	
	Car tax, insurance, service and maintenance	
	Children's expenditures and presents	
	Credit card, loan and other personal debt repayments	
	National insurance	
B	**Total costs (£)**	£
C	**Estimated income**	**Monthly income (£)**
	Income from family/partner	
	Part-time job	
	Working tax credit	
	Child benefits	
	Other benefits	
D	**Total income (£)**	£
E	**Total survival income required** (Total costs–Total income £)	£
Backup plan		

You now need to consider how much income can be generated through your business idea or how much funding is required to deliver your business, depending on what your focus is. Again, this is not an easy task and would ideally be achieved through looking at the organisations' historical data … but you don't have any. In this instance, you need to consider the potential demand of your business, taking into account the fact that the first 6–12 months of a business being up and running can be the most challenging. If possible,

	Feb	Mar	Apr	Totals
Sales Income				£0.00
Own Funds				£0.00
Dragons loan				£0.00
Grant				£0.00
Total Incoming	£0.00	£0.00	£0.00	**£0.00**
Rent & Rates				£0.00
Wages				£0.00
Utilities, phone, internet				£0.00
Insurances				£0.00
Motor Expenses				£0.00
Marketing/Advertising				£0.00
Print/Stationery				£0.00
Training				£0.00
Loan Repayments				£0.00
Capital Spend				£0.00
Professional Fees				£0.00
Other				£0.00
Total Outgoing	£0.00	£0.00	£0.00	**£0.00**
Incoming less outgoing	£0.00	£0.00	£0.00	**£0.00**
Opening Bank Balance				
Closing Bank Balance	£0.00	£0.00	£0.00	**£0.00**

FIGURE 13.2 Cash flow forecast

complete a cash flow forecast, as shown in Figure 13.2. This will not only allow you to consider all costs coming in and out of your business, but it will also give you more of an understanding of when this will happen.

Funding

There are so many ways to fund a community start-up business. Most entrepreneurs don't realise that there are more ways to get funding for your start-up than going to an angel investor or bank. Angel investors are a growing community of wealthy investors encouraged by generous tax reliefs. Angels typically each invest between £5,000 and £100,000. Sometimes they'll do this in a group that invest together or will act as a syndicate of half a dozen or so that has been constructed specifically for an investment in one business. Either way, they are likely to demand an 'Investor Director' to represent them on your board. If you are fortunate to have a choice of investors, you may be able to go for a mix of investors that have and are willing to share expertise and contacts within your sector.

You can find angels independently – using LinkedIn – but also from local community groups, organisations and businesses already established. But be prepared for the time needing to be spent meeting angels and pitching your story. An angel investor is useful for a small, local business if they are struggling with expertise in a particular area.

Crowdfunding

Crowdfunding is very different from angel investors in that it involves many people or organisations. In crowdfunding, significant amounts of capital are raised from different individuals, organisations and so on. There are several sites devoted to crowdfunding: Crowdcube, SyndicateRoom, Seedrs, Kickstarter and GoFundMe are just a few. With these platforms, entrepreneurs can ask for funding from practically anyone. An entrepreneur is capable of raising hundreds to millions through crowdfunding. Investors generally invest between £100 and £50,000 through crowdfunding, and this could involve a large number of shareholders for the business; a positive in regard to advocates for the business.

Self-funding

Self-funding (this can also be known as bootstrapping) is definitely an effective way of funding a start-up in some situations. It enables you to manage your business yourself without relying on investors. It also saves you the time and energy involved in looking for investors. However, the disadvantage of self-funding is that you cannot run your business if you do not have enough money to start it. More so, you might risk your money if your business plan is not good enough. This is a risky option personally as a start-up, but will allow you complete control.

Grants

There are a number of options available here depending on the entrepreneur themselves, and/or the nature of the business and/or location. There are also grants available from a sport/physical activity perspective to develop activities and the benefits they may bring. Grants are available from a number of different sources. The UK government currently supports a number of programmes available to support the development of new business. These can change on a regular basis, so the best advice would be to access online support for the most up-to-date funding options. Alternatively, many UK universities run incubator schemes that support students with new start-ups.

Within sport, there is considerable support through organisations, such as Sport England, to develop entrepreneurial activity within communities. This is a way of ensuring that needs are being met of local communities, and, therefore, they offer a number of funding options, from small grants (£500–£10,000) to community and volunteering grants.

Loans

Normally from a bank, business loans are straight loans based over a pre-agreed period of time and set to various interest rates. These are a more expensive method of funding, but there are still options here. Governments have supported loans that are available with a reasonable interest rate, alongside offering support and mentoring through the process. The value to the economy of having new and successful businesses operating (whether commercial or not-for-profit) is sizeable and, therefore, of interest to the government.

In the UK, The Prince's Trust offers an exclusive Enterprise programme that lends grants and mentors to young individuals to help them start their own business. They must be 18–30 years old in order to apply for The Prince's Trust grants, however, it offers a bespoke personal support programme dependent on your business.

Enterprising delivery

It could be that you are already involved in an organisation in community sport and wish to increase your memberships or to generate more income for example. There are some great examples of how this can be achieved, and it mainly focuses around the stages that have been discussed within this chapter. If you understand the values of your organisation, and are clear in what it is that you hope to achieve, then follow the steps within the chapter, and listen. Listen to your local partners in what the issues are and in how they can support you; listen to your potential customers, why they would like to attend some activities and what is stopping them. Listen to your community, how you can support them and what it is that they need.

CONCLUSION

The idea behind this chapter was to give you an insight into the enterprising nature of sport. The changes that have occurred over the last ten years may encourage change within some sporting organisations, but in a way that fundamentally grows the reach and customer base within local communities. Ultimately, it is about the customer; the way in which we seek out sporting and physical activity opportunities is changing, the way in which we communicate is changing and the way in which we view sport is changing. And so, sporting organisations on a local level need to ensure that they are aware of their customers' needs and are reacting to it appropriately. It was also hoped that this chapter would give you the initial nudge into considering your own enterprising capabilities and some guidance into how to develop that. New ventures and enterprises do not need to be multimillion-pound, income-generating machines; they can work alongside school, part-time or full-time work. If anything, this chapter should have given you an appreciation that developing your own enterprise within sport could be possible. The skills do not all need to be present from the start; they will develop throughout the enterprise journey; all you need right now is the enterprising mindset.

Throughout this chapter, there has been a series of tips that can help support the development of your own enterprise. We can summarise these neatly:

- Start with what the purpose of your enterprise would be. Is there an issue that you want to address through the vehicle of sport and physical activity, e.g., unemployment, homelessness, health and well-being education in disadvantaged communities, etc.?
- Do you have a unique set of skills, and how could they relate to the enterprise?
- You don't have to do this by yourself, so know your strengths and weaknesses. Who else would you need to make it happen?
- Define your mission and core values. This will help be your road map and keep you heading in the right direction.
- Like any business, ask yourself 'Why would somebody want to buy your product/service?'
- Research, research, research! Thoroughly research your market, your competitors and your customers.
- Ask for help! The power of the crowd can help you achieve your ambitions faster, more efficiently and can make the whole process even more enjoyable! There is a lot of support for enterprises, from local councils, to university enterprise teams and even social enterprises that support start-up social enterprises.
- Finally, network! There are plenty of enterprise social events where you can meet like-minded individuals working in a similar area to you. These are great places to pick up tips, receive advice or simply be inspired to carry on the work you want to do.

REVIEW QUESTIONS

1. Can you name two successful sporting entrepreneurs? Why do you think they are successful?
2. What are the factors that had an impact on Mel in the case study to set up on her own?
3. Consider Mel in the case study. What skills, behaviours and attributes do you think made her successful?
4. What values do you think are important to Mel in the case study that has encouraged her success?
5. What potential challenges do you think are facing Mel in the case study?
6. Consider Mel's promotion and method of communication – what are the strengths and potential weaknesses?

REFERENCES

Ball, S. (2005). The importance of entrepreneurship to hospitality, leisure, sport and tourism. *Hospitality, Leisure, Sport and Tourism Network*, 1(1), 1–13.

Bolton, B., & Thompson, J. (2013). *Entrepreneurs: talent, temperament and opportunity* (Third ed.). Oxon: Routledge.

Drucker, P. (1999). *Managing for results: economic tasks and risk-taking decisions*. Oxon: Routledge.

FSB. (2016). *Women in enterprise: the untapped potential*. Federation of Small Businesses. Published online: www.fsb.org.uk/docs/default-source/fsb-org-uk/fsb-women-in-enterprise-the-untapped-potent ialfebc2bbb4fa86562a286ff0000dc48fe.pdf?sfvrsn=0.

Gibb, A. A. (1993). Enterprise culture and education: understanding enterprise education and its links with small business, entrepreneurship and wider educational goals. *International Small Business Journal*, 11(3), 11–34.

Kelley, D., Brush, K., Green, P., Herrington, M., Ali, A., & Kew, P. (2015). *Women's Entrepreneurship*. Global Entrepreneurship Monitor. Published online: www.babson.edu/Academics/centers/blank-center/global-research/gem/Documents/GEM%202015%20Womens%20Report.pdf.

McClelland, D. C. (1961). *The achieving society*. Princeton, NJ: Van Nostrand.

Mintel. (2017). *Hobbies and interests*. UK: Mintel Group Ltd.

Nichols, G., et al. (2016). *Motivations of sport volunteers in England. A review for Sport England*. Available online: www.sportengland.org/media/10205/motivations-of-sport-volunteers.pdf.

ONS. (2017). *UK business; activity, size and location: 2016*. Retrieved from ONS: www.ons.gov.uk/businessindustryandtrade/business/activitysizeandlocation/bulletins/ukbusinessactivity sizeandlocation/2016.

Rae, D. (2007). Connecting enterprise and graduate employability. *Education + Training*, 49(8/9), 605–619.

Ratten, V. (2011). Sport-based entrepreneurship: towards a new theory of entrepreneurship and sport management. *International Entrepreneurship and Management Journal*, 7(1), 57–69.

Shane, S., & Venkataraman, S. (2000). The promise of entrepreneurship as a field of research. *Academy of Management Review*, 25(1), 217–226.

Sport England. (2016). *Towards and active nation*. London: Sport England.

Sport England. (July, 2017). *This girl can*. Retrieved from Sport England: www.sportengland.org/our-work/women/this-girl-can/.

CHAPTER 14

Monitoring and evaluation

Maxine Gregory and Jayne Wilson

SUMMARY

This chapter explores the role of monitoring and evaluation (M&E) in the delivery of community sport programmes within the context of government priorities. You are provided with the key concepts and a range of tools to help you, as a manager, design community programmes, which, through effective M&E, have a *clear line of sight* to the required social impacts with supporting evidence. This – in common with other chapters – further develops your skills in planning, decision-making and control. The chapter will help you to answer key questions:

- What is 'M&E', and why do I need to do it?
- What type of M&E should I do?
- How will M&E support and benefit my project?

We will consider different approaches to evaluation and discuss the challenges of evaluating community sport programmes, supplemented with illustrative examples of good practice from the Street League charity. The requirement to demonstrate the impact that sport can make on wider social issues has never been greater and is a major driver of government investment in community programmes.

AIMS

By engaging with this chapter, you will be able to

- Understand the current policy context for investment in sport and the importance of demonstrating impact,
- Understand the key concepts and terminology,
- Consider a range of options and approaches to measure and evaluate projects, including practical data-collection tools,
- Appreciate how effective M&E can add value and improve the delivery of community sport programmes and
- Reflect on good practice, drawn from case study examples.

THE COMMUNITY SPORT LANDSCAPE AND ITS IMPLICATIONS ON MONITORING AND EVALUATION

A 'mixed economy' of providers

The structures for delivering sport are complex and varied including local government and the educational, voluntary and charitable sectors (such as National Governing Bodies and Sport Clubs). Historically, the largest provider of community sport has been Local Authorities, principally through their provision of sports facilities and services delivered by sport-development teams. However, reductions in Local Authority funding in recent years has resulted in more community sport services being delivered by the other sectors, further increasing the 'mixed economy' of provision (by both public and private sectors). To add further complexity, there is the growing *'sport for development'* sector, largely representing charitable or non-governmental organisations. These are organisations that are characterised by their ability to use *sport as a hook* to deliver social good. They generally share the objectives of more traditional providers, such as increasing participation or removing barriers to participation, but also use sport to address broader social issues such as youth offending, unemployment or substance misuse, as shown in a number of previous chapters in this book.

New strategies for sport and physical activity

In addition to the mixed economy of community sport providers, there has also been a shift in the recent policy context. This is predominantly as a result of the publication of the government's new national strategy for sport and physical activity *Sporting Future* in 2014 and the responses to this from other organisations, including major funders. *Sporting Future*, and the subsequent Sport England strategy *Towards an Active Nation 2016–2021* (Sport England), highlights a range of Key Performance Indicators (KPIs) against which success can be assessed and provide direction on how projects should be monitored and evaluated.

Sport and physical activity initiatives are increasingly required to go beyond providing opportunities to just play sport, for example, demonstrating improvements to an individual's personal development and physical and mental health. This requires a greater emphasis on evaluation, which measures social impacts, and the need to go above and beyond the monitoring of performance indicators, such as attendance, throughput and programme retention, to assessing benefits at a societal level, such as improving social cohesion, regenerating communities, reducing crime and antisocial behaviour and creating economic benefits.

Increasingly, individual outcomes are measured, such as increased confidence and self-efficacy (self-belief) and improved employability and increased subjective well-being. The outcomes of successful community sport-development projects are both 'hard' (e.g., numbers of participants) and 'soft' (e.g., changes in attitudes and behaviour), and successful M&E will capture both these aspects.

The *Sporting Future* strategy has shifted the priority from measuring *outputs* (e.g., **who** has been accessing a particular project or service, **how** they are involved [frequency, duration etc.] and **what** they think about it) to an *outcome*-focussed model of evaluation with the emphasis on what the **impacts** of involvement are and how these can be measured and maybe even valued.

Sport England Monitoring and Evaluation Toolkit (2017)

There are some important principles that underpin the need for effective M&E across the sector for all organisational types. Some of the core principles of current M&E have been recently summarised in Sport England's Monitoring and Evaluation Toolkit (2017). This toolkit describes the three core roles of measurement and evaluation as follows:

1. To understand the impact of activity on the strategic priorities for community sport and physical activity,
2. To ensure continuous learning and improvement and
3. To support advocacy; demonstrating impact, specifically the benefits of participation in sport and physical activity and making the case for investment nationally and locally.

Through this chapter, we will explore approaches to monitoring and evaluating community sport and physical activity programmes in line with these key principles.

WHAT IS MONITORING AND EVALUATION?

Defining monitoring and evaluation

This section will help you to understand the key terms relating to M&E. This will lead to discussion of the process and options for designing and implementing M&E.

MONITORING...

> ... is the regular, systematic, collection and analysis of information related to a planned and agreed programme of action.
>
> (Coalter, 2006)

Monitoring is *systematically* collecting information that will help you to answer questions about your project. It focusses on providing evidence of the extent to which the programme is being delivered as planned, meeting its targets and making progress towards the achievement of its objectives. Collecting 'monitoring' data is about keeping the project on the right track and evidencing the development of the project to key stakeholders.

Through general operational processes, such as having meetings amongst staff, planning work and giving/receiving feedback, it is likely that most organisations undertake some form of monitoring regardless of whether this is done formally or informally, or recognised as 'monitoring'. The process of monitoring a project can be very simple (keeping a record of what is delivered, counting attendances, tracking participation, recording training and volunteering experiences), but this data collected over time can be valuable in helping to demonstrate project impacts and provide both internal and external accountability. Furthermore, the collection of monitoring information helps you to *evaluate* your project.

EVALUATION...

> ... is the process of undertaking a systematic and objective examination of monitoring information in order to answer agreed questions and to make judgements on the basis of agreed criteria. Evaluation is also an ongoing process and provides the basis for learning and organisational and programme development.
>
> (adapted from Coalter, 2006)

Evaluation takes the collection of data to the next level by considering, assessing, judging or appraising the project. It helps you to design or redesign projects, ask the right questions, gather evidence, interpret the evidence, communicate important information and take informed decisions. There are many varied strands to a project that can be evaluated, and ultimately, the first stage is often to consider to what extent the project or programme is meeting its objectives. Evaluation will help to demonstrate a project's value and accountability to stakeholders and funders, but the usefulness goes far beyond this. Evaluation data can identify the extent to which changes and adaptations are required, e.g., if things aren't working or could be improved.

PROCESS OR IMPACT EVALUATION?

Evaluations can have different priorities; they can be designed specifically to measure and showcase impact, to learn and showcase good practice and to inform future project design or to achieve all of these factors. An evaluation can be a *'process'*, an *'impact' evaluation* or both of these. A process evaluation generates insight into *how* a project or programme is being implemented, whereas an impact evaluation focuses on the *effectiveness* of a project and its outcomes.

FORMATIVE OR SUMMATIVE EVALUATION?

Evaluation can demonstrate the effectiveness, efficiency and impact of a project. Evaluations can also be described as *formative* or *summative*. *Formative* evaluation goes beyond demonstrating accountability (showing how resources were used) to play a central role in learning and development, leading to both organisational and programme improvement. *Summative* is usually a more retrospective or end-of-project review that summarises the impact. Ideally, where and when possible, formative evaluation should be undertaken, as this is done on a more 'real-time' basis and can help to inform delivery and development during the life course of the project, rather than reporting its impact at the end.

QUANTITATIVE AND QUALITATIVE DATA?

Traditionally, much M&E in sport has been about quantitative data collection – focusing on **inputs** and **outputs**. A simple example of this can be found in the public leisure facilities where, historically, monitoring focussed on the number of visits to centres and the subsidy per user provided by the Local Authority. There was no consideration of the impact of the visit on the individual's health and well-being, just the need to provide the most visits (output) at the least cost (input).

The measurement of statistics and KPI data are vital but do not always tell us the whole picture. We need data to **tell the stories** and to illustrate what change has occurred and how this was achieved. Quantitative and qualitative methods complement each other by providing key learning points and helping to identify success factors; quantitative data are focussed on 'number crunching', metrics and statistics to demonstrate the scope, scale and reach of a project, whereas qualitative data involve asking questions, listening to and observing project participants to understand the difference that the project made to them. By using a 'mixed methods' approach (collecting quantitative and qualitative data), M&E becomes a tool that enables people to **learn** and **develop** from their experiences. To contrast with the earlier example relating to measuring 'subsidy per user', we now need to consider a shift to the measurement of outcomes and the ability to demonstrate the impact of taking part. Examples of such outcomes could include an individual's improved sense of well-being or an improvement in a specific health condition arising from increased activity levels.

KEY PERFORMANCE INDICATORS AND TARGETS

A KPI is a measurable value that demonstrates how effectively an organisation is achieving its objectives. These can be used at an organisational level, an individual project level and at multiple levels within a project to enable effective M&E. A performance indicator describes the change required; the examples below, taken from *Towards an Active Nation 2016–2021* (Sport England), illustrate this and also demonstrate how a series of indicators can be developed to measure change from a number of customer perspectives:

KPI 1: Increase the percentage of the population taking part in sport and physical activity at least twice a month
KPI 2: Decrease the percentage of people physically inactive
KPI 6: Increase the percentage of young people (11–18) with a positive attitude towards sport and being active

A target is simply the amount of change required in the indicator over time and brings into play the importance of being able to set a baseline (to show the start position prior to any project being implemented). Most projects will have KPIs defined by external funding streams or organisational priorities, and the skill in developing an effective M&E framework is ensuring that the right ones are selected and baselines are established for these. Collecting the right data to inform each KPI will be considered later in this chapter. When choosing KPIs for M&E, you should consider the following issues:

- Do they reflect the project objectives?
- Do they have a purpose and focus; are they relevant to the project/organisation, and do they give a balanced view of performance across the elements of the project?
- Are they clearly defined and understood, with an appropriate methodology for data collection?
- Are they ambitious but achievable targets?

WHY IS MONITORING AND EVALUATION IMPORTANT?

M&E is vital in demonstrating the **impact** of community sport programmes. Without a strong evidence base, it can be difficult to communicate to funders why they should continue to fund programmes. It can be easy to describe what has been delivered as part of a programme – How many sessions took place? What was the project timescale? Who was involved? What experience did they get? Did the project represent value for money? But the key is to communicate to funders or project commissioners: 'What was the impact?' Help them to understand: What difference did the project delivery make to participants, to stakeholders (such as other partners or organisations), to volunteers and to local communities? Through implementing M&E, it becomes possible to explain to funders:

- What is happening/has happened as a result of a programme?
- Why has the programme worked (or hasn't worked)?
- How can the programme (or similar programmes) be improved for the future?

A common question posed by funding bodies is 'What works?' This is important knowledge to help with reviewing and revising delivery and supporting projects to improve and develop. In addition, it is important to consider the supplementary questions: What works …'for who?', 'How?' and 'In what context?' This takes into account the individual differences, settings and varied circumstances that are likely to exist within projects. It supports the fact that there is no 'one size fits all' approach to engaging and retaining individuals in sport and physical activity and that approaches to measuring impact need to be tailored to suit individuals and their needs.

> We have been able to use our evidence base to engage in really meaningful conversations with partners and funders to explain particular business decisions, areas of under-performance and success.
>
> (Managing Director Street League, Interview)

The shift from outputs to outcomes at a national strategy level, as discussed previously, has had an immediate impact on the type of M&E needed to measure success across the sector. For this reason, the structure of this chapter follows the core principles of Sport England's Measurement and Evaluation Framework (2017). This framework provides a toolkit to guide the sector and suggests mechanisms that measure the outcomes highlighted in the national strategy *Sporting Future*.

Start with the objectives

The starting point for any M&E is to define your objectives for the evaluation, often prescribed by the specific funding regime or project stakeholders. You may also have specific performance indicators that you are required to report, and there may be specific questions to be answered, relating to processes and outcomes. Typical examples include

- How many new participants are involved?
- How has the project attracted them?
- Is this project improving employability? and
- Are people increasing their physical activity levels?

It is important to decide and agree on the purpose of the evaluation and who the audiences will be so that an appropriate method can be selected that will answer the required question(s).

Once the objectives and audiences are determined, then it is possible to identify the best method to approach the evaluation. The following section provides a practical guide to lead you through this process.

IMPLEMENTATION

Developing a logic model

Sometimes referred to as a logical framework, theory of change or programme theory, a logic model is a visual representation of the rationale for projects that helps to demonstrate the relationship between project inputs, activities, outputs and the outcomes. The underlying purpose is to assess the relationships between elements of the programme. They are also a good tool for engaging partners and stakeholders in the design of a project and building consensus in terms of the desired outcomes and processes for delivering the project. A logic model should be dynamic in that it is continually reviewed and developed, therefore, it can be a valuable tool for planning and delivery.

Coalter (2006) identifies three further reasons for the use of logic models in relation to M&E:

- They provide the basis for identifying sufficient conditions and managing outcomes. A logic model helps you set out how and why programmes are supposed to work so that they can be managed to ensure the desired outcomes are achieved.
- They can assist where there are difficulties in defining what is to be measured, or controlling other factors that may be impacting on participants, or where there is lack of resource or expertise in M&E.
- A logic model approach increases the ability to disseminate best practice and to communicate how and why a programme worked or did not work. This is important in the context of building the evidence base for sport and physical activity, and to promote learning within the sector.

KEY STAGES IN DEVELOPING A LOGIC MODEL

The generic logic model in Figure 14.1 illustrates the required elements and examples of content.

The starting point is always to consider 'What outcomes do you want to achieve?' These are usually the longer-term strategic outcomes and will be aligned the current policy priorities. For example, *improving physical well-being* would be a primary outcome for many sport and physical activity programmes. It is useful to think of the approach to developing a logic model as *reverse engineering*, e.g., starting with the outcome and working backwards to design the project in a way that evidence suggests will deliver the outcome. In terms of product design, using an outcome-focussed approach prevents the development of programmes that are activity led and cannot demonstrate the required impact to external funders.

It is very likely (and desirable) that there will be multiple outcomes from a project. In terms of effective monitoring, it is important to decide what will be the main 'primary outcome' and to also identify the short-term, 'secondary' or 'intermediary' outcomes that you may want to monitor on the way to achieving this. Intermediary outcomes will be indicators of your progress towards achieving the ultimate longer-term goal (which may be described as a 'final outcome' or 'hard outcome').

Our Street League case study illustrates a hierarchy of outcomes. The primary outcome of the programme is to get young people who are not in employment, education or training (NEETs) into sustained work, education or training (for a period of at least six months). Street League describe this as their *hard outcome* by which the organisation measures its impact. It is possible that a project may have other outcomes such as improved mental well-being, but it is important to consider these as secondary outcomes that contribute towards achieving the primary outcome.

The important point is to be clear on what you want to achieve and the changes your intervention needs to deliver. It is then possible to develop the outcome indicators that will measure that quantifiable change is taking place and contributing to delivering the overall outcome.

Once the outcomes are agreed, you can work backwards to construct the model by agreeing on what the other elements should be. This is best done in collaboration with

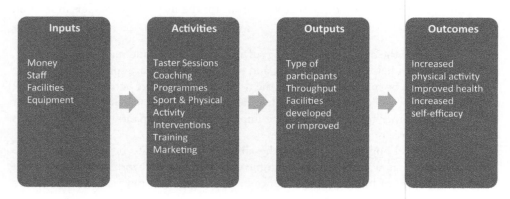

FIGURE 14.1 Generic Logic model

all project stakeholders with a vested interest or understanding of how the project is designed to work.

OUTPUTS

These are the elements of the project that are tangible and the easiest to quantify and measure and can include the

- Number of participants attending (often broken down by demographic profile),
- Number of activities or session delivered and
- Number of people volunteering, in receipt of training and/or receiving a qualification.

This section of the logic model identifies the key output indicators that will be monitored to ensure the project delivers the required impact. These indicators form part of routine monitoring to ensure that the project has the required throughput and is delivering the quantity of activity required to ensure the project's *effectiveness*.

ACTIVITIES

This is the intervention, or the product, and what it does. In this section of the logic model, the focus is on what is being delivered and how that links to the outputs. This section of the logic model is linked to the rationale for the project and will articulate the key features and assumptions relating to the delivery. There may be specific elements of the activity that must be delivered to achieve the change required. This may go beyond the products on offer to explore less tangible issues such as social climate and specialist skills required by staff involved in the project such as skills in mentoring and behaviour change and even the evaluation itself.

INPUTS

Inputs are the various resources that are required to deliver the activities. This can include money, staff, equipment, facilities and expertise. The relationship between project inputs and outputs relates to the concepts of *economy* and *efficiency*, e.g., the cost of the project resources (economy) in relation to the level of activity provided (efficiency). A consideration for many funders is the cost-per-project benificiary and whether that represents value for money in relation to the planned outcomes.

ATTRIBUTING CHANGE

Having identified the elements in each section of the logic model, it is important to examine the assumed relationship to ensure it is *logical* and not merely a leap of faith. Whilst the purpose of logic models is to ensure a focus on impacts, which are often longer-term, a logic model also identifies the key processes that support the delivery of the programmes and ensure that the desired change is achieved. This is built on the premise that it's not just 'doing sport' that may be delivering the outcomes. As discussed earlier, it may be the way that the sport or physical activity intervention is provided and experienced, which is the key to having an impact. This is the concept of 'necessary and sufficient conditions' (Coalter, 2013). Taking part in sport and physical activity is a necessary condition to achieve the outcome of increasing physical activity. Sufficient conditions refers to the processes that help achieve the required outcome. Our case study of Street League identifies the additional elements of the programme that create the *conditions* that support the young people into employment, education and training, which would not be achieved just by playing Football or taking part in Dance Fit.

Following the process of developing a logic model will make it easier to identify appropriate indicators and to develop your measurement framework.

Data collection

Tools

The selection of the most effective tools to carry out M&E for any project is determined by the design of the evaluation. Earlier in this chapter, we discussed the core elements of any evaluation design and the need for clarity and purpose in these areas:

- Establishing clear, realistic and achievable objectives
- Understanding the evaluation audience(s) and their requirements
- Using a logic model approach/creating an evaluation framework to understand the project inputs, activities and outputs – and the outcomes to be measured (primary and secondary, if relevant)
- Setting or agreeing on performance indicators (KPIs)

The next stage is to assess the skill set, interests and partner/stakeholder requirements, taking note of any previous evaluations that have been done, the infrastructure to support these and what worked well. It will be easier to engage your workforce (or to motivate yourself) if you choose data collection methods that fit with the project and your skills, e.g., if somebody is interested in videos or photography, then this could be incorporated into a qualitative data-capture tool. Alternatively, if there is a way to collect data in a way that is incorporated within project delivery, then this minimises the workload for deliverers and makes life easier for participants.

Parklife project: effective data collection

An example of incorporating data collection into delivery would be to embed the mechanisms to collect the required monitoring data into the registration process for a project, rather than having to do this as a separate task to collect baseline data. It may be possible to use technology to collect some of the necessary data. Sport England and the Football Association's Parklife projects, which have been piloted in

Sheffield and Liverpool, have taken this approach. Parklife Hubs offer a new central venue format for Football facilities, designed to provide a more cost-effective and higher-quality offer. This generates the opportunity to stimulate broader social benefits through widening community usage, co-locating a range of facilities on-site and strengthening community links. The registration system for anybody wishing to use a Hub requires the completion of an online form, which creates a QR code for participants, who then use this code to access the Hub. Participant-tracking data is subsequently generated, along with a system that enables easy follow-ups with clubs, parents and individuals.

Table 14.1 summarises some of the main quantitative and qualitative tools that are commonly used for data collection and the pros and cons and rationale for using each. Collecting the right data to inform each KPI that you have agreed should be a deciding factor in your choice of method. The list below is not intended to be comprehensive, however, the further reading at the end of this chapter will signpost you to further information. You may not always need to create data-collection tools from scratch; there may be existing tools you can adapt, or use, to develop ideas.

Also consider how new innovative technologies can assist with data collection and provide new ways to monitor and evaluate. Given the pace of change, our advice would be to research apps to support M&E or data-collection technology at the time that you are considering which methods to use. Examples of how to use digital data (Outdoor Recreation Network, 2016) can be found in the further reading section. It is important to remember that not everybody has access to technology or smartphones, therefore, your data-collection methods must be suited to your target respondents and be inclusive. The choice of tools also needs to be informed by the ability to provide the right data for each KPI.

SAMPLING

Consider the following issues in your planning:

- What data do you need to collect before the initiative begins? ('baseline' data)
- When will you collect data while the project is underway?
- How often will you collect data?
- What data do you need to collect at the end of your project?
- When are the best times for data collection? (do you have any good opportunities, e.g., events?)

There are some data that you might aim to collect from all participants, whilst other data may be collected from just a sample of participants. Ensure that any sample is as representative as possible, e.g., inclusive of participants from different demographics, with different perspectives and at different points in time.

The same applies to project stakeholders who may be able to offer differing perspectives on both the process and impact of the project. It may not be feasible to speak to everyone, so it would be advisable to prioritise and determine who it is 'essential' to

TABLE 14.1 Quantitative and qualitative tools for data collection

Tool	What is it?	Why?/How?	Advice/'top tips'
Paper-based surveys (in person, by post or completed via telephone interviews)	Surveys enable standardised data to be collected quickly and easily through asking a series of questions. Surveys can be used to identify opinions, attitudes and behaviours at a single point in time, or to track any changes by undertaking a follow-up survey.	Surveys are easy to use, inclusive and usually gives a good response rate. In person, during project sessions or at events, or completed and returned by respondents.	Surveying works well with 'captive groups' (e.g., event attendees during 'downtime'). Simple, clear and concise questions are needed. Prioritise what you REALLY need to find out.
Online surveys	A series of questions that can be routed (adapted) to suit individuals based on their previous answers. Can be completed using a range of devices (mobile phones, tablets, laptops, desktops, etc.). Online surveys offer flexibility to complete a survey in a place and at a time that is convenient to the recipient.	Free or low cost to use. Some data analysis and reporting (tables, graphics, etc.) may be automated. Can be distributed to participants via email or social media after a session or event.	Identify appropriate channels to disseminate and promote the survey. Share real-time response rates to encourage further responses from the population or by specific target groups.
Group discussions/ focus groups	Asking a series of questions to a group of people to encourage discussion and to gather a range of perspectives on a topic or experience. These can be more formal-style 'focus groups' or informal discussion groups.	More detailed insight possible. Identify a suitable environment to put participants at ease. To minimise inconvenience, cost and to put participants at ease, it is recommended that you go to participants in their own local environment.	Encourage all participants to get involved in discussions; try to bring people into the conversation. Offer a suitable environment and refreshments, etc.

Interviews	Asking a series of questions to an individual (or more commonly, numerous individuals) to gain more detailed insight into a project, topic or experience. Used with participants and project stakeholders in a variety of ways.	To develop personal understanding of how a project works for an individual. Telephone Interviews can be low cost and are resource efficient, although it is more difficult to establish a rapport than during face-to-face conversations.	Strike a balance between enabling the interviewee to talk openly and have the opportunity to express themselves, whilst having (and explaining) a clear aim for the interview. Sending questions in advance can help individuals to feel more comfortable.
Observation	Gain valuable insight within a natural environment/in 'context'. Can be done as a one-off or as multiple visits. Can be 'ethnographical' where the researcher engages/immerses themselves in the activity or purely observational. A visit may involve a mix of observation, surveying, interviews and discussion groups.	Get a real feel for the project. Quotes, stories, photos and videos may all form part of the data collection. Introduce yourself, ensure that you follow ethics guidance and do not get in the way or make people feel uncomfortable.	Work in partnership with project deliverers to ensure that you select the best project/session to visit/participate in. Be clear about your aims and what insight you wish to gain.
Participatory methods/ interactive data collection	There are a range of participatory methods for collecting data such as interactive quizzes, video diaries, group challenges and activities and mapping. Methods can be inclusive and a great way to gather and make use of a range of views. See the link in further reading for more details.	Using a participatory approach, you can involve many people and give everyone a sense of ownership. It should be an ongoing process of planning, action and reflection.	Tools should be used flexibly and adapted to suit.

speak to (project managers, key deliverers, beneficiaries and partners) and select a range of additional people to consult with. However, there is no definite rule for how many people you should include; ideally, the more the better, until the point at which you feel that you have an in-depth understanding and are not identifying any new data.

PRIORITIES AND PROPORTIONALITY

The resource invested in M&E should be appropriate and proportionate to the needs of stakeholders. You should consider factors such as the capacity of the organisation and the complexity of the project and determine what the key priorities are. If project delivery is via a tried and tested approach, then the evaluation can be more basic. However, if the project is new and innovative, then the funders will expect more detailed evaluation to demonstrate change and maximise the opportunities for learning and development.

Sport England's Measurement and Evaluation Framework incorporates 'five levels of impact measurement', which offers guidance on the extent and level of evaluation expected, ranging from basic descriptions to evidencing change; see: https://evaluationframework.sportengland.org/design-phase/decide-the-level-of-evaluation/.

A quote from Street League's Managing Director helps to emphasise importance of not over-evaluating:

> [Key challenges include]…staying focused and ensuring that our M&E processes are proportionate and purposeful. It is quite easy to measure 'everything' but that puts unnecessary pressure on delivery teams and can confuse analysis and insight.

ATTRIBUTION

A core principle adopted by Street League is 'do not over-claim'. They understand that impact needs to be evidenced in a robust way. It is highly likely that any behavioural change by an individual is influenced by a variety of factors, rather than a single factor, e.g., 'participation in your project'.

> To start at a realistic place for where you are and measure what you absolutely must, ensure it is accurate and evidenced. We hope it would also help to adopt our three golden rules: 'Don't over claim, don't use vague percentages and have evidence for the outcomes you report'.
>
> (Managing Director Street Leagues)

ANALYSIS AND REPORTING

There are a number of considerations when planning for the analysis and reporting of M&E data. The priority for analysis and reporting is clear – to maximise the impact of what you have collected. A summary report or infographic will only reach its potential if it is tailored to meet the needs of the specific audience. It is vital at the outset to discuss and agree stakeholder requirements.

The analysis phase may include processing a range of both quantitative and qualitative data. Reporting statistics, such as the number of participants, demographics, throughput, retention and dropout rates, will help to set the scene and provide understanding of who accesses the project and how. The metrics reported should match up with the objectives and KPIs agreed at the onset. Excel or SPSS (Statistical Package for the Social Sciences) are usually recommended for quantitative data analysis, however, if online surveys have been used, some of the analysis may already have been undertaken automatically by the survey software.

Qualitative data are descriptive and can be resource intensive to process and analyse. The process of analysis can involve the need to transcribe recorded conversations and is, to an extent, dependent on the consistency and skill of the researchers undertaking the analysis.

Qualitative data can be difficult to generalise and standardise but can be analysed via a content analysis or thematic analysis approach. Systematic analysis helps to quantify and organise participant feedback and draw out the main threads and core messages. Qualitative data is often used to 'tell the stories', provide richer insight and to illustrate project impact, including contributing to the production of case studies. For larger amounts of data, there are also software options for managing qualitative content such as NVivo and Tableau. The software options cited are simply illustrative examples, and individuals should do their own research to identify which options offer the best solution for them.

There are also various 'real-time' online data-management platforms that could be accessed or subscribed to at a cost (such as Sportworks, Substance's Views and Upshot) that will help to process and combine both quantitative and qualitative data. The following summarise what you need to achieve through the analysis and reporting process:

- Fulfil any stakeholder requirements.
- Provide useful information that helps you make decisions.
- Identify things that enable you to make improvements to your funding stream or project.
- Show you where things might be going wrong so you can fix them.
- Give updates on the impact you are having (i.e., progress towards your outcome indicators).

(Sport England's Measurement and Evaluation Framework, 2017)

BEST PRACTICE CASE STUDY: A CLEAR FOCUS ON THE HARD OUTCOME

Street League is the UK's leading Sport for Employment Charity, which operates in 14 cities in the UK. Participation in sport (Football and Dance Fit) is integral to what Street League does, but its programmes are focused on achieving the hard outcome of getting young people into employment, education or training:

Sport is integral to making Street League work - it brings people together, creates fitter bodies and fitter minds, teaches key skills like discipline, communication and team work and is one of the most powerful engagement tools when working with young people particulary those who are hardest to reach.

(www.streetleague.co.uk/about-us)

Street League provides opportunities within communities for young people who are NEETs to join a sport and employability training programme. This brings together daily participation in sport combined with life and employability skills development, mentoring, qualifications and work experience, which provide routine and structure. Football and Dance Fit are the activities that provide 'the hook' to enthuse young people to get involved. Young people can progress to the training programme once they can demonstrate they are ready to take advantage of it and can operate within the social climate demanded by the project.

In 2014–2016, the Charity engaged with 2,177 young people through Football and Dance Fit and achieved an outcome of employment, education or further training for 1,281 young people. The latest figures for 2016–2017 (yet to be published) show that this figure has increased further still to 1,553 young people.

Using the generic logic model, the Street League has developed its own, as illustrated in Figure 14.2.

The charity's approach to M&E is underpinned by 'three golden rules': (1) Never overclaim what they do. (2) All percentages are to be backed up by absolute numbers. (3) All outcomes are to be backed up by auditable evidence. This is illustrated in Figure 14.3.

Street League has developed a comprehensive approach to M&E that tracks data relating to delivery of the programme and baseline assessments of young people when they

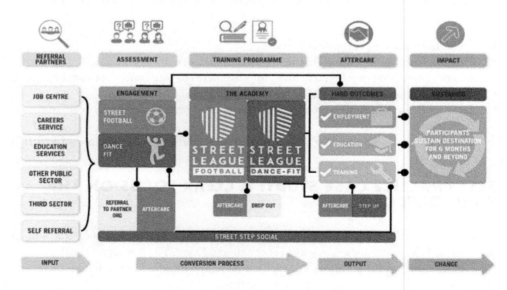

FIGURE 14.2 Street League Logic model

FIGURE 14.3 The Street League's Three Golden Rules

enter the programme. The evaluation can evidence, for example, the number of participants entering the progamme without qualifications and the barriers that they have to employment. This is important in demonstrating overall impact and the journey made by young people in the programme.

All participants are tracked regularly through the programme to ensure they are progressing in line with their Individual Learning Plan. Beyond this, the programme will assess whether they have sustained the hard outcome of employment, further education or training for a period of six months or longer. The outcomes for the project are rigourously audited, and evidence is provided for every individual achieving the outcome.

STRENGTHS OF THE STREET LEAGUE APPROACH

- A clear focus on one hard outcome related to employment education and training with secondary achievement outcomes relating to the formal qualifications
- A systematic monitoring system (Hanlon) that tracks individuals from the point at which they engage with Street League and records their progress throughout the programme
- Comprehensive socio-economic data on each participant to evidence the barriers faced by participants at the start of the programme in relation to the hard outcomes achieved
- Rigorous auditing of the data to ensure that there is evidence to support the achievement of the hard outcome by each project beneficiary
- Transparency in terms of those participants who joined the scheme but didn't progress to employment, education and training or could not be contacted. Street League does not claim outcomes for individuals that cannot be evidenced.

The infographic shown in Figure 14.4 summarises the impact of Street League projects in 2014–2016 by focusing on the key indicators used to monitor the participants at the

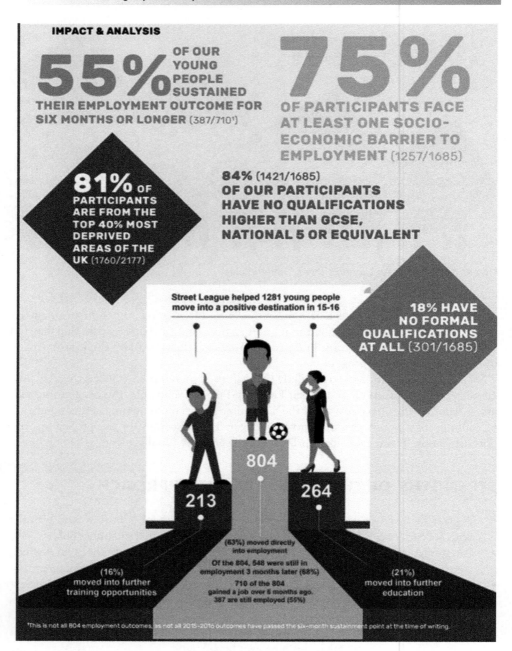

IMPACT & ANALYSIS

55%
OF OUR YOUNG PEOPLE SUSTAINED
THEIR EMPLOYMENT OUTCOME FOR
SIX MONTHS OR LONGER (387/710[1])

75%
OF PARTICIPANTS FACE
AT LEAST ONE SOCIO-
ECONOMIC BARRIER TO
EMPLOYMENT (1257/1685)

81% OF
PARTICIPANTS
ARE FROM THE
TOP 40% MOST
DEPRIVED
AREAS OF THE
UK (1760/2177)

84% (1421/1685)
OF OUR PARTICIPANTS
HAVE NO QUALIFICATIONS
HIGHER THAN GCSE,
NATIONAL 5 OR EQUIVALENT

Street League helped 1281 young people
move into a positive destination in 15-16

**18% HAVE
NO FORMAL
QUALIFICATIONS
AT ALL** (301/1685)

804

213

264

(16%)
moved into further
training opportunities

(63%) moved directly
into employment
Of the 804, 548 were still in
employment 3 months later (68%)
710 of the 804
gained a job over 6 months ago.
387 are still employed (55%)

(21%)
moved into further
education

[1]This is not all 804 employment outcomes, as not all 2015-2016 outcomes have passed the six-month sustainment point at the time of writing.

FIGURE 14.4 Street League Project Impact

start of the project and the number of participants achieving the hard outcome. It also demonstrates the effective use of infographics to communicate the impact of their work to partners and stakeholders.

RECOMMENDATIONS AND GOOD PRACTICE

This final section draws together our thoughts relating to good practice drawn from our experience of supporting M&E for a wide range of projects.

Overcoming challenges: facilitating engagement

The key challenges commonly experienced whilst carrying out project M&E is to engage the required people in the process and to collect the right data in the right ways and to maximise its impact. The good practice principles, which follow, provide suggestions of how to engage project deliverers and stakeholders in the M&E process and, in doing so, to increase the quality and impact of the evaluation. It is also necessary to encourage participants to engage with the process of data collection. Whilst offering some form of incentive can be useful, it is not usually necessary (although as a minimum, any costs incurred should be reimbursed). Keeping the process simple, ensuring that it is quick and not burdensome and explaining the purpose of the data collection and what it will help to achieve are usually sufficient to motivate participants to get involved. The timing of the data collection is also important; if it can be done at convenient times (e.g., during downtime at events) or with captive audiences with a vested interest, this should help to boost response rates. The data collection tools must be appropriate to the project and its context and proportion to it, e.g., if someone has had a short engagement with an event or project, then they should not be expected to engage with lengthy/detailed/extended evaluation. Support should be given where appropriate, and data collection should always be with over 18s, unless prior parental or school consent has been given.

Effective planning: consult, involve and integrate

Many people see M&E as a chore or burdensome and something that is separate to their 'day job', 'work' or 'project delivery'. Evaluation can sometimes be perceived as a process just to 'tick boxes' or check up on people, or something that is done for somebody else's benefit. To break down this perception, we would recommend consulting with all those involved in the M&E process to find out what would be feasible for them and would help them to do their job more effectively. This will start to address the perception that M&E is something that takes resource away from their 'real job' and is done for somebody else, to demonstrating the benefits of M&E for them and their project.

Evaluation should begin with some exploratory conversations or focus groups to understand how a project is delivered and what the intended impacts are. Constructing a logic model in partnership with project stakeholders helps to review how the project is designed and to link the inputs, activities, outputs and outcomes to the work programmes of the people delivering it. If project deliverers can understand what their role in the project is, and how they are contributing to the 'bigger picture', then this can help to encourage engagement with the evaluation process. Making the evaluation meaningful for those involved can help to create a culture within the delivery team that is focussed on impact and not just delivering the service that has been funded. Sharing examples of previous evaluations, which clearly demonstrate how the evidence was used and the impact, would also be helpful.

Good communication and a clear line of sight between the purpose of the M&E and the benefits generated are essential. It is necessary to facilitate understanding of the intended impact of your project and the context in which it will be delivered, including understanding local need and the project's fit with policies and priorities.

It is also desirable, where possible, to embed some of the evaluation principles and processes into existing systems; this can help to address resource concerns and increase efficiency. M&E should be 'bolted in, not bolted on' to projects. Essentially, it should be an integral part of project design and delivery, rather than an afterthought or something that does not fit with how the project is delivered.

Implementation: ensuring a good 'fit' with individuals and existing systems

Whilst there is a strong argument for standardised M&E to enable greater comparability between projects and to create a stronger voice for the sector, this needs to include flexible elements to ensure the feasibility and practicality of its use. The key to successful M&E is to find the right approach. In M&E terms, there should not be a 'one size fits all' approach in all cases – pragmatism is often required. There has been a long-standing issue within the evaluation of sport projects – that there is no standardised framework or set of indicatives to measure performance against. These will usually be determined by the project funder; therefore, if a project has multiple funders, it is likely that they may have to report different data, in different formats, to each funder. However, tools like Sport England's Measurement and Evaluation Framework help to address this and to offer standard measures.

Try to select a series of performance indicators that are consistent with other similar projects, e.g., existing evaluations for local comparability or national surveys such as Active Lives or the new Sport England measures. Once these key indicators are established, there can be flexibility in the ways in which they are collected to suit the needs of the project team and participants. The new Sport England framework also includes question banks and indicators as part of the toolkit to help increase consistency and, in doing so, enhance advocacy for the sector. Consideration of the following principles may be useful to aid your selection and guide your use of appropriate KPIs:

- A range of outcome indicators that demonstrate that change/impact are required. You need to consider the use of process indicators related to inputs and outputs to help monitor that the project is working as it should, e.g., the right participants (target groups).
- You need to ensure proportionality. M&E resource must be balanced with the project resource needed to deliver the activities. Do not paralyse the project delivery because the M&E suggested is too onerous.
- Use standard evaluation tools and frameworks that have been developed in the sport and sport for development sector where possible, but apply this in a bespoke way to suit your project.

- Develop a simple hierarchy of outcomes, identifying the primary outcome and indicators that will evidence that this outcome has been achieved (plus any secondary outcomes and indicators).
- Flexibility may be required as projects change and develop over time. Don't be afraid to review and reconsider your measurement of indicators and to make the necessary changes to ensure that they remain fit for purpose.

Using a combination of data collection methods (quantitative and qualitative) helps to understand and capture project impacts, going beyond the 'number crunching' to appreciate the real-life changes that may be attributable to the project.

Making it real: review and revise

The logic model and resultant evaluation plan will help to guide your M&E, but it is always good practice to review this over time. Your logic model should be dynamic and able to be changed in response to changes in delivery, new priorities, new people or opportunities that arise. The following principles will help to guide this approach to learning and reflection:

- Projects evolve and develop over time; therefore, evaluations need to do likewise. There should be some flexibility/adaptability and a mechanism for reviewing the evaluation on an ongoing basis and making changes to ensure that it remains fit for purpose.
- The timing of the data collection needs to be right. Whilst it is important to collect some data at the start of the project to establish a baseline, the follow-up data collection needs to allow sufficient time for the programme to have established itself and started to have an impact with its target groups. Many projects experience delays, and the evaluation needs to be flexible to ensure that these are accommodated and data collection does not begin too soon or too late.
- Consider use of specialist resource, e.g., M&E experts to advise or to carry out all or part of the evaluation. If the level of evaluation required exceeds the capacity of the project team or is outside their skill set, this may be a good option.

Despite Street League's achievements in showcasing high-quality M&E, they too acknowledge the need for continuous improvement and strive to enhance their approach yet further. This quote also highlights the need for a culture of supporting and valuing M&E at the executive level to ensure that M&E is sufficiently prioritised:

> We have sought to continually learn and improve our M&E processes and approach. We certainly don't have all of the answers but endeavour to get better each month, quarter and year. We also benefit from having a Board and leadership team who are wholly supportive of robust M&E and a culture across the organisation that reinforces its importance. Data is fed back to delivery teams to highlight successes and opportunities for learning, which makes it far more engaging and relevant.

> (Managing Director, Street League)

CONCLUSION

M&E is extremely important but can also be challenging, especially due to the current climate and policy shift from presenting outputs to measuring (and maybe valuing) social outcomes. However, despite the additional complexity, the longer-term benefit of this changing emphasis will be a stronger evidence base, which underpins and guides delivery and illustrates the potential value and impact of community sport projects. The M&E landscape is changing quickly, and the timing of this book has enabled current best practice to be showcased. M&E is not just about evidencing impact, but should also be about celebrating success and enhancing future delivery. If M&E is viewed by an organisation as a tool to add value, rather than an obligation to fulfil, there can be significant positive impacts on delivery and efficiency.

M&E can be resource intensive and needs careful consideration, without reinventing the wheel. It will be beneficial to look at examples of M&E reporting, logic models and to investigate tools you can adapt and develop to guide your evaluation. The consistent use of developing techniques, such as Social Return on Investment, and standardised success measures and performance indicators, such as the new Sport England guidance, will have the long-term effect of demonstrating the impact of the sector as a whole. A strengthened evidence base will position the sector well to engage in more cross-departmental projects, accessing a wider range of funding streams. This, in turn, will benefit society as a whole through using sport and physical activity to deliver on health, education and community outcomes. Finally, ensure that good practice and learning is disseminated as widely as possible to contribute towards the goal of continuous improvement.

REVIEW QUESTIONS

The following questions should be considered after reading this chapter to help put learning into practice. Consider a project that you have knowledge of, and think how you would start designing an evaluation. Focus on what you would do within three key areas: planning, implementation and reporting/dissemination.

1. Who needs to be involved in the evaluation? How can they be identified and engaged?
2. What resources (time, money and expertise) will be needed for the evaluation, and how can they be obtained?
3. What will success look like? What do you want to achieve from the evaluation?
4. What methods would work best, and what measures or indicators will be used?
5. How will emerging findings be used to inform delivery? How will you maximise the impact of the evaluation?

FURTHER READING

M&E guidance

Coalter, F. (2006). *Sport-in-Development: A Monitoring and Evaluation Manual*. University of Stirling and UK Sport, London. Accessed at www.toolkitsportdevelopment.org/html/resources/56/56853A82-146B-4A3F-90D6-5FC719088AE5/Manual%20monitoring%20evaluation.pdf.

Inspiring Impact. http://inspiringimpact.org/listings/.

Sport England. (2017). Measurement and Evaluation Framework. Accessed at https://evaluationframework.sportengland.org/.

Taylor, P. (2013). Torkildsen's Sport and Leisure Management – Chapter 17.

Using digital data and participatory methods

Outdoor Recreation Network (ORN). (2016). Digital Data and Outdoor Recreation: Research, Tools and Applications. www.outdoorrecreation.org.uk/events/orn-research-seminar-digital-data-and-outdoor-recreation-research-tools-and-applications/.

Sport Scotland and Social Value Lab. (2013). Participatory Tools for Community Sport Hubs and Sport Clubs. Accessed at www.triathlonscotland.org/files/clubdevelopment/Club%20Evaluation%20Tools.pdf.

Analysis and presentation of data

MEASURE Evaluation. www.measureevaluation.org/resources/training/materials/basic-data-analysis-for-health-programs.

REFERENCES

Coalter, F. (2006). *Sport-in-Development: A Monitoring and Evaluation Manual*. Stirling University and UK Sport, London.

Coalter, F. (2013). *Sport in Development: What Game Are We Playing*. Routledge, Oxon.

Index